Dan Blythe is an international speaker, content creator and Global Youth Director for Alpha International.

Rocky Nti is an artist and songwriter who helps to lead Amplified Arts Academy, a performing arts school for talented youth in inner-city London.

FACING FEAR 365

Daily reflections
for hope, peace
and courage

Dan Blythe
& Rocky Nti

FORM

First published in Great Britain in 2023

Form
SPCK Group
Studio 101
The Record Hall
16-16A Baldwin's Gardens
London EC1N 7RJ
www.spck.org.uk

Scripture acknowledgements can be found on p. 398.

British Library Cataloguing-in-Publication Data
A catalogue record for this book is available from the British Library

ISBN 978-0-281-08800-3
eBook ISBN 978-0-281-08801-0

1 3 5 7 9 10 8 6 4 2

Typeset by Fakenham Prepress Solutions, Fakenham, Norfolk NR21 8NL
First printed in Great Britain by Clays Ltd

eBook by Fakenham Prepress Solutions, Fakenham, Norfolk NR21 8NL

Produced on paper from sustainable sources

CONTENTS

INTRODUCTION

Are you fearless? The chances are, given that you've chosen to journey with this particular devotional, that your answer is the same as ours: No! We don't write this book as people who don't feel fear but as those who have, over time, chosen to face our fears: heart beating, hands sweating and knees shaking. We feel fear, but we also have faith.

For both of us – Dan and Rocky – our faith has given us the courage to face our fears daily and see them become stories of God's goodness. This has not been an instantaneous thing, but rather something we have had to work on day in and day out, which is why we decided to write this book in the first place. Our heart and hope are that this devotional will give you the daily courage and confidence to step out of the grip of fear, and step into everything God has for you.

Nearly every fear has a lie behind it. Throughout the next year we will engage with the truth of Scripture daily to expose the lies, so that together we will experience more and more freedom from fear. We hope that reading a short, truthful reflection every day will help you to cultivate a rhythm of regular Bible reading and develop a faith that can help you face whatever the day throws at you – the highs, the lows and everything in between.

We learn our rhythms from the healthiest human who ever lived: the person of Jesus. Jesus knew the Scriptures well and declared them often. It is for this reason that throughout this book we share some of the same truths, told in different ways – sometimes even the same scripture explored from a different angle. These messages need to become as dear to us as our very breath. Jesus also made a regular practice of Sabbath – a day of abstinence from work; a day to rest, recharge and refocus on God – knowing the importance of living from a place of rest and trusting God as the One who is ultimately in control. He practised silence and solitude and, in a world as noisy as ours, these practices have become more vital than ever before. It is for this reason we have factored in intentional pauses – *selah* moments – to reflect more deeply on how the content we are reading is forming us and strengthening our faith as we seek to apply it in our lives.

Before we dive in further, let's start by owning the areas in which fear is currently holding us captive. What are the spaces, situations and places we run from because they intimidate us and make us shrink back? Write these things down today, giving them to God so that at the end of this year we can look back and see what he has done, how things have changed, how we have changed and how the way we see the people and situations around us has been transformed.

This book is not about dispelling all fear but learning how not to be paralysed, derailed or bound by it; to learn to live life with more freedom, freedom that is already ours for the taking.

- On a scale of 1 to 10 (feeling fearful being 1 and feeling fearless being 10) write down a number for where you feel you are right now.
- What is one area of your life where you would like to have less fear and more faith?
- What is one thing you could initiate this year that you were too intimidated to do last year?
- What would you try tomorrow if you knew you couldn't fail?

Acknowledging where we are, let's press on to more hopeful days ahead.

FACING
FEAR
365

JANUARY

1. BEGINNING AGAIN

Sing to the Lᴏʀᴅ a new song;
sing to the Lᴏʀᴅ, all the earth.
Sing to the Lᴏʀᴅ, praise his name;
proclaim his salvation day after day.
Declare his glory among the nations,
his marvellous deeds among all peoples. **Psalm 96:1-3**

There is nothing quite like New Year celebrations: the bright lights, fireworks, the whirlwind of positive vibes and enthusiasm. Being amid the noise and glorious chaos is always a moment of reflection for me. It's the beginning of a new chapter, the start of a new season.

I can often find myself sitting down at the back of the celebrations, reflecting on what has gone before and what now lies ahead. If I'm not careful my mind can drift to the realm of pessimism, and a time of joy turns into an evening of dread. *What if I try something and fail? What if I reach out to someone and they reject me? What if what lies ahead isn't good?*

We can get so caught up in the days gone by that we forget to celebrate the very breath in our lungs. The breath that was unearned and freely received, which gave birth to the cosmos and yet still fuelled us to get out of bed this morning. While we have that breath in our bodies, coursing through our lungs, we have hope.

Although it's not always easy, sometimes we have to choose joy, we have to choose gratitude, we have to celebrate the gift of life we have been given and be thankful for the opportunity to go again.

RN

2. JESUS FACED FEAR

They went to a place called Gethsemane, and Jesus said to his disciples, 'Sit here while I pray.' He took Peter, James and John along with him, and he began to be deeply distressed and troubled. 'My soul is overwhelmed with sorrow to the point of death,' he said to them. **Mark 14:32-4**

For many years, I (Dan) have spoken a message titled 'Fearless' - coupled with the hashtag #TheFearlessGeneration. The message wasn't a bad one, but it wasn't a totally *accurate* one.

It's taken me a decade to realise that, as impacted human beings in a broken world, we will never actually reach a state of being completely fearless until we get to heaven. Fear is a thorn in the flesh for us all and is unfortunately a part of everyday life for every human on the planet.

When Jesus was on earth, he experienced fear. However, he didn't let it stop him doing what he was here to do: rescue humanity. In today's verse, we see Jesus in fearful anguish as he prepares for his death on a cross - a moment that is recorded in all four Gospels. Jesus faced fear as a human, so we could know that we too can face fear and overcome it. There is no fear in life that we will experience that Jesus has not already overcome.

Jesus demonstrated consistent and complete confidence in God. He felt fear, but he was not confined or constricted by it thanks to his faith, trust and dependence on his heavenly Father. We may never be totally fearless, but with faith and trust in God, we can learn to fear less.

DB

3. YESTERDAY HAS GONE

Forget the former things;
do not dwell on the past.
See, I am doing a new thing!
Now it springs up; do you not perceive it?
I am making a way in the wilderness
and streams in the wasteland. **Isaiah 43:18-19**

'Let us begin again, brothers, for up until now, we have done little or nothing.' These incredible words have been attributed to Saint Francis of Assisi. Said to have been spoken near the end of his life, these bold and challenging words become even more so in light of all that he had accomplished.

Saint Francis, who left behind a life of comfort and wealth in pursuit of honesty and truth, founded the Franciscan order and in doing so revolutionised the Catholic tradition. It's humbling to see someone who achieved such heights, or rather journeyed to such great spiritual depths, not afraid to wipe the slate clean and go again - not fearfully building an empire that would retain his legacy and make him famous for generations to come, or erecting shrines to the past.

No matter where we find ourselves today, we must honour the past, but not become lost in yesterday's glory, because God is inviting us into the present, where a new day is dawning.

RN

4. ORIGIN OF FEAR

'I was afraid because I was naked...'
And he said, 'Who told you that you were naked?' **Genesis 3:10–11**

In today's reflection we read about Adam and Eve turning their backs on God in the garden of Eden. As soon as they did, we read, they became aware of their nakedness, their disobedience and their failure. With their disobedience in eating the forbidden fruit against God's will, fear entered their stories for the first time, and they would now live with it, as we do, every day.

God asked Adam and Eve, 'Who told you that you were naked?' This question is key to facing and fighting fear. Many of the things causing us to fear come from *somewhere*, a source other than ourselves or our heavenly Father. It can be social media, magazines, friends, teachers or even family. It is important for us to identify where our fears are coming from. Which negative voices have spoken into our lives? What lies might be leading us further into fear?

My wife Charlie and I often take breaks from using social media, and we choose to spend the most time with people who build us up, because we are aware of the power of negative words on our lives. We would love to be bullet-proof, but we are human, and so identifying the lies that can be believed through words spoken and deciding where to invest time and friendship are healthy things to do.

What lies have resulted in you living in fear? Where are they from? If the source is not godly or trustworthy, then maybe it's time to detox that voice and listen to what God has to say instead!

DB

5. A NEW DAY HAS DAWNED

Therefore, if anyone is in Christ, the new creation has come: the old has gone, the new is here! **2 Corinthians 5:17**

Prayer is one of the most important tools we have to ground ourselves in God. Throughout these devotionals there will be psalms and scriptures for us to meditate on, but true-life transformation is not attained by simply reading words and hoping for the best. We must also create time and space to come face to face with our maker.

Take the passage above, for example; it's one thing to read it, but quite another to spend time asking God to help us grasp the truth of these words and what they mean for our lives. A new day has truly dawned for all those who are in Christ. When we spend time reflecting on that promise, when we allow those words to be the anchor of our prayer to God, it can transform our lives. Speaking it over ourselves daily, reminding ourselves of who God says we are, a new creation with an endless horizon ahead of us, can begin to quiet the voices of doubt in our minds that tell us otherwise.

When you read these reflections, there may be a word, an idea, a verse or a theme that jumps out to you. I urge you to capture that moment, to still yourself, to bring it before God in a quiet place and to pray it over yourself. Day by day you will begin to build the courage to live your life the way God designed you to.

RN

6. QUIET VOICE OF THE SPIRIT

The world cannot accept him, because it neither sees him nor knows him. But you know him, for he lives with you and will be in you. I will not leave you as orphans; I will come to you. **John 14:17-18**

This is not a book of answers. We write as those bound by our contexts and our human understanding. We can't tell you where the Spirit of God will take you tomorrow (if we could, perhaps our own lives wouldn't be filled with their own questions, disappointments and wonders!). The one thing we can tell you is that the Spirit only ever brings us closer to God.

The Holy Spirit is intertwined within the Trinity. Just as Jesus could only speak words and do acts that he saw the Father doing (John 5:19), the Spirit can only blow and move in the direction of sacrificial love.

The Spirit leads us towards unmerited favour, grace and peace. Now that doesn't mean that the sun will always be shining – literally and metaphorically – but Jesus says that the Spirit 'remains with you *continually* and will be in you' (John 14:17 AMP).

The very truth of the universe is buried within your rib cage, flowing through your veins, coursing through your imagination and staring right back at you in the mirror. When was the last time you quieted the noise in your mind to allow the smallest voice within you to rise up and remind you that you carry that Spirit?

RN

7. *SELAH* – BE STILL AND KNOW

Today, create some space to be still and focus on God at the start of this year.

Let's write down some of our hopes and desires for the year and thank God for new opportunities in him! Let's also write down any fears we may have. What is that fear telling us about ourselves? I'm not good enough, I'm alone, I'm a failure...?

Now consider the fact that you are a new creation in Christ Jesus. The past is the past and our future is secure. What does a future with less fear look like for you and me?

Give your hopes and fears to God and ask him to speak into them over this next year, that you might be transformed by his truth and love. You may want to pray the following prayer:

Jesus, at the start of this new year, I give you my hopes and dreams, my challenges and fears. Please help me in my journey of facing my fears to confront them with your truth and love for me. As I draw closer to you, transform me into your likeness, for your glory. Amen.

8. LEAVING THE PAST BEHIND

*Brothers and sisters, I do not consider myself yet to have taken hold of it.
But one thing I do: forgetting what is behind and straining towards what is
ahead, I press on towards the goal to win the prize for which God has called me
heavenwards in Christ Jesus.* **Philippians 3:13-14**

We often need to draw a line under what has gone before in order to move
forward. Otherwise we can idolise the way things have been, so much so that
we become paralysed in our present.

This is not to render the past irrelevant – we are thankful for the trials,
triumphs and trophies that have led us to this moment right now – but fear
can make us think that the golden days have been and gone. We cling to the
glimmering nostalgia because the future looks uncertain, dark and scary.

The unknown can be so intimidating that instead we remain on the island
we have become too familiar with. That island, which perceivably keeps us
safe from danger, is stifling the growth that is necessary for us to reach our
God-given potential and find the peace we so desperately long for.

We are promised that the future ahead is brighter than we could ever imagine.
Through our lives, through the seasons of unknowing, through the doubt and
uncertainty, God is pulling us towards the next chapter. Do we dare risk leaving
our places of comfort and trusting God as we swim out into the ocean of
possibilities and opportunities?

RN

9. COURAGE REQUIRED – COURAGE ACQUIRED

He said to them: 'It is not for you to know the times or dates the Father has set by his own authority. But you will receive power when the Holy Spirit comes on you; and you will be my witnesses in Jerusalem, and in all Judea and Samaria, and to the ends of the earth.' **Acts 1:7–8**

When did we last require courage?

If it was ages ago, chances are we're living in our comfort zones! God often leads us out by asking us to do something that relies on his power, strength and the kind of courage that only comes from him. If we have no need to call on God's power, we're probably not dreaming big enough.

I learned to drive at seventeen and it took me six attempts to pass my test! Three-point turns had me stumped (power steering wasn't even a thing back then!). When we live life in our own strength, it's like learning to drive without power steering – clunky, hard and (for some) easy to fail. When we rely on the power of the Holy Spirit, it's like driving through the curves and corners of our lives with power steering, using God's strength, rather than our own, to do what he is calling us to do.

Have we been striving or struggling to live day to day in our own strength? Let's wait on the Holy Spirit and ask for God's strength and power to assist us in all we put our hands to.

DB

10. GO!

The LORD had said to Abram, 'Go from your country, your people and your father's household to the land I will show you.' **Genesis 12:1**

'Go where?' We can imagine Abram asking when God tells him to go. And God's answer? 'Don't worry, I'll show you on the way.' I have quite the nomadic spirit, but even for me, walking blindly into my own future is a terrifying proposition. I'm also a (relatively!) spring chicken, but Abram was seventy-five years old when he set out from Harran, his home town, into the unknown.

By the time God is telling Abram to 'go', he has built a whole life in Harran: family, friends, a career. After seventy-odd years in a space, the roots he had built would have been far reaching, so this 'call' into the unknown would not have been a light one. Abram was leaving behind everything that he had built his life on, that he had grown to love, that he had formed his identity around and rooted his purpose upon. Not to mention that Abram wasn't even given a clear destination by God.

Abram was given a direction without a destination. No Google Maps or Uber, no clear pathway; he was armed with just a promise. Bold. Courageous. Abram might have been seen as a little naive or even reckless by the locals and family members surrounding him. But we would do well to remember that some of what seems wise to the world could be foolishness in the eyes of God, and what might seem absurd to our human comprehension could well be wisdom beyond our understanding.

RN

11. THE COURAGE OF ABRAM

I will make you into a great nation,
and I will bless you;
I will make your name great,
and you will be a blessing. **Genesis 12:2**

Abram's bold decision to surrender his plan in exchange for the adventure
God had planned for him, and to obey God's invitation to a new chapter, had
profound ramifications.

His courage led to God changing his name from 'exalted father' to 'father of
many', and the newly named Abraham is now considered the founding father
of some of the most established religious movements the earth has ever seen,
in Christianity, Islam and Judaism. I'm sure he would never have guessed
that his step of faith would lead to billions of people over thousands of years
stepping into fellowship with the Creator. Like Abram, our private devotion can
have a significant impact on ourselves, others and our environment, but the
first step can be the most difficult.

God will never invite you down a path only to then abandon you. If you feel the
Holy Spirit is taking you in a direction, whether that's a new job, relationship,
friendship or deeper spiritual experience, go. Sometimes we procrastinate,
trying to limit the risk we're taking, but seventy-five-year-old Abram didn't wait
until the fog had cleared, he walked the path presented to him, and by doing
so fathered the whole nation of Israel.

What dream is waiting to be birthed in your life? There is a dream that lies just
the other side of you taking that first step. Go.

RN

12. FEAR OF LOSS

The LORD is close to the broken-hearted
and saves those who are crushed in spirit. **Psalm 34:18**

In 2020, when Covid-19 caused much of the world to lock down, many children's outdoor parks were also closed. Heavy-duty padlocks were brought in to stop the little ones getting in. I am sure that many of you were not affected by this at all, but my son Knox, then two years old, could see the swings and slides and couldn't understand why he couldn't play on them.

Breaking into tears, Knox was experiencing loss. Now, I could have told him about all the other people in the world who were experiencing much greater losses than him during this time – loss of health, loss of livelihoods, even loss of loved ones – but that wouldn't have helped. Loss is personal, and loss hurts, whoever we are and whatever age we are. Often, knowing someone else is facing a much 'greater' loss, doesn't prevent us from feeling ours.

Jesus, today we pray for every reader experiencing loss. May you meet them where they are and give them a peace that outweighs the pain. Give them hope for tomorrow. May they grieve well and heal from the loss and, in time, move forward without the fear of loss. Amen.

DB

13. RESET AND LOOK AHEAD

Let your eyes look straight ahead;
fix your gaze directly before you. **Proverbs 4:25**

I commend any human being who has not already broken their New Year's resolution.

I normally last about twenty-four hours before I slip back into some habit or routine that I was convinced I would eradicate this year. I don't know how many times I've momentarily transformed into a marathon runner or a five-fruit-a-day consumer, only to fall flat on my face one January morning when confronted with Netflix and a packet of Jammie Dodgers.

Into the season of establishing the new, come setbacks. We are going to drop the ball at some point – it happens to us all. Being human means being vulnerable to moments of weakness.

We all know the awkward 'one step forward, two steps back' shuffle. Moments that can throw our momentum off balance. However, in those precious moments, we are confronted with a choice: to throw in the towel or to extend compassion to ourselves and give it another go.

We can choose today to fix our gaze directly before us, extending compassion to our weaknesses but refusing to dwell there. The future we look towards is built on top of those moments of failure and inconsistency. Head high, shoulders back, you got this.

RN

14. *SELAH* - PAUSE AND TAKE STOCK

Today, pause, breathe slowly and take stock.

Do you feel ready to move forward with courage, leaving the past behind? Do you feel hindered by the past, feel you've failed, believe you've let yourself, others or God down? Remember, while you have breath in your lungs and Jesus in your heart, you have opportunity to dust yourself off and try again.

Whether you've failed or fallen once or a hundred times, Jesus' forgiveness covers it all. It's important to receive his full forgiveness by forgiving yourself too, so all weight is lifted off and you're free to be who God made you to be!

Consider the heroes of the faith in the Bible that God called into the unknown who dared to step out one step at a time. Is God calling us forward into the unknown? Ask the Holy Spirit for the right next step, then fix your eyes on Jesus and step out; you may want to say these words as you do:

Thank you, Jesus, that your blood covers every one of my failures and mistakes, and restores me to who you made me to be. Give me courage to step out of my familiar ways to respond to your call on my life. Show me my first step and help me make space for creativity, awe and wonder today. Amen.

15. ANOTHER ONE

Be devoted to one another in love. Honour one another above yourselves.
Romans 12:10

One thing I have learned is that it is very hard to love people we fear.

Often, we try to avoid people who intimidate us, scare us or make us feel small. This is a survival mechanism which humanity has used for centuries. However, there is another way to survive and even to live with those who consistently bring others down: by loving them.

Love is the strongest, most powerful survival mechanism God has given us.

When, with God's help, we love the unlovable, speak well of them, forgive them or even serve them, something supernatural takes place. The love we show them not only has the power to affect and influence them, but it also changes our heart towards them.

They say hurting people hurt people, in an ongoing cycle of pain and rejection. When we respond to others with God's love, we break the cycle and turn the world upside down. How can we show love to someone who intimidates us, to break the cycle of fear and conflict?

DB

16. WHAT IS LOVE?

Love is patient, love is kind. It does not envy, it does not boast, it is not proud. It does not dishonour others, it is not self-seeking, it is not easily angered, it keeps no record of wrongs. Love does not delight in evil but rejoices with the truth. It always protects, always trusts, always hopes, always perseveres.
Love never fails. **1 Corinthians 13:4-8**

What is love? These three simple words might cast your mind to the 1993 classic by Haddaway (unless this comment is just showing my age...). We say we love fried chicken, and we love our best friend. We say we love our partner, and we love chocolate. We use the word so flippantly that it feels like it has lost its power. We say it so often that we're not always sure when it counts.

We see from today's verses - love is patient, love is kind - that love is so much more than a feeling. What's more, this scripture is not just a description of how we are meant to love one another; it's a demonstration of how our heavenly Father loves us.

He is patient with us, he forgives us and his love for us will never fail us. The closer we are to God, the more we understand the power of his love - that it always trusts, always hopes, always perseveres.

Spending time dwelling on this love gives us daily confidence and courage to face whatever battles lie ahead, and also gives us the ability to show love to a hurting world around us.

DB

17. PERFECT LOVE

Perfect love drives out fear. **1 John 4:18**

Have you ever been in love?

At sixteen, I told my first girlfriend over MSN Messenger that I loved her! (For younger readers, MSN was like WhatsApp, but you had to meet on the internet at an agreed time.) I didn't have a personal phone, it was on the family computer, so if I wrote, 'Love you,' and the family saw it, everyone gathered around the computer in banter, which was pretty embarrassing. Looking back, I realise that I didn't even know what love was when I first typed those words. I thought it was a feeling. However, I've come to learn that love is much more powerful than just a feeling.

Perfect love is everything when it comes to fighting fear.

As human beings, we cannot give perfect love to anyone, as we all have imperfections. However, Jesus is perfect, and he showed us perfect, sacrificial, fear-facing love on the cross. It is his love alone that has the power to rid us of fear. Not 'some' or 'occasional' fear, but *all* fear.

Spend some time thinking about God's perfect love for us rather than focusing on the love we desire from others. How might that reshape the things that you are facing today?

DB

18. LEAVING THE 'SAFE HOUSE'

So do not throw away your confidence; it will be richly rewarded.
You need to persevere so that when you have done the will of God, you will
receive what he has promised. **Hebrews 10:35-6**

In times of disorientation, we can retreat to people, personas, patterns or places that make us feel comfortable. For a while, hiding in these comfort zones - our 'safe houses' - can feel amazing! There's nothing terrifying to be experienced because we've already explored all the rooms of the house; we know what is around the corner and who might be dwelling on the stairs. But we were not made to live our lives indoors, trapped in self-made cages hiding from the world.

Retreating in fear rather than running towards sacrificial love can undermine the invitation of transformation offered to every single one of us. We must remain bold and courageous as we walk towards the horizon of heaven, where love awaits, fixing our eyes on God every step of the way.

The same warmth we experienced in the 'safe house' is calling us outside, hoping to encounter us again, helping us through to the other side of the inevitable pain and discomfort of change. Let's rest in the confidence that everything we need to take the next step in the relationship, opportunity or activity we are facing is buried within us; by weathering the storm we will find a way.

RN

19. CLOSE

'Don't be afraid, I've redeemed you.
I've called your name. You're mine.
When you're in over your head, I'll be there with you.
When you're in rough waters, you will not go down.
When you're between a rock and a hard place,
it won't be a dead end -
Because I am GOD, your personal God,' Isaiah 43:1-2 (MSG)

The Bible doesn't say that we won't experience hard times. It is clear that there are rough waters and overwhelming times to go through in our lives here - no matter our background or situation. Throughout history and throughout Scripture, humanity has always had to face difficult times. From war and famine to sickness, pain, suffering and loss, hardship is normal for human beings. It is often in these hard times that we cry out to God as if to say, 'Where are you when I need you?' and feel the weight of his silence. Maybe you're feeling like God is on mute when it comes to what you're facing right now?

In today's verses we read that even though the situation or circumstance we currently face may cause us to feel fearful, God is with us and close to us. As leader and author Christine Caine is quoted as saying, 'Being faithful doesn't mean you are fearless. It just means that your faith is greater than your fear.'

God is with us in this moment and will not leave us to face things alone. Let's pour out our troubles to him and take confidence and courage in the fact that he is with us, right in the midst of what we are facing, whether we feel him with us today or not.

DB

22

20. CLOSER

Come near to God and he will come near to you. **James 4:8**

In today's short quote, James is writing to the church in Jerusalem, encouraging them to spend time with their heavenly Father.

I am the father of two young sons, and I have noticed that there are times when I want to be with them but they don't want to be with me! The other day my eldest hit his baby brother. I addressed his behaviour and made him apologise for what he had done. Afterwards, I said, 'Let's carry on playing,' but he hid behind the door, not wanting to play with me. When I asked why, he said it was because I had told him off. I proceeded to assure him that just because I'd told him that hitting wasn't acceptable, it didn't mean I didn't love him or want to be with him. I said that I'd told him off to help him, not hurt him – like any good father, I want him to learn right from wrong. I went to hug him and said there was nothing he could do that would ever stop me wanting to be with him. I realised in that moment that his guilt was stopping him wanting to be near me.

Perhaps our guilt stops us drawing close to our heavenly Father?

Know today that there is nothing we can ever do, say or think – past, present or future – that will stop our heavenly Father loving us and wanting to be with us.

DB

23

21. *SELAH* – COME NEAR TO GOD

Pause and come near to God, and he will come near to you! There is no barrier between you since Jesus covered all your failings and gave you his righteousness when he died on the cross for you.

Focus on his unconditional, unpunishing love for you. Ask him what he loves about you, and note down what you first think, see, feel or hear! Thank him for your unique attributes!

Think of someone you know who needs to know God's unconditional love today. Ask God what he loves about them and write down what you receive. Think of some creative way of letting them know or showing them, and pray that God would use that to draw close to them.

Jesus, thank you that when I draw close to you, you always draw close to me. Thank you for your unconditional love and acceptance and for the unique things you've created in me [list them out]. Help me use these gifts to show others, particularly [write or say their name], your love. Amen.

22. BOUNCEBACKABILITY

Give careful thought to the paths for your feet
and be steadfast in all your ways. **Proverbs 4:26**

For those who are not avid fans of football, I warn you, there will be one or more sporting metaphors on this page (I apologise for nothing!).

The term 'bouncebackability' was made famous by Iain Dowie, former Crystal Palace Football Club manager (who seemed to have made it up on the spot). This word beautifully describes the mentality we need to adopt when faced with a momentum-breaking experience, such as a phone call from a loved one sharing news that breaks us in two, or exam results that firmly shut the door to the progression we've been dreaming of. Bouncebackability is the ability to bounce back after a defeat, after things don't go to plan; it is the capacity to be flexible and to find another solution. The spirit of perseverance, especially early on, in navigating the fragility of a new pattern.

After an early fumble, we have the propensity to spiral into apathy or even shame for failing ourselves and God. That shame and guilt, frustration and disappointment can derail us and leave us feeling that the goals or transformation we desire are beyond us, and we'd be better off throwing our new pattern in the bin. As difficult as it may seem, the challenge is to lift our head up and go again. Reset our alarm, delete their number, stretch out of our comfort zone, do whatever it takes; the best place to begin again is where we find ourselves right now.

RN

23. AS BOLD AS A LION

The wicked flee though no one pursues,
but the righteous are as bold as a lion. **Proverbs 28:1**

When we take a leap of faith and jump into the vast ocean of opportunity, our first instinct when the seas get rough, or doubt begins to creep in, is to swim back to the boat we just jumped from. To retreat to the old places or people or things that once provided us comfort and stability. But the truth is, the 'yesterday' we so deeply desired, the golden years of old, the boat that we just left, no longer exists. That ship has sailed. The present is the only thing in our hands. The only way to achieve a new order, to reach a new 'promised land' and achieve something that we haven't been able to achieve before, is by doing something we have never done before.

The stability we seek is not in the past but can be found in the place where we presently float. The peace we seek can be embraced if we choose to swim through the waves and boldly navigate the current disorder we're experiencing.

Boldness is defined as willingness to take risks and exercise innovation. The 'new thing' we are hoping for often calls for us to use new tools to experience it. We may need to awaken parts of ourselves that we have left dormant for years, traits that we dismissed, gifts we've overlooked, courage we didn't think was ours. Boldness, my friend, is part of your DNA. You may just need to awaken the inner lion that's been sleeping for a bit too long.

RN

24. NOTHING IS WASTED

For we know in part and we prophesy in part, but when completeness comes, what is in part disappears. **1 Corinthians 13:9-10**

At the dawn of a new chapter, we can be tempted to look back and think, what was the point?

In hindsight, we can perceive the relationship struggles we've endured, the failed businesses, the unfulfilled dreams or time spent in wilderness seasons, as wasted time. We can fear that we now carry too much baggage to be free to forge a new path or have too many skeletons in our closet to start anew. The truth is, nothing is wasted with God.

Every moment of our past - the dead-end roads, the rejections and the triumphs - have led us to where we are now, and everything, no matter how destructive or painful, can lead us deeper into God's perfect plan for us and all creation.

What I've found, during the short stay I've had on this planet so far, is that time and healing have given me perspective and allowed me to be thankful for the things that broke me. That's because on the other side of that breaking was new life, transformation, the birth of a deeper understanding of love and of sacrifice, and inevitably joy. Right now, trapped in time and space, in your room, on the train, you can't see where this moment or journey is going, but trust that God is leading you there.

Everything can be redeemed, and nothing is wasted.

RN

25. GOD IS OUR REDEEMER

And we know that in all things God works for the good of those who love him,
who have been called according to his purpose. **Romans 8:28**

A 'redeemer' can be defined as someone who repays, recovers, saves or
exchanges something for something else.

God, the originator of sacrificial love, the author of the universe and the
mystery behind creation, is our redeemer. Essentially, this means that God has
the power to bring the gold out of the very things that we perceive as rubbish.
Whether it be moments, events or even our own perspective of ourselves, we
can believe things are too far gone, are not worth saving or are too damaged
to be repaired. But where we see an expiration date, God sees a birthday. The
depth of darkness is the perfect environment for the miraculous to happen,
even if that same space feels like a void to us.

The apostle Paul says in the letter to the church in Rome that 'in all things
God works for the good of those who love him'. Everything. Not just in the
areas, moments or people we believe to be good, but in everything we have
experienced. It's important to note that not all things that happen to us are
good or are necessarily God's plan or purpose for our lives; some things that
have happened to us may have been positively evil. However, once those
things have happened, the Divine Alchemist invites us to bring our fear and
anxieties and to walk with him day by day on a transformational journey. He is
able to turn our pain into peace; we just have to trust the process.

RN

26. WE WILL NEVER KNOW EVERYTHING, AND THAT'S OK

And I will ask the Father, and he will give you another advocate to help you and be with you for ever. **John 14:16**

Venturing into uncharted territory is a daunting task; it takes courage to step out in faith. The alarm bells begin to ring and the questions start flying out of our subconscious with force. *Is this the wrong move? Is this another dead end? How do I know I'm on the right path?*

Not to put a dent in your ego, but you will never truly know. It's extremely rare in life that all the facts, hurdles and potholes are laid out before us. Inherent in life is 'not knowing', but instead of procrastinating while trying to gain a 360-degree clarity that is unachievable, we must embrace the fact that we see only a part of the puzzle. But our God, who sees all, knows all and created all, has not left us here in time and space to flail in mystery alone.

Jesus talks in John 14:16 about 'another advocate', the Holy Spirit, who has been given to us like a spiritual compass to guide our steps and beckon us deeper into our destiny. The questions may never all be answered, but we can move in uncertainty with peace. Unlocking this level of trust requires us to be sensitive, to still ourselves and to listen to the One Who Knows All.

RN

27. FOLLOWING THE WIND

The wind blows wherever it pleases. You hear its sound, but you cannot tell where it comes from or where it is going. So it is with everyone born of the Spirit. **John 3:8**

Following the wind requires us to be present – and I'm not just talking about being somewhere physically but about being in a state of hyper-awareness of the infinite nature of *now*. To truly and humbly behold the moment that we sit in, not to be lost in our thoughts nor occupied with the image of ourselves that we are trying to project, or slaves to the shame placed on our shoulders.

To be present is to quiet ourselves to the point of stillness, so we can notice the subtle shifts as the Holy Spirit works within us. Jesus Christ, speaking to the inquisitive Nicodemus, likens the Spirit of God to the wind. We are invited to become 'wind whisperers', to train ourselves in stillness and openness and to surrender to the Spirit of God, the Divine Wind, to take our part in this mystical dance that has been moving for billions of years.

The Holy Spirit is the creative force behind the universe. Just as the Spirit knows every hair on our head intimately and every blade of grass in Hyde Park personally, he also knows the path that will lead to our deepest dreams and desires. So we can follow this Spirit boldly, knowing our steps are guided by someone who truly wants the best for us and loves us more than we love ourselves.

RN

28. *SELAH* – FEEL THE SPIRIT

When the Holy Spirit first filled the disciples, they were on fire with boldness (Acts 2)! He led them into the streets to share the goodness of God with others.

How bold would you say you are? If you need more courage and boldness, you can ask the Holy Spirit to keep filling you!

If God works all things for good for those who love him, those who are called to his purposes, we can proceed full of Holy Spirit courage, boldness and expectation, trusting that all will be well. What next step is the Holy Spirit guiding us to take? Can you spend time waiting on the Spirit today?

Jesus, thank you for asking the Father to send the Holy Spirit to teach, counsel, guide and fill me with your presence. Thank you for the gifts released to me, and through me, to others. Let the fire of the Holy Spirit burn in me, making me courageous and expectant whenever I share your love and the good news of Jesus. May I boldly go where you are calling me to go. Amen.

29. FEAR OF OTHER PEOPLE

'So do not be afraid, Jacob my servant;
do not be dismayed, Israel,'
declares the LORD.
'I will surely save you out of a distant place...
Jacob will again have peace and security,
and no one will make him afraid.' **Jeremiah 30:10**

Jeremiah was a prophet who heard the word of God and gave the message to others. In this message we see God's heart for his people, and it's still his heart for us today. Fear not, and don't be dismayed, whatever the situation.

God says, 'No one will make him afraid.' I love that! In my own life it's been more like 'many' have made me afraid. This has led to unhealthy behaviours, like people-pleasing and avoiding situations that I know will be awkward, painful or potentially uncomfortable for me and others. Here, there is a call to lose the fear of other people, to live each day unintimidated or unafraid of those around us.

This is a journey, not a strapline. It takes time, but throughout this year, as we keep drawing close to our heavenly Father, the fear of others will shrink.

Who or what is intimidating us or making us afraid? Where do we feel fear – work, home, school, university? God wants us to be free to live unafraid, and, as we grow in God's protective love and power, the power other people have over us will diminish, and we can begin to live life to the full.

DB

30. FEAR OF GOD

The fear of the Lord is the beginning of wisdom,
and knowledge of the Holy One is understanding. **Proverbs 9:10**

What do we think of when we hear the word 'fear'? What images come
to mind?

It might remind us of an event in our past, or a challenge we are facing. It may
make us feel helpless and vulnerable, or throw us off guard in some way. The
word 'fear' usually reminds us of negative things, our deepest worries and the
things we are most afraid of. It may surprise us, however, that there is one
unique instance where the word 'fear' is actually overwhelmingly positive. I'm
talking about the 'fear of God'.

Today we read that the fear of God is the beginning of wisdom. As we begin to
understand what fearing God means, we become wiser! In this context, 'fear'
means 'great reverence' for God. Fear of God does not mean being petrified,
but rather being in awe of his goodness and greatness.

The more we understand how mighty and powerful God is, the less we fear
others. Fear of God is the antidote to the fear of other people. It is the
ability to see and appreciate God as he really is - full of truth, love, wisdom,
power, justice, mercy, grace, forgiveness, patience, holiness, righteousness,
omnipotence, omniscience, omnipresence and immutability, to name but a few!

Let's ask God to increase our knowledge and positive fear of him so we lose the
fear of people.

DB

31. 365/360 REFLECTION

In this first month of the year we have reminded ourselves that we are unconditionally loved and accepted by God, and uniquely gifted by him to step out into new opportunities this year.

Our past is fully forgiven, and the future awaits us as we step forward in the power of the Holy Spirit.

Are we assured of our position in God through Jesus, and ready for our next steps?

We don't forge ahead alone, but in the power and love of God. With every step we decrease in fear and increase in faith in the One who cheers us on.

As this month draws to a close, set aside an amount of time and sit in silence, simply listening to God, asking him to search you wholly and to bring to light any areas of your mind, body or soul that he wants to restore or transform anew.

FEBRUARY

1. OUR FATHER
Our Father in heaven. **Matthew 6:9**

When I first became a dad, something in me changed. I found myself connected to this little baby, and ever since my son was born I've always wanted to be with him. I've always wanted to spend time with him, regardless of what he does or doesn't do (and trust me, some days his character is more aligned with the Avenger Hulk than Jesus...).

This realisation helped me begin to understand just how much more my heavenly Father wants to be close with me, regardless of how good or bad I may have been. My son relies on me and is confident in my love, care and protection. He's not afraid when he is with me.

Jesus taught us to pray to our Father in heaven, using the Aramaic *Abba* for 'father'. This word, unrelated to the 1980s Swedish pop band, means close, relational and intimate father. The word is still used today by some communities to mean 'close and present daddy'. Sometimes we don't understand our heavenly Father's love and desire for us; we can think him distant and remote. We think we have to be good for him to draw close.

Know today that the Father wants to draw near to you and longs for you to draw close to him in return. Know, too, that in his care we will increasingly fear less as we live our lives in light of who God says we are, and not just what we think of ourselves.

DB

2. MAY YOUR NAME BE HONOURED

May your name be honoured. **Matthew 6:9 (NIRV)**

Older translations of the Lord's Prayer say, 'Hallowed be thy name,' meaning, 'Holy is your name; honour and glory to your name.' Jesus shows us that when we pray, we ought to start by drawing close to our heavenly Father and giving him praise, not a shopping list of needs!

In instructing us to say these words, Jesus shows us that worship is an important and powerful part of prayer. To worship means to give someone or something adoration and devotion. All humans worship something or someone, whether Christian or not. Sometimes we worship people, possessions, fame and fortune, our partner or our parents. This causes a problem, because God did not create us to worship people or things. He created us to worship the One who made and loves us – himself!

When we worship anyone or anything other than Jesus, that person or thing can take from us, deplete us and even have the potential to destroy us. When we worship Jesus, he builds us up, restores us and empowers us. We become like the things we worship, and when we worship God at the start of our prayer times, it gives us a clear perspective on his magnitude and greatness; it also makes us more like Jesus, and more able to face and conquer our fears.

DB

3. GOD'S KINGDOM COME

Your kingdom come,
your will be done,
on earth as it is in heaven. **Matthew 6:10**

In the next lines of the Lord's Prayer, we are encouraged to pray for God's kingdom to come here on earth as it is in heaven. And for us to pray this prayer authentically and faithfully, we need to know what heaven is like.

Heaven is perfection. There is no war, no hatred, no tears, no famine, no poverty, no sickness, no pain and no disease. There is no racism, no terrorism and no narcissism, where people focus only on self. There are no eating disorders, mental health problems or suicidal thoughts.

When Jesus was on earth, he went about his days not fearing the problems in culture, but instead bringing touches of heaven to earth, boldly and confidently stepping into earthly situations and lives, bringing transformation and restoration.

In the same way, if we, or someone else, are experiencing something that would not exist in heaven, we can boldly pray for God's kingdom to come on earth, in our sphere of influence, in our situation or in our circumstance. Today, let us surrender our fears to God and ask for his kingdom to come and bring change for his glory.

DB

4. DAILY BREAD

Give us today our daily bread. **Matthew 6:11**

The Lord's Prayer is not a formula, but rather a framework within which we talk to our heavenly Father in a real, raw and authentic way - not out of worn-out religious or weary duty.

Up until now the focus of this age-old prayer has been on God - who he is, what he is like - lifting our eyes, changing our perspective. Now the prayer shifts more to our needs and shows us that it's OK to pray for 'daily bread' - in other words, for God's provision.

So often our greatest fears surround provision; we fear lack. God promises to look after our needs because he loves us. Just a gentle reminder: it refers to our needs, not our greeds! I love my children and give them what they need to thrive. I also give them gifts as blessings so they can learn to be generous to others. I don't answer their every request for chocolate, cake, ice cream or toys because I am their loving dad who cares about their physical and emotional health, not just their wealth. In the same way, our heavenly Father will give us all we need.

Think about your present needs, or the needs of others you know; give them to our Father and ask for his provision for these people or circumstances today.

DB

5. THE F WORD

Forgive us our sins,
as we have forgiven those who sin against us. **Matthew 6:12 (NLT)**

In the next line of the Lord's Prayer, Jesus throws a spanner in the works!

Jesus moves on to say that as part of our regular prayer times, we should also bring our selfishness, wrongs and failings to God. As we receive his grace, love and mercy, we too can dish it out to the people who have hurt us. This means that forgiving ourselves, and others who have wronged us, should be part of our regular lives of prayer.

Forgiving others does not mean that they deserve it, any more than we deserve the love and grace we receive from God! Forgiveness is about freedom from bitterness, anger, rage, hatred and fear.

Forgiveness is about our hearts being healthy and our lives being Christlike. It's about handing the ones who cause us pain to God, and trusting him to deal with them as he chooses.

Nelson Mandela, the late former prime minister of South Africa, was wrongly put in prison for standing up against injustice. After he was released from prison, he said that if he hadn't forgiven the people who put him there, he would find himself in another prison. Who do we need to give to God in forgiveness today?

DB

6. DELIVERY

Lead us not into temptation,
but deliver us from the evil one. **Matthew 6:13**

There is an enemy trying to pull us down to his level; his level of hating, cheating, instilling fear and lying. Often, it's his lies that cause the fears we carry. His temptations try to draw us away from God, hoping we will hurt ourselves or others, causing guilt, shame and regret. Guilt is felt when we know we've messed up. Shame is felt when we think we are a mess-up. Jesus tells us to pray to be protected from temptations and from the one who brings them. God never lets us experience any temptation that we cannot overcome with his help. So we pray, 'Deliver us from the evil one.'

To 'deliver' means to take something from one place to another, like a postman delivering mail, or it can mean to come through on hopes and expectations, like a doctor delivering a baby or a football striker scoring a penalty. God is the ultimate deliverer. He takes our shame and guilt and gets rid of it by putting it on Jesus on the cross and replacing it with grace and mercy. He comes through for us, having already defeated the enemy; there is no evil he cannot overcome.

Let's be honest and open with our Father about our temptations, so he can deliver us, for our good and for his glory.

DB

7. *SELAH* – THE LORD'S PRAYER

Pause and contemplate how the prayer Jesus gave us covers all bases. It stresses our position as adopted sons and daughters of our heavenly Father, who has the whole world in his hands and whose powerful kingdom is advancing on the earth! It covers our basic need for provision and protection, reminding us that we are forgiven and delivered from the enemy's power.

How can you incorporate this prayer into your daily life? Maybe you could consider setting an alarm to remind you to pray regularly through the Lord's Prayer in the middle of the day. Or add it to your diary so it is as visible and noticeable as all your other meetings and appointments!

Spend some time meditating over the Lord's Prayer today and asking God to reveal more of himself and his will for you as you do.

Jesus, thank you for this wonderful prayer that reminds me who you are, and who I am because of you! It reminds me I am deeply cared for by you. You will meet my every need and I am secure in you. Thank you that it reminds me I'm a child in your kingdom, which has conquered the kingdom of evil. Help me advance your kingdom every day. Amen.

8. THERE IS NO FEAR IN LOVE

There is no fear in love. Instead, perfect love drives away fear. **1 John 4:18**

I went on a safari with the family when I was ten. After Disney's *The Lion King*, my youngest brother was fixated with lions. As we drove past the other animals all he talked about was lions - their teeth, their claws and how they had taken human lives.

When we finally drove though the lions' section, I decided to make it more exciting. I lowered his window a little - not enough to let a lion in, but enough to scare the life out of him. He let out the loudest scream and leapt into the arms of my stepdad, the strongest and biggest human in the car.

This to me is a perfect picture of faith. We will always have fears to face, but we can have faith in the strongest, most trusted Father to save us - our Father in heaven.

Faith is running into the arms of our heavenly Father right in the middle of the storm. When we face fears, do we rely on our Father or seek the solution ourselves? An experience of God's presence can eradicate a lifetime's fears because God is perfect love; it's who he is. Faith is realising that it is better to be in the storm with Jesus than on the shore without him.

DB

9. BREATHING DEEPLY IN THE FACE OF THE FLOOD

But I have calmed and quietened myself,
I am like a weaned child with its mother;
like a weaned child I am content. **Psalm 131:2**

When we are faced with chaos and our brain's defence system is on red alert, our normal processes can shut down. Our lives can feel like standing at the foot of a sharp cliff that we are being forced to climb without a harness. Or staring at an oncoming tidal wave rising in the distance, and we know that, whether we like it or not, we're about to be swept off our feet. These intense situations, events or feelings can be completely paralysing and isolating.

And yet, sometimes we don't feel isolated; we feel *surrounded*.

The sheer volume of advice or opinions about what to do next can add even more panic to the situations we face. *Which is the right step? Is there a one-size-fits-all answer to every situation?* Sometimes even Scripture seems to add to the dilemma: one verse says run, another says attack, and the message we just listened to says don't move an inch!

Sometimes there is simply too much noise. In the midst of the frenzy, when you feel frozen in the face of difficult circumstances, choose to quiet your soul by taking five deep breaths to centre yourself. Present yourself to God, like a child to its mother, without agenda, and breathe deeply in him.

RN

10. COURAGE THAT COUNTS

Have I not commanded you? Be strong and courageous. Do not be afraid; do not be discouraged, for the Lᴏʀᴅ your God will be with you wherever you go.
Joshua 1:9

Have you ever walked down a street late at night with little streetlighting and people lurking in the distance? The fear we feel in such a circumstance can cause us to change direction. We can be tempted to go back the way we came or to take another, safer route.

This is the power of fear; it reroutes us like a satnav changing our direction. In this case, fear may have worked as a survival mechanism, saving us from danger. But in our walk with God, the enemy uses fear to disorientate and derail us, to stop us going where God asks us to go or reaching those he wants us to reach with his love, goodness and mercy.

Joshua had been given the role of leading God's people after Moses. They were big shoes to fill, so understandably Joshua felt afraid. God commanded Joshua to be strong and courageous. It wasn't a recommendation or an optional extra; it was an *order*.

The focus for us today, as it was for Joshua, is that God says he will be with us wherever we go. As he was with Joshua, Almighty God is with you to encourage and strengthen you today.

DB

11. ONE SIZE DOES NOT FIT ALL

Israel, put your hope in the Lord
both now and for evermore. **Psalm 131:3**

As children before God, by looking up to our Maker, who birthed us into this wonderful reality, we can still our hearts and sift through the noise in our minds.

Sometimes the noise isn't within us but in our surroundings. There are so many thoughts, explanations, self-help experts, but there is rarely one right action for every situation we encounter.

Life is too nuanced to have a simple answer for every situation.

The wisdom required in the spectrum of circumstances we face in life can seem extremely contradictory; one day the antidote to vanquishing our fears will be to be brave, take a risk and go for it. Other days the wisest course of action may be to sit in silence and self-reflect. Our job is to create enough space in our busy lives to know what our heavenly Father is asking of us.

To see the range of colours in the skyline, sometimes we need to drive slowly, and it is the same with learning to discern what God is asking of us. With the Bible as your guide, can you make time to sit in contemplative silence at some point today?

RN

12. WHAT HAPPENS NOW?

He has also set eternity in the human heart. **Ecclesiastes 3:11**

I remember during my last week of university being on a beach in Cornwall, asking those 'What happens now?' questions as I looked towards my future. We've all been there in some capacity, faced with the end of something that grounded us and gave us a sense of purpose.

Looking upwards, I was greeted by a clear night sky, free from the light pollution of London, free from the relentless noises of the hustle and from everyday distractions, car alarms and sirens.

The more I surrendered my attention to the sky, the more I was rewarded with stars and satellites emerging one by one as I reflected in gratitude, and I was able to set aside the chaos of my own thoughts. I set myself among the rest of creation, and in that moment I was reminded of the size of my doubt against the scale of the universe. As insignificant as I am among the rest of the universe, the paradox remains that I am infinitely loved by God.

The Author of my destiny has not forgotten what he promised, so I too should hold on to the hope that what is ahead is in the hands of the One who sculpted the universe. Incredibly, the limitless potential that created all things is sitting within me too.

RN

13. THE LORD IS OUR STRENGTH

For the LORD *your God is the one who goes with you to fight for you against your enemies to give you victory.* **Deuteronomy 20:4**

Lord, you give me the strength to hold this, and to know that I am not alone. That is often my prayer in my day-to-day life when I feel overwhelmed, when I feel like my arms are being stretched so far apart because I'm holding on to two ideas that are running in opposite directions.

Whether you're praying to the God who heals but you're still waking up in pain every day, or you're rooted in a community that has always been a sanctuary for you but is now causing you heartache and you don't know what to do next, it's not easy to hold life's tensions. The good news is, we do not have to hold them alone.

Even in the midst of the tension, God is the one who goes with you. He fights for you; he can bear the weight. Today, find some time to sit with the following prayer:

Lord, thank you that you give me the strength to hold this. I am not alone; you are the God who stands with me and helps me to fight my enemies. Protect my peace and bring me to victory. Amen.

RN

14. *SELAH* – GOD, MY PROTECTOR

Pause and think about how God fights for you and protects you. He does not sleep, get weary or throw in the towel when it comes to you! Consider times you know God fought for you and write them down. If you can't remember, just ask him to reveal these to you now.

God knows you. He knows you deeply – your thoughts, actions, fears, hurts, joys. He knows you better than you know yourself, and he knows your potential to do mighty things for him. Your Father is with you now and knows what you need. Do you need comfort, inspiration, healing, encouragement? He knows!

Father, thank you that you fight for me, even at times when I'm unaware I'm in danger! Thank you for always having me in your thoughts and never giving up on me. I lay before you my anxious thoughts and my insecurities. Will you take them and give me instead your encouragement, wisdom, strength and power? I love you and I'm so thankful you love me! Amen.

15. SLEEPING IN THE STORM

Let us then approach God's throne of grace with confidence, so that we may receive mercy and find grace to help us in our time of need. **Hebrews 4:16**

A paradox is a seemingly absurd or contradictory proposition which when investigated may prove to be true – and the Bible is *full* of them. Though we've established that fear cannot be eradicated from the full spectrum of human emotions, throughout Scripture we are constantly being invited not to fear. From the command to cast our cares on Jesus (1 Peter 5:7) to being told to not worry about tomorrow (Matthew 6:34), the Bible frequently assures us that God has it all sorted ahead of time. Fear is an inevitable human experience, but God has not given us a spirit of fear (2 Timothy 1:7)... and therein lies the paradox.

We must grow to live within that tension. Jesus fell asleep in the middle of a storm, exhibiting an inner stillness in the abundance of movement, displaying peace in the midst of chaos. I often ask myself, 'If this situation doesn't change, how can I find peace in it?' If Christ can find *shalom* in storms, then we can too.

Fear is not an enemy that needs to be beheaded, a part of our existence that needs to be lobotomised. Joy comes by embracing the darkness that we too often fear God is absent from, yet this 'darkness' is often where God does his best work.

RN

16. BECOME A FOOL

Do not deceive yourselves. If any of you think you are wise by the standards of this age, you should become 'fools' so that you may become wise.
1 Corinthians 3:18

In today's reflection we are seemingly faced with another paradox. The apostle Paul, in his letter to the church in Corinth, is saying that if we want to be wise, we must first become fools. Wait. What?

At first, I was scrambling to my study books, thinking that perhaps the word 'fool' held different connotations in Paul's time. Alas, it meant exactly the same! The Greek word here for 'fool' is *mōrós*; it's where the word 'moron' comes from. This seems to be the worst advice you could give to someone before a job interview. *Don't worry mate, just act moronic, you'll nail it!* But Paul and the other biblical authors are constantly inviting us to use a framework for living that is by and large not accepted as 'wise' by the cultural norms of their day – or indeed, ours!

Today, begin the ascent into wisdom by accepting foolishness as your starting point. The beginning of knowledge and wisdom is to humbly accept that you know very little and still have a lot to learn.

RN

17. IMPOSTER SYNDROME

But he said to me, 'My grace is sufficient for you, for my power is made perfect in weakness.' Therefore I will boast all the more gladly about my weaknesses, so that Christ's power may rest on me. That is why, for Christ's sake, I delight in weaknesses, in insults, in hardships, in persecutions, in difficulties. For when I am weak, then I am strong. **2 Corinthians 12:9-10**

I worked as a youth leader in Canterbury at the age of twenty-one. I remember feeling high levels of imposter syndrome – I felt like I didn't belong, that I didn't deserve to be there at all. I'm not sure if you've ever felt this way.

I remember thinking that the leaders were all so well educated and intellectual. They were Bible scholars, and when talking theology with them, I felt out of my depth, on edge, fearful and, well, pretty dumb. But looking back on those uncomfortable moments, I realise they were instrumental in my journey. Those wise leaders encouraged me to press in to understanding the Bible in its context. If it weren't for them, I would not enjoy preaching and teaching as much as I do now. My confidence came from pushing through the discomfort of having imposter syndrome and into God's word, and – importantly – who he says I am.

All the way through the Bible, God calls people who don't believe they are up to the task; they have imposter syndrome too! Over the last fifteen years, every time I have stepped into a new role, I have felt imposter syndrome, but I didn't need to fear. God put me there, and if I am to see fruit in any new situation, I have to press into him and trust his power to be made perfect in my weakness!

Is there somewhere you are feeling imposter syndrome today? Can you bring it before God and ask him to reveal why he has put you in that situation?

DB

18. FLIP THE SCRIPT!

The fear of the Lord is the beginning of wisdom,
and knowledge of the Holy One is understanding. **Proverbs 9:10**

As we have seen, in the upside-down kingdom of Jesus Christ, our journey into wisdom begins with foolishness. Yet it's one thing to be a fool in private, quite another to be seen as a fool for Jesus! No one wants to put 'aspiring moron' on their CV or update their Instagram bio with 'voluntary fool'. If we're really honest, the image that we show to the world is far too important to us.

Today's reflection reminds us that we should not be lulled into the false wisdom we see all around us, the portrayal of power and success that is actually rooted in fear, greed and self-preservation.

True wisdom is rooted in knowledge of the Holy One. He might ask us to do things that may look foolish to those around us: to give to those who cannot return the favour, to lead by following, to love those who hate us.

If you find yourself at a point where the framework you've been using to navigate life is not bearing the fruit of inner peace, then maybe it's time to ask God to help you flip the script?

RN

19. THE POWER OF SELF-TALK

The tongue has the power of life and death,
and those who love it will eat its fruit. **Proverbs 18:21**

As a storyteller at heart, I love a metaphor. My brain makes sense of complexities by dragging ideas into storylines and putting thoughts into miniature narratives. As much as I may like casting myself in the starring role of my own life, I know I am not the director. Our decisions matter, but ultimately God's decisions matter infinitely more. And yet, we do daily get to choose our script.

Our words are the scripts for our lives. Our self-talk can be a feedback loop of destruction or of freedom. I'm so often guilty of descending into the depths of despair on a bus journey because I've let a negative thought run loose and spiral out of control.

The daily choices we make, the words we speak over ourselves and others and those mundane moments we deem to be insignificant actually have infinite weight and impact. They can transform our lives as words and thoughts shape our realities into horror movies or love stories.

We must take charge and acknowledge the power in our words. We can be careful to monitor what we utter with our mouths and, in doing so, begin to direct the desires of our hearts.

RN

20. GOD'S PLAN IS NEVER ON HOLD

But the plans of the LORD stand firm for ever,
the purposes of his heart through all generations. **Psalm 33:11**

Though our own plans play a big part in the trajectory our lives take, ultimately the responsibility for holding the whole universe together does not fall into our hands. Thank the heavens! We do not have to be indestructible, perfectly articulate, infallible creatures. God is the one who stands firm, and he has been standing firm since way before time even began.

As participants in the unfolding of God's purposes, this tapestry is being rolled out in real time.

There is space for us to get it wrong. Where we are fragile, God is firm. Where we fall short, God is faithful. God doesn't cancel plans, for he knows what will come to pass ahead of time. God is not shocked or shaken. God's firmness, and the assurance of his plans of love to be established, should free us to authentically and boldly walk our lives.

It takes time to learn how to trust in God's character, and this trust can only be built through experience, through the discipline of dying daily to our own obsessive, controlling thoughts, and by falling into his arms. To paraphrase a famous song lyric, he holds the whole world in the palm of his hand. He has plenty of room to carry you.

RN

21. *SELAH* – RESET THE SELF-TALK

What has your self-talk been like this week? Rooted in how God sees you (as in his word), or rooted in the words of the world or in our insecurities?

Who we are is who God says we are, because he is Truth! Who the world says we are, or what our insecurities tell us, may be very different!

If God has called or placed you somewhere, you can never be an imposter, so although you may sometimes feel imposter syndrome, remind yourself that you are in that space because God put you there! Ask him how you can use your position for his glory. It may lead to small acts of kindness or some creative solution that builds relationships and support in your situation, ultimately making you feel more a part of things and a valuable contributor!

Jesus, thank you that you direct us into spaces and places that stretch and grow us, even if we feel out of our depth. Assure me that you have placed me there for your purposes and glory. Give me opportunities to build relationships and to make my contribution. Go with me and make me bold! Amen.

22. LIFE OF HARD KNOCKS

The LORD is good,
a refuge in times of trouble.
He cares for those who trust in him. **Nahum 1:7**

The year 2020 brought a rude awakening to many people, including young adults.

We live in a time where the culture says, 'Life should be easy; less work and more play.' More Instagrammable brunches and more holidays abroad. Social media platforms send a message that our once-a-year holiday of sun and sand, cocktails and coffee, should be a weekly experience, and if we are not living that life then we're not living our *best* life, and we're failing.

When we look throughout history and through the Bible, however, we see that easy, carefree living isn't the norm. Normal life for humanity in a broken world involves going through hardships, times of lack, sickness, death and natural disasters.

As much at it pains me to say it, persecution, war and injustices have been present since the very first time we decided we could manage life without God (see Genesis 3). The key to getting through the hard times is not to fear them, but to know that God is our stronghold on any day of trouble, and that we can take shelter in him.

What challenge or situation do you need to invite God's power and kindness into today?

DB

23. DEBILITATING ANXIETY

Do not be anxious about anything, but in every situation, by prayer and petition, with thanksgiving, present your requests to God. And the peace of God, which transcends all understanding, will guard your hearts and your minds in Christ Jesus. **Philippians 4:6-7**

I used to think that all anxiety was bad and that we should do everything we can to get rid of it. I've since learned that there are two types of anxiety – facilitating anxiety and debilitating anxiety.

Facilitating anxiety is a type of survival instinct which gets us to run away from enemies; it helps keep us from danger. It also helps us think about the safety and well-being of others. Debilitating anxiety stagnates or freezes us, causing us to give up and run from our destiny. This is the anxiety we need to take hold of. It can have physical effects, causing a tight chest, sweating, shaking and panic attacks. We can label it stress, tension, unease or feeling uncomfortable. Whatever we label it, we can overcome the fear of it by telling someone we love and trust about what we are facing.

Many are embarrassed about their weaker moments, but they are normal; we just don't talk about them enough to realise that everyone goes through them! Sharing what we are going through with a trusted friend and allowing them to pray and support us will help us break the power of whatever it is we are facing and help us on our way to overcoming it.

We can be there for others too, helping them overcome debilitating anxiety.

DB

24. IT'S OK TO BE AFRAID

After this, the word of the Lord came to Abram in a vision:
'Do not be afraid, Abram.
I am your shield,
your very great reward.'
But Abram said, 'Sovereign Lord, what can you give me since I remain childless
and the one who will inherit my estate is Eliezer of Damascus?' **Genesis 15:1-2**

'Do not be afraid' is a phrase that is used in the Bible 365 times, depending on the translation you're reading, and on the first of these occasions, God says these famous words to Abram.

Abram is plucked out of obscurity, promised generational greatness by the God of the universe and then sent onwards into the wild. Sounds wonderful! Yet, even though God has given Abram the vision, Abram's day-to-day reality hasn't changed. Despite being promised descendants who will be blessed because of his faithfulness, Abram still has doubts, concerns and fears as to whether or not those words are too good to be true.

This tension of living in between the promise and its fulfilment is one we all face daily. It's tough when we know we've been promised a 'good life', but it's been a while since we've even had a 'good day'. God's word to Abram is the same word for you today. Do not be afraid of the questions or the frustrations.

Abram wasn't kicked out of God's presence for asking questions, or even for doubting his goodness or faithfulness, and neither will you be. But take heart; he *is* faithful and he *is* good.

RN

25. WHEN THE PRESENT DOESN'T LOOK LIKE THE PROMISE

And Abram said, 'You have given me no children; so a servant in my household will be my heir.'
Then the word of the LORD came to him: 'This man will not be your heir, but a son who is your own flesh and blood will be your heir.' He took him outside and said, 'Look up at the sky and count the stars - if indeed you can count them.' Then he said to him, 'So shall your offspring be.' **Genesis 15:3-5**

Our heads can be so focused on the ground beneath us that we completely ignore the spectacle unfolding around us.

The guilt we feel in response to our doubts can keep our heads locked to the floor, under the weight of our stress, overwhelmed by thoughts about the practical outworking of God's promises. Abram responded to God's promise with, 'How on earth am I going to have blessed descendants when I don't even have children?!' The promise and his present reality were polar opposites.

I am relieved that, like Abram, my questions do not lead to conviction; it brings me great comfort to know that I can always enter into conversation with God. Buried right at the heart of the Christian tradition is the space to be human, to feel fear, to have doubts, and to bring all of that to God. In the face of Abram's fear, God invited him to look at the stars. So, too, you can take your eyes off the impossible before you and trust that God will make the impossible possible.

Our task is not to figure it all out for ourselves; it's simply to trust God and marvel at the mystery.

RN

26. OUT OF OUR TENTS, INTO GOD'S HANDS

He sits enthroned above the circle of the earth,
and its people are like grasshoppers.
He stretches out the heavens like a canopy,
and spreads them out like a tent to live in. **Isaiah 40:22**

We must leave the tents that we have erected to encompass our lives, emotions, thoughts and relationships, and enter into the tent God stretches out, which encompasses all created things.

'Look up at the sky and count the stars - if indeed you can count them... So shall your offspring be.' God reminds Abram in that moment, 'I haven't forgotten you. I, who created the heavens and the earth and stitched together every atom and cell in your body; I, who spent thirteen billion years crafting your smile, meant what I said, even though the promise is yet to be fulfilled.'

'We should not believe every word, or every impulse,' Thomas à Kempis writes in *The Imitation of Christ*.[1] Our minds, thought patterns and inner environments can become very small spaces, and can turn into restrictive rooms where we ruminate on negativity. Our human thoughts, emotions and limited understanding of reality can never truly represent the fullness of God's creation or God's grace-fuelled universe; they are only valid within the walls of our earthly tents.

Sometimes we have to take the opportunity to step outside our metaphorical tents and look upwards to get the heavenly perspective.

RN

[1] Thomas à Kempis, *The Imitation of Christ* (Penguin Classics, 2013).

27. PRISONER OF HOPE

For I know the plans I have for you... plans to prosper you and not to harm you, plans to give you hope and a future. **Jeremiah 29:11**

'Hope means expectancy when things were otherwise hopeless,' says the renowned theologian G. K. Chesterton. Fear can make us hopeless, but with God there is always hope!

Sometimes we lose hope because we think there is only one plan, and somehow we've missed it or messed it up. One Yellow Brick Road that leads to our destiny, and we have simply come off track.

We can experience so much fear through worrying about making the right or wrong decision. Be encouraged that God has a plan for our lives and is committed to helping us see it through when we walk with him. If we make the wrong decision, like choosing the wrong university, career or relationship, God can still turn everything around and help us make better choices moving forwards. Rather than walking a Yellow Brick Road, our journey is more like using a satnav!

Heaven is our destination and, as we listen to the Holy Spirit for direction, we should be encouraged that even if we sometimes go the wrong way, if we turn to him for help, he will simply reroute us.

Have we become hopeless in a situation? Bring this scenario to God and let him rekindle our hope and confidence in his plan for our lives.

DB

28. 365/360 REFLECTION

Looking back on the month, we can see that we are a people of hope because we have a heavenly Father who is immeasurably great and powerful, and yet he cares for us down to the smallest detail of our lives. He provides for us. He protects us. He positions us.

Do you know you are provided for, protected and positioned by the Creator of the universe, who also happens to be your Dad? How does being assured of this family bond diminish your fear and fuel your faith?

Why not spend some time today reflecting on the past month. Where are you physically? Emotionally? Spiritually? In the silence, ask God to highlight anything he wants to bring into the light for the sake of healing.

MARCH

1. SCARED OF THE CALL

The word of the LORD came to Jonah son of Amittai: 'Go to the great city of Nineveh and preach against it, because its wickedness has come up before me.'
Jonah 1:1-2

Jonah is given a clear mission brief by God. Go to Nineveh and preach to the people there, because their wickedness is keeping me up at night. The message is received; it's not ignored, but it is rejected. Ignoring a call is one thing; to actively do the opposite is quite impressive.

We all love to run away - from our responsibilities, from stupid mistakes or from burning truths that we don't want to face but which are fighting to reach the surface of our consciousness. There may be a host of reasons why stepping away is easier than stepping up.

Maybe we're too comfortable in the ways things are, and a change to our landscape would prove problematic. Maybe it's because we struggle to obey authority figures, and rebellion is our natural go-to. It seems easier to run than to embrace responsibility; it seems easier to numb than to confront the pain. But the truth is, it's not that easy to keep running...

Whatever is at the heart of our retreat, the reason for it will undoubtedly point to an underlying fear. Facing that desire to run away means we have to ask ourselves, 'What am I truly afraid of? Who am I scared of becoming? What am I afraid to lose?'

RN

2. SCORCHED PLACES

*And the L*ORD *will guide you continually*
and satisfy your desire in scorched places
and make your bones strong;
and you shall be like a watered garden,
like a spring of water,
whose waters do not fail. **Isaiah 58:11 (ESVUK)**

How often, in moments of flight, do we run for the place that once gave us a firm footing?

In moments of panic or fear we can reach out for familiarity in order to regain perceived control. The 'places' we run to aren't always geographical locations. These 'scorched places', as described in Isaiah, can be patterns of behaviour, substance misuse, toxic forms of sexual gratification or unhealthy thinking patterns that hold our minds captive. But often those things numb the quiet voice that beckons us towards truth, towards our heavenly Father.

But if, somehow, we can spot the pattern, we have every chance of breaking the cycle. And the Holy Spirit is always on hand to help us identify our deepest needs.

Jonah chose Tarshish, on the edge of his known world, as his exit strategy. Yet, even en route to disobedience, Jonah was not forgotten. Even though, like Jonah, we may deviate greatly from the course God planned for us, God's patient love never fails, and he will always give us a chance to turn around and get back on the right track.

RN

3. LIFE IN THE DESERT, PLANTS IN THE CONCRETE

The desert and the parched land will be glad;
the wilderness will rejoice and blossom.
Like the crocus, it will burst into bloom;
it will rejoice greatly and shout for joy. **Isaiah 35:1–2**

Often I walk the streets of Soho, and I marvel when I stumble upon a plant in a peculiar location.

Among the concrete slabs, discarded takeaway boxes and cigarette butts, forcing its way through the paper-thin gaps in the pavement, life emerges. In a place where I expected no fruit whatsoever, a gift of beauty has appeared. Birthed in a place I thought unsuitable, new life is present. Hope only needs a paper-thin gap to flourish. God only needs a seed of faith to birth a mighty tree.

Below the deck, as the ship rocked from side to side and the storm raged above him, Jonah would never have dreamt that anything good would take place in this situation. In the heart of the mess he had single-handedly orchestrated, this would surely be the place of his demise?

And yet...

This spot was the birthplace of redemption, the crucial moment that changed the trajectory of a whole city full of humans. The place where you are might seem desolate, but in that very spot a seed can be sown, which in time will burst into bloom. There is no terrain so dry that God cannot water it back to life and birth something new.

RN

4. A MOMENT FOR THE SAILORS

Then they took Jonah and threw him overboard, and the raging sea grew calm.
At this the men greatly feared the Lord, and they offered a sacrifice to the Lord
and made vows to him. **Jonah 1:15-16**

In focusing on the person of Jonah, it's so easy to overlook the other humans involved in this story. Let's think about the sailors present on the ship, unknowingly written into our sacred history.

The sailors were minding their own business, and then chaos erupted. They panicked and then prayed to their own gods, which ended up with them throwing a human overboard as a sacrificial offering. And yet, in response to witnessing God's power and might over their environment, these men were transformed. Their eyes were opened to the Lord, and they made vows to 'the God of heaven, who made the sea and the dry land' (Jonah 1:9). Talk about an eventful day at work! In the midst of the storm, a relationship was born. They unexpectedly came face to face with the living, all-powerful God. I'm sure their lives were never the same again.

The point is, the call you are being invited to isn't just for your own personal well-being.

Our self-centredness can have us calculating how a new pathway will benefit us directly, and if it doesn't, we can be tempted to write it off as void. Instead, this story prompts us to question. Are we willing to pay the cost? Are we willing to sacrifice our own personal comfort, reputation, well-being or finances in order for those around us to have an encounter with the Divine?

RN

5. MIND 'THE GAP'

From inside the fish Jonah prayed to the Lord his God. He said:
'In my distress I called to the Lord,
and he answered me.
From deep in the realm of the dead I called for help,
and you listened to my cry.' **Jonah 2:1–2**

Like Jonah, we have to be honest about the place that we find ourselves in. No more pretending or projecting a false image. We must acknowledge the gap that exists between where we are and where we've been invited by God to be.

The 'gap' may be metaphorical or it may be literal. It could be the gap in our spiritual development, the level of authenticity within our friendships, or pursuit of the passion that points us towards a deeper purpose; the list goes on.

This 'rerouting' prayer, presented in Jonah's moment of surrender, can be drawn upon no matter what depths we find ourselves in. We can run to these verses and cry out, like billions of humans have before us, in the knowledge that God is listening.

Jonah doesn't hold anything back in his prayer; he details the perils he has faced and how far off track he's found himself. But then, in a moment of remembrance, he embraces the return journey, opening the way for redemption and restoration.

Prayers like this one can be the public announcement that mark the inner transformation we so desperately need.

RN

6. YOU ARE A CATALYST OF CHANGE

This is the proclamation he issued in Nineveh:
'By the decree of the king and his nobles:
Do not let people or animals, herds or flocks, taste anything; do not let them eat
or drink. But let people and animals be covered with sackcloth. Let everyone call
urgently on God. Let them give up their evil ways and their violence. Who knows?
God may yet relent and with compassion turn from his fierce anger so that we
will not perish.' **Jonah 3:7–9**

When Jonah finally decided to rock up to Nineveh and declare the message
God had instructed him to preach, the unthinkable happened. Everyone, from
the king to the animals, the whole nation, was transformed. Even the animals
were called to wear sackcloth. Do you know how wild a scene it was that every
human/animal in the nation was wearing sackcloth?! It's akin to every cow in
the country donning funeral attire during a period of national mourning!

This wild scene became even more remarkable because this was the fruit of
a disobedient, begrudging prophet, who went the long way round to deliver a
message he had tried to avoid. Never underestimate the power of your path.

You may be a catalyst of change on a scale you could never fully appreciate.
Rarely will our paths be forged for our benefit alone. Our lives are inextricably
linked with all of creation. Running towards God's plan can shift toxic cultures,
tear down relational barriers and set in motion changes that we never
dreamed possible.

RN

7. *SELAH* – TIME TO STOP RUNNING

Consider Jonah's story and be encouraged that he had the same struggles as you and me, and God still used him! Have you been running from what God is asking of you?

Take time to connect with your feelings and identify the fears and beliefs that are holding you back. Acknowledge them to God and listen to his response. Maybe a Bible verse, a picture, a word or a thought will instantly come to mind to reassure you – write them down. Ask further questions and share your concerns; God will not be shocked or disappointed. Often, we don't respond to God's call because in our mind we assume the worst will happen: False Expectations Appearing Real.

What would it look like to assume the best of God and to see the future with hope?

Jesus, thank you for Jonah, an example of someone who struggled and wrestled with the same fears I have. I pray for courage to listen to your direction and to follow where you lead me, trusting you for my protection and for good outcomes for me and many others. Amen.

8. FEAR OF THE FUTURE

But those who hope in the LORD
will renew their strength.
They will soar on wings like eagles;
they will run and not grow weary,
they will walk and not be faint. **Isaiah 40:31**

In our current culture, waiting is not something that is encouraged. Patience is not something many people practise. We want it all, and we want it now, and if God doesn't make it happen in our timing, we will make it happen ourselves.

When I do the school run, there are days when Knox, my five-year-old, tries to cross the road even though the green man isn't showing. From his perspective, the road is clear. However, from my five-foot-nine perspective, I can see further than he can, and I can see that there is a car playing some drum and bass that's about to race around the corner. I don't tell him to wait to make him late or to stop his fun; I tell him because I love him and want the best for him.

In the same way, God asks us to place our hand in his and to trust that he sees exactly what's ahead of us. He'll say, 'Go,' when the time is right – all we need to do is take his hand.

DB

9. GOD STRONG

My flesh and my heart may fail,
but God is the strength of my heart
and my portion for ever **Psalm 73:26**

We know that at times we will fail, but that doesn't make us failures, so we must live free from the fear of failure.

If we have this fear, we will often make excuses as to why we can't do something. We assume the worst outcome rather than the best, and therefore we avoid trying. Like many, I have a fear of public speaking. It's crazy when I think about it because I have spoken in arenas with up to thirty thousand people! It's not crazy to God because he always asks people to do things that lie on the other side of fear, so he can show off his power in us, rather than us depending on our own self-confidence.

Here, we are told that even though we may fail, God is our strength. If we want to keep living our life in our own strength, then we will stay in our comfort zones. However, if we want to depend on God's strength, we will need to step out without the fear of failure.

When someone challenges us to face our fear or asks us to do something we find intimidating, let's check to see if we are making excuses and limiting ourselves. If it is fear of failure, then let's face it with God and do it anyway.

DB

10. FAILURE IS NOT OUR IDENTITY

Do not gloat over me, my enemy!
Though I have fallen, I will rise. **Micah 7:8**

Failure is a bruise, not a tattoo; an event, not a permanent label. Failing at times does not make us failures. It means we had a go. The key is to get up and try again. We can do that if we allow failure to teach us rather than to define us. This way, we win or we learn, but we never lose.

The Bible is full of stories of people who failed; it is also full of stories of people who overcame their failures. In life, we will have some small fails and epic fails. Some we forget in a day; others we carry around for a lifetime if we don't allow God to lift the weight from us.

The question is, do our failings make us stronger and wiser, or fearful to step out and go again? There is much hope in today's verse. To be aware of a failure but focused on the comeback is a beautiful thing – even if the comeback is simply getting up off the ground and standing firm again. It's important we don't let failures label us or let the fear of failure stop us in life.

Our failure is not our identity; our label is not 'addict', 'divorcee', 'unemployed', 'failed parent or friend'; our label is 'child of God'. Can you spend time reflecting on this identity today?

DB

11. FAILURE IS A FERTILISER

Make a clean break with all cutting, backbiting, profane talk. Be gentle with one another, sensitive. Forgive one another as quickly and thoroughly as God in Christ forgave you. **Ephesians 4:31 (MSG)**

If we want to know if it's OK to fail within our relationships, we just need to listen to the words spoken around us. Do we constantly hear the blame game? If people are shifting the blame and pointing fingers, that is not a culture where failure can be moved through. If people jump in and help out regardless of who's at fault, that's a community where it is OK to sometimes fail.

Some jobs have zero tolerance for failure, and rightly so - for pilots and heart surgeons, for example - because lives depend on them. However, it is important to remember that they previously had years of practice and training, a period in which they could fail without serious consequence. Heart surgeons had dummy bodies to practise on; pilots had simulators and test flights. These were platforms where they could fail many times, allowing them to grow and hone their skills.

When it comes to our walk with God, no one is perfect. We are works in progress, on a journey, and failure along the way will happen. Let's embrace it, learn from it and prevent it from holding us back from God's good plans for us.

Have we let failure restrict us? God still believes in us and is ready to restore us from all our brokenness.

DB

12. CULTURE CREATORS

Don't pick on people, jump on their failures, criticize their faults - unless, of course, you want the same treatment. Don't condemn those who are down.
Luke 6:37 (MSG)

Criticism can cause such fear that it confines our God-given dreams, limiting what he can do through us. In the Bible, it wasn't what God said to people, but criticism from others that affected them. If we are going to say, do or try something for God, there will be critics, but let's not stop creating.

Albert Einstein once wrote on a chalkboard: 9x1=9, 9x2=18, 9x3=27, 9x4=36, 9x5=45, 9x6=54, 9x7=63, 9x8=72, 9x9=81, 9x10=91. Chaos erupted in the classroom because Einstein made a mistake. Obviously, the correct answer to 9x10 is 90, so his students ridiculed him.

After their mocking, Einstein said, 'Despite the fact that I analysed nine problems correctly, no one congratulated me. But when I made one mistake, everyone started laughing. This means that even if a person is successful, society will notice his slightest mistake.'

If we want to create a culture that does not create fear or destroy people for their mistakes, we must celebrate when people get things right. Who can we encourage today?

DB

13. V IS FOR VICTORY

But thanks be to God! He gives us the victory through our Lord *Jesus Christ.*
1 Corinthians 15:57

As a teenager, I was football obsessed. I played every Saturday and listened to the Premier League scores on the radio. On Saturday evenings, *Match of the Day* played the highlights of the games from that day. I watched each replay with anticipation, even though I knew the final score and the winner!

This verse says victory is ours through Christ Jesus. This means that even though we might be going through a situation or season where it feels like we are losing hope, we know the final score. We win! Jesus has already paid the price and won the battle for us.

Knowing God's victory doesn't mean pretending everything is awesome when it clearly isn't; this way of thinking is not ignoring or overlooking the reality or severity of our situation. Rather, it is looking to the sovereignty of our King in all things. Knowing Jesus is with us now in our hard times and knowing we will be with him in eternity is comforting and strengthening.

God gave us victory through Jesus so we wouldn't be crippled by the fears of life or overwhelmed by the fear of death. Jesus died and rose again so we could live each day to the full.

DB

14. *SELAH* - COMPLETE IN CHRIST

Sometimes we fail in life, as many did in the Bible, but we are never beyond redemption. Jesus' blood is enough to cover every sin, mistake and failure we have made, or will ever make. Failure may be an occasional event, but it's not who we are and it doesn't define us, so never expect to fail!

You are not your failures or mistakes; you are in Christ. Because he is victorious, you are victorious. Because he is triumphant, you are triumphant. Because he is an overcomer, you are an overcomer. Whether you feel like this or not, this is your identity in him.

Take time to ponder these things. You may want to take Communion - eating a bit of bread and drinking a bit of wine or non-alcoholic red juice - to remember the body and blood of Jesus that was sacrificed for you. As you do so, remember Jesus has made you righteous.

Jesus, thank you that your grace and mercy covers all my guilt and shame. You forgive my wrongs, eradicating all trace of them; you redeem all my mistakes and failures and use them for your glory. I give you my fear of failing again; I receive your forgiveness and let myself off the hook, so I can go again with fresh passion and expectation. Amen.

15. TRUST GOD

Trust God from the bottom of your heart;
don't try to figure out everything on your own.
Listen for God's voice in everything you do, everywhere you go.
Proverbs 3:5–6 (MSG)

There are many books on the market today on how to be successful. Perhaps we fear looking like a failure in the world's eyes, or maybe the advent of social media has just meant we feel the pressure to do and feel and be more. Either way, few of us stop to ask what is actually meant by success.

The dictionary defines success as the accomplishment of an aim or a purpose, and humanity seems to desire this success so much that if God does not give us the kind we want, when we want it, we trust in something or someone else to supply this sense of purpose for us. The truth of the matter is, however, that only one purpose will truly satisfy the desires of our hearts.

Biblical success is about becoming the person God has called us to be, which is more like Jesus. It requires us to trust and follow his lead, no matter how scary or intimidating that might seem, and to trust his timing, no matter how long it takes.

Milan is an hour ahead of London, but that does not make London slow. If we are thirty-five and a professional footballer, we are considered old, but if we are thirty-five and a politician, we are considered young! There will always be people ahead of us and behind us. The key to biblical success is not to compare ourselves to or compete with others, but to stay in our lane, running our race and stepping into all God has for us, in his timing, being successfully formed into the likeness of Christ.

DB

16. THE ARCHITECT OF DREAMS

The Lᴏʀᴅ is not slow in keeping his promise, as some understand slowness. Instead he is patient with you, not wanting anyone to perish, but everyone to come to repentance. **2 Peter 3:9**

How many of us have seen a vision for our lives, or experienced a dream born in our hearts, and instead of running towards this new dawn, buried our heads in the sand?

Something about the enormity of the vision we have been given can have us acting like a deer in headlights, jumping back into the forest from which we emerged, pretending it was all a dream. Some sprint for the nearest exit or drown themselves in procrastination. Fear has us suppressing our dreams, essentially turning our inner notifications to silent, deleting the app, hitting 'unfollow'.

Do you believe that God, the patient Architect of Dreams, would plant a dream in your heart that would lead to your ruin? Do you really think that the One who is faithful to his promises would let you down and not follow through on his promises to you?

He is patient as we learn more and more about his trustworthy nature. Spend some time today asking God what aspect of his character he'd like to reveal to you or remind you of today.

RN

17. FORGIVENESS IS A FRUIT

I am the true vine, and my Father is the gardener. He cuts off every branch in me that bears no fruit, while every branch that does bear fruit he prunes so that it will be even more fruitful. You are already clean because of the word I have spoken to you. Remain in me, as I also remain in you. No branch can bear fruit by itself; it must remain in the vine. Neither can you bear fruit unless you remain in me. **John 15:1-5**

'Fruit' in the Bible is used to describe the visible evidence of God at work in our lives.

One of these spiritual 'fruits' that is often cultivated in us as we encounter God's love and spend more time with him is the gift of being able to forgive others. Because he has forgiven us, we receive the power and ability to forgive others. It's hard, if not impossible, to do this when we are not in relationship with God, as the world, the flesh and the devil will often tell us never to forgive, never to forget. Today's verses say that if we are to bear fruit, we must remain in him, and when it comes to our ability to hear God's voice and heart on the topic of forgiveness, this is no exception.

Fear pushes us to take control, take revenge and retaliate, which escalates the situation until even more pain is inflicted on both parties. Faith in Jesus produces fruit that empowers us and enables us to forgive ourselves and to forgive others, setting us free from hurt, pain, rage and bitterness. It also shows a broken world the crazy, unlimited love of Jesus and its power to restore.

What may you need to forgive yourself or another for today?

DB

18. GOD IS NOT TRICKING YOU

I will instruct you and teach you in the way you should go;
I will counsel you with my loving eye on you. **Psalm 32:8**

We are never called by God towards a future that will not increase our capacity for joy; a joy that the Bible tells us can be experienced in all circumstances.

Now, that road will not be free from trouble, or from suffering – joy is very different from transient happiness – but we must remember that God isn't trying to hoodwink us into going down a path that is of no benefit to us; in heaven with the angels, plotting our downfall. God isn't a sadist or a cosmic killjoy. God is Love. Only ever calling us back towards unity, love is the destination of our walk with him, no matter what hurdles, pitfalls and risks have to be faced along the way.

Even if the road ahead looks like an assault course that we're going to have to do blindfolded, his eyes are upon us. Our part is to trust that the call to step out into the unknown isn't a hoax, isn't a trap. In fact, it is for our benefit, no matter what direction we're facing. His eye is upon us. The Spirit who lives within us equips our souls to endure, and eventually to flourish.

RN

19. FEAR IS A LIAR

In the desert the whole community grumbled against Moses and Aaron. The Israelites said to them, 'If only we had died by the Lord's hand in Egypt! There we sat round pots of meat and ate all the food we wanted, but you have brought us out into this desert to starve this entire assembly to death.' **Exodus 16:2-3**

Fear makes us think the worst. FEAR can stand for **F**alse **E**vidence **A**ppearing **R**eal. When our children get sick, we think it could be fatal. When we fall out with our friends, we think it is forever. When we hear our parents arguing, we think it will end in divorce.

Fear makes us imagine a future without hope. If we want to conquer our fears, we must stop ourselves imagining the worst and ask God to bring about the best outcome. What if our children's bodies fight their illness and build immunity? What if our friendship fallout leads to a much deeper understanding, and our parents' verbal wrestle leads to a stronger bond?

The Israelites questioned God's goodness and feared the future. They allowed fear to dictate their present reality, so they wanted to turn around and go back to where they came from.

Have we been in a situation when we wondered whether God would come through? Moses encouraged the people to stand firm to see God's deliverance. God's message is the same to us: don't flinch, don't let fear dictate our reality, stand firm, and we will see God move.

DB

20. THE DARKNESS IS NOT DARK TO GOD

If I say, 'Surely the darkness will hide me
and the light become night around me,'
even the darkness will not be dark to you;
the night will shine like the day,
for darkness is as light to you. **Psalm 139:11-12**

Even in the darkest place we can run to, even in the most Godforsaken corner of the universe we can find, where we think there is no light in sight, God can still show up. Not only *can* God show up, but God is present, and is prepared to reveal his compassion and kindness to us, always.

We can be so focused on engineering environments to 'bring' or summon God's presence that we sometimes fail to understand that the very place where we stand has all the criteria needed for the miraculous to occur. The best place to pray, if we feel distant from God, is in the hole that we've run into. God is always present, even if the darkness limits our view.

If you think that God can't work with where you're at, then think again. The Spirit of God has flourished in harsher environments. Flowers can grow in concrete jungles, intimacy can be uncovered in moments of perceived separation, and God has the power to reframe the darkest day into a date with destiny. Hope is on the horizon.

RN

21. *SELAH* – DREAMING AGAIN

What dreams have we given up on because our fear spoke louder than our faith?

Have we agreed with fear's lies or with God's truth about us?

Is unforgiveness holding us back from communing with God or others?

Take time today to be in God's presence. Sit in silence or put on a worship song and remember how forgiven and restored you are in Jesus. Ask the Holy Spirit to reveal any lies you have been believing about yourself or others, or any unforgiveness you are holding on to. Offer these to God and ask him to reveal his perspective and truth. What does he want you to know about the person who hurt or offended you? Does this change anything and enable you to give them to him to help you deal with what you are facing so you can move forward?

Jesus, you are known for your love and forgiveness. My hope is that my life can mirror your love and forgiveness to others. I give you those who have hurt me and ask you to bring healing and restoration to me. As I receive from you, may I also overflow with love and forgiveness to others. Amen.

22. ROLE MODELS

Goliath stood and shouted to the ranks of Israel, 'Why do you come out and line up for battle? Am I not a Philistine, and are you not the servants of Saul? Choose a man and let him come down to me.' **1 Samuel 17:8**

Who we follow will determine what we fear. If we follow someone who is fearless, we will fear less; if we follow someone who is fearful, we will have more fear.

Fear is a learned trait – from parents, role models and our bad experiences. But the good news is that if fear can be learned, then it can be unlearned too! We can choose who to follow, and by doing that well, we can help conquer our fears.

When David saw Goliath intimidating the Israelite army, paralysing them with fear, he boldly stepped out and defeated the giant. Later, in 2 Samuel 21, we read how David followed God, which made him fearless when others were fearful and inspired his mighty men to show similar courage in taking on the giants. We can fear less by following God, and that can have a ripple effect on the people around us, helping us to defeat the giants we face too: whether they be anxiety or depravity.

Our friends, our children, our partner, our work colleagues – how do they see us respond when a giant comes our way? In a financial recession, in a world pandemic, when sickness hits, do they see us full of fear, full of worry or full of faith? When intimidation comes our way, do they see us running?

Let's run to God and, in doing so, begin to see our giants fall.

DB

23. DON'T BELIEVE THE LIE

For we have made lies our refuge,
and in falsehood we have taken shelter. Isaiah 28:15 (ESVUK)

We have all told, and believed, lies. What we don't understand is that even after we know the truth, some lies still affect us - spiritually, emotionally and even physically. Sometimes they become a cop-out for poor choices and behaviours, as this verse shows. If someone were to tell me that my friend had told them I was untrustworthy and a liar, I would be devastated - and furious! Then, if they were to say, 'Only joking, got you!' the emotion and pain from that lie wouldn't just vanish instantly. Even after hearing it was a lie, I would most probably check in with my friend, just to make sure. The lie could still have an impact on us through knocking our confidence or causing anxiety that lingers.

My point is, fear comes from lies, and although the answer is to believe the truth, the ongoing effects of lies can still have an emotional impact on our lives as if they were true.

Even though we know the truth through knowing Jesus, what fears and lies still connect to our felt emotions? Have we hidden behind those lies and checked out in some way? Which lies in our hearts do we need to ask Jesus to heal? Pray these through - maybe with another trustworthy person for support.

DB

24. LOST IN THE MATRIX

Finally, brothers and sisters, whatever is true, whatever is noble, whatever is right, whatever is pure, whatever is lovely, whatever is admirable - if anything is excellent or praiseworthy - think about such things. **Philippians 4:8**

Netflix has to be one of the greatest innovations of the twenty-first century - and yet it could also be said to be one of the biggest agents against progression. That, coupled with a sprinkle of Instagram and TikTok (I cannot even venture on to TikTok for fear of losing myself), has a generation of us running away from our purposes without even realising it. I love the access, innovation and ingenuity of social media platforms, but we have such a tendency to over-indulge.

With attention spans reduced to three-second iPhone scrolls, and brains screaming for dopamine hits that our real lives cannot give us, we have too often become a people of procrastination. When we're invited by God to forge our own path, to create our own business, to write a new chapter in our own lives, the bright lights and hashtags of the internet can prove a beautiful distraction, preventing us from asking ourselves, 'Who am I? What am I meant to be doing with my life?'

How might we be able to limit digitally 'running away' from the voice of God today?

RN

25. BREAK'S OVER, GET BACK IN THE GAME

The one who calls you is faithful, and he will do it. **1 Thessalonians 5:24**

When was the last time you sat and daydreamed?

When was the last time you stopped distracting yourself, pulled your head out from behind a screen, or wherever else you may have been hiding yourself, and opened yourself to being led by the Spirit?

Practically, when was the last day you spent without a screen, without any notifications screaming for your attention? It is so important, now more than ever, to provide space for ourselves to actually address some of those inner nudges we feel. To give life to those dreams we may have left dormant in the edges of our hearts, to bring to life some of those moments of inspiration we've put on the shelf.

The truth is, it's easier to watch someone else's hard work than to engage in hard work ourselves. It's safer to observe someone fulfilling their own dreams than to chase after our own.

Accepting a call on our lives, stepping out to forge our own path, is a risk. But a life lived in fear of the consequences is a passive existence watching from the sidelines. Put your phone/laptop/tablet down, dare to look at your life. On the other side of our distractions can lie our destiny.

RN

26. A MOMENT OF PRAYER

I sought the Lord, and he answered me;
he delivered me from all my fears.
Those who look to him are radiant;
their faces are never covered with shame. **Psalm 34:4-5**

The Bible contains stories, songs and prayers from millennia ago, collected orally and bound together meticulously. And they still resonate with humans thousands of years later.

The locations may be different, but the hearts of the people who raise those prayers – upwards and inwards – have not changed. The Spirit that unites us all is timeless. When we pray, we are closing the perceived gap between ourselves and God. Even if only for a moment, the walls shatter, the problems dissipate, we step outside ourselves and stand hand in hand with our Maker.

Those who look to him are radiant; their faces are never without shame. Spotless in the light of the Lord, blameless in the shadow of his grace. If you've delayed or you've denied the call on your life for this reason (or heard God call and hung up a thousand times), let go of the shame or guilt you may be holding over yourself. Today is as good as any to find a quiet place and pray.

RN

27. CONTENT CREATOR

For you created all things,
by your will they were created
and have their being. **Revelation 4:11**

'Content Creator' is the job title of a person who spends their time making memes for Facebook, vlogs for YouTube, photos for Instagram or choreographing dance moves for TikTok (or whatever other combination of infinite activities and platforms are out there). There are many gifted creators on the planet using something to create something else – an app, a piece of software, a phone or a camera. And yet this creation is just a glimpse of the One who created us.

God is the ultimate creator because he's a continent creator, a creature creator and the creator of the Church. He creates something out of nothing.

Sometimes fear gets the better of us and diminishes our creativity, causing us to shrink back from the perceived darkness or nothingness – whether that be a blank page or a new roll of film in the camera. If we focus on God, who he is and what he does, we realise we are connected to an unlimited source of creativity, a wellspring of imagination. We just need to choose to step into it.

God spoke the heavens and earth into being without a Pinterest board for inspiration! He created us without Instagram for direction. Have we put God in a box? Have we lost our wonder and awe? Spend time today thinking about his magnificent creation. Let's hear what he reveals to us through the places we go to and the people we see today. Let's give him our future and see what he will do.

DB

28. *SELAH* – TAKING TIME

Take time today to consider God's creation.

His attributes are celebrated in the skies, the mountains, the trees, the flowers, the birds – everything speaks a message of his greatness, his creativity and his imagination. You are made in God's image; your redeemed imagination is a visionary gift from God!

Take one aspect of nature and let it speak to you of God's character and nature, his sovereignty and power, his creativity and care, his encouragement to you!

Thank you, God, for your magnificent creation and for your messages of love and care in your created world. Thank you that I'm a creative being, made in your image. Help me find creative ways to encourage others and creative solutions for the world's needs. Amen.

29. EAT, SLEEP, PRAISE, REPEAT

About midnight Paul and Silas were praying and singing hymns to God, and the other prisoners were listening to them. Suddenly there was such a violent earthquake that the foundations of the prison were shaken. At once all the prison doors flew open, and everyone's chains came loose. The jailer woke up, and when he saw the prison doors open, he drew his sword and was about to kill himself because he thought the prisoners had escaped. But Paul shouted, 'Don't harm yourself! We are all here!' **Acts 16:25-8**

These verses shock me! Paul and Silas were battered and bruised and put in prison. I don't know what you would do in this situation, but I'm sure I would probably be screaming to get out of there rather than singing my favourite worship songs at the top of my lungs.

Paul and Silas knew that if they were going to be released, it had to start by trusting God from within. In the midnight hour, the darkest hour, as they lifted their voices, an earthquake shook the foundations, giving them an opportunity to escape. Surely, they ran, right?

Not Paul. He was convinced that God wanted to use the situation for good and for his glory. He shouted to the prison guard not to harm himself because they were all there. Paul put his own future on the line to save someone else's.

Praise is a powerful weapon; it invites Jesus into the situation and gives him access to do what only he can do. Here, a man's life was saved. What situation are we in right now? We might not feel like praising God, but it's a key to seeing the situation turn around. We never know what God wants to do until we invite him in.

DB

30. THE GREAT ESCAPE

The jailer called for lights, rushed in and fell trembling before Paul and Silas. He
then brought them out and asked, 'Sirs, what must I do to be saved?'
They replied, 'Believe in the Lord Jesus, and you will be saved - you and your
household.' Then they spoke the word of the Lord to him and to all the others
in his house. At that hour of the night the jailer took them and washed their
wounds; then immediately he and all his household were baptised. The jailer
brought them into his house and set a meal before them; he was filled with joy
because he had come to believe in God - he and his whole household.
Acts 16:29-34

This is a story of salvation, of family transformation, and it all ends in a great
celebration. A party 'til the early hours of the morning, dancing to classic
1980s electro music. Well, maybe not - but there was a good old shindig.

I love this story because it starts with two people in prison, who should
have been paralysed by fear, and it ends with them released and the jailer
encountering the love of Jesus and his whole family experiencing freedom.

Overcoming fear isn't just about us. It has a ripple effect on others around us
at the time.

What are we facing today that is making us cower under the weight of the
problem, rather than looking to and praising God?

Let's put on some worship music, sing out and pray for a miracle. The Bible
tells us that because of Jesus, we are free. Can you let that sink in today? Even
if your brain or body *feels* like it's in prison right now, you are free indeed!

DB

31. 365/360 REFLECTION

If this last month has shown us anything, it's not only that we are fully forgiven for every wrongdoing we will ever have made, but also that God is able to redeem our failures and will never stop trying to bring about his purposes through us. God never gives up on us! This enables us to persevere with others, forgiving their mistakes and not taking lasting offence.

God also restores our identities as creative 'chips off the old block', and longs to bring creative solutions to the challenges of the day through us. We are creative because he is creative.

Are you living in the fulness of grace and forgiveness that renders you forever unpunishable? Are you carrying any unforgiveness towards yourself or another? Are you ready for God to reveal creative solutions for the challenges you or others face?

Take time to reflect on these questions with God before continuing onwards, knowing God is by your side. Remember also that God has designed us for relationship and community with other believers, so you may want to invite a trusted friend or family member to help you journey with these questions too.

APRIL

1. COUR-AGE

Be strong and courageous. Do not be afraid or terrified because of them, for the Lord your God goes with you; he will never leave you nor forsake you.
Deuteronomy 31:6

If we research the word 'courage,' we find that it is rooted in the Latin word *cor*, which means 'heart'. Back in the day, the word was used to describe someone who was unafraid to share what was truly on their heart. Over time however, this word has evolved. 'Heart' is often used to mean 'inner strength', as in to 'take heart', with another word for inner strength being 'valour'. Valour is an inner strength of heart and mind that enables us to meet danger and trouble without fear. The question is, where do we take heart, or valour, from?

In *The Wizard of Oz*, the character of the cowardly lion was on a mission to find a heart because he wanted courage. Today's verse clearly describes from where our heart or courage comes. It comes from God: 'Do not be afraid or terrified because of them, for the Lord your God goes with you.'

Knowing that Jesus is with us and that he will never leave or forsake us gives us heart, courage and the ability to meet trouble without fear. Where do we need heart or courage today? Perhaps you want to actually list these things down on your phone or write them on a piece of paper. Let's spend time with Jesus today, going through each of these areas or scenarios and surrendering our fears to him afresh. Once you do so, you may want to delete or cross out these worries one by one, or else pray this verse over them: 'Be strong and courageous... for the Lord your God goes with you.'

DB

2. HEART TIME

In their hearts humans plan their course,
*but the L*ORD *establishes their steps* **Proverbs 16:9**

We love making plans! Plans for our life, our education, career, holidays, business, what we are going to eat or do or wear. Even if you don't really consider yourself a planner, I am sure you plan some things that mean a lot to you, because the truth is that what we *care* about, we plan for.

In our heart we make plans, we decide how we will spend our time. In fact, if we want to see where our heart is, we just need to look at where we spend most of our time. For many, most of our time is spent at work. Some of us may think our heart isn't necessarily in that, but rather we have to work to pay the bills and live a certain lifestyle. Well, that may be the case, but does that not show us that our heart is in survival through our own strength?

How we spend our time reveals a lot about our passions and heart. Sometimes I check my screen time to see which apps have taken the most of my time, and sometimes I get a rude awakening!

Today's verse says we plan our course in our hearts, but God establishes our steps. This encourages us to hold tightly to Jesus and, in doing so, to hold to our plans loosely. He is in control, and he has the best plans for us. We can try to plan our course, but ultimately, he has our next step sorted.

Where do you find yourself spending most of your time? What does God think about this? Where might he be asking you to invest a little more or less time today?

DB

3. HEART TREASURE

For where your treasure is, there your heart will be also. **Matthew 6:21**

Saint Augustine is often quoted as saying, 'Where your pleasure is, there is your treasure; where.your treasure is, there is your heart; where your heart is, there is your happiness.'

If we want to see where our hearts are, we need to look at where we spend our money, or who we spend it on. If we love our football team, perhaps some of our money goes on a season ticket or a Sky Sports subscription. If we love fashion, our bank account may show us that we're spending a good chunk of our resources on clothes. And if we love someone else, we might spend a lot of money on them.

When we gaze at our bank statements, we might be pleased that we have been generous, helped the poor or blessed others. Or we might see that we've bought things we didn't really need, with money that we didn't have, to make ourselves feel better or to impress others we don't need in our lives. Fear of not fitting in, or of feeling different, causes us to do all sorts of things with our treasure.

Jesus doesn't need our money, but he does want our hearts, and he wants us to be generous to others. Spend some time in prayer, asking your heavenly Father if there is any area of spending, giving or saving that he wants you to do differently, knowing that every gift comes from him.

DB

4. HEART THOUGHTS

For as he thinks in his heart, so is he. **Proverbs 23:7 (NKJV)**

God has given us the gift of thought. He does not control, or contain, our thinking. He has given us free will and we can think about what we want, when we want, whether beneficial or not, whether it honours him or not.

Our thoughts are a direct reflection of who we are, because, as this verse shows, they come from our heart. So if we want to know where our hearts are today, we need to stop and consider what we are thinking about the most.

Did you know that we can't think two thoughts at the same time? We can go from one thought to another quickly, but it is impossible to have two thoughts simultaneously. This means if we are thinking too much about something that is causing us fear, worry or anxiety, if we can begin to focus and dwell on God's word instead, we will begin to see things change.

Let's give Jesus our hearts today and, as we do, his thoughts will become our thoughts. Let's surrender our concerns to him, asking what he says about them, and declaring his words as the ones we want to think and dwell on. Before long, these godly thoughts will begin to replace the negative ones.

DB

5. HEART TALK

For the mouth speaks what the heart is full of. **Matthew 12:34**

If courage comes from having a heart full of God's love and truth, we need to do a regular check-in on what our heart is full of, analysing the things we love or the people it longs for.

Going to the doctor for a heart check-up is quite a normal thing to do, so why shouldn't completing a regular spiritual heart check also be our new normal?

One of the ways I check on my heart and courage levels is by looking at the words I'm speaking to myself and others throughout any given day. When I say things that show that I want to run away, I know fear is in my heart. When I want to give up rather than go again, I know fear is in my heart. I don't want my heart to be a home for fear, so when I hear the language of fear, doubt and hopelessness, I know I have to make time to go to God. Once I've recognised this negative pattern, I find a quiet space and pray a sincere prayer asking for help; I listen to some worship music and begin to declare bold, courageous truths over my life.

What words are we saying to ourselves and others today? Are our hearts full of fear, or full of faith? Living the life God calls us to live will always need us to evict fear from our hearts. There's no better way than speaking out his truths. What declarations do we need to speak out today?

DB

6. HEART INTEGRITY

I know, my God, that you test the heart and are pleased with integrity.
1 Chronicles 29:17

When listening to people's questions about life, I realise they often have two big ones! 'How can I be happy?' and, 'How can I be successful?' There is a real fear of being unfulfilled, or of not belonging, or of failing in whatever we put our hand to.

In today's passage, the writer reminds us what our heavenly Father values above the other things we chase after: integrity of heart. It is said that integrity is who we are when no one is looking, and it should be the same as when everyone is looking! We hold fast to the truth of who God made us and don't change like a chameleon to fit the presenting situation.

If we want successful relationships and friendships or a thriving career, we need to make sure that we don't allow a gap to grow between our actions and our words, and that we do everything we can to keep them locked tightly together.

I have seen many relationships in the workplace, in school and in personal lives break down because of a lack of honesty and integrity – words not matching actions. How can we be a person of our word?

Let's pause and ask the Holy Spirit to reveal any area in our life where we have a gap between our words and our actions. Ask that they be tightly locked together by God's power rather than by human strength.

DB

7. *SELAH* – FOUR TS

Looking back at the four Ts – Time, Treasure, Thoughts and Talk – where is your heart right now?

What do you spend most of your time on? Who do you speak about the most, think about the most? Where do you spend or place most of your treasure? Is your heart wholly God's?

When you go to the doctor, they check your heart is healthy. Would you say yours is spiritually healthy, or are there some things you need to adjust to make it so? Ask God, and he will let you know what he wants to do in and through you (with conviction, and never with condemnation).

Jesus, thank you that you went all in and gave everything to win my heart. In response I give you my whole heart. I surrender all aspects of my life to you now. Show me any places where I need to adjust my time, treasure, thoughts and talk, because I want to love you wholeheartedly. Amen.

8. THE TRINITY

May the grace of the L<small>ORD</small> Jesus Christ, and the love of God, and the fellowship of the Holy Spirit be with you all. **2 Corinthians 13:14**

God is relationship. God, Christ, Holy Spirit. Father, Son, Spirit. Creator, Redeemer, Advocate.

Three Persons intertwined, in a dance-like interchange since the beginning of time. A grand mystery that gave birth to the universe and everything in it. Mutually submitting, mutually glorifying one another, mysteriously creating space to abide in one another. The church fathers used the word *perichoresis* in an attempt to encapsulate this mystery, which speaks to the three Persons of the Trinity continuously outpouring to one another in this divine interchange.

It melts my mind thinking about how it all works, and humanity has been wrestling to understand what is going on between the 'Big Three' for thousands of years. This communion between the Trinity, this intertwined love triangle, explains why humanity has buried within us this innate, deep yearning for connection. When we lack this connection, it feeds anxiety as we become aware of disconnection from God, from each other, from creation and from ourselves.

If we can understand that the very God who created us is a relational God who has a deep desire to be in relationship with us, we can be confident that being in connection with God, with ourselves, with others and with creation around us is the best thing for us, because it's part of our DNA.

RN

9. JOINING THE DANCE

My prayer is not for them alone. I pray also for those who will believe in me through their message, that all of them may be one, Father, just as you are in me and I am in you. May they also be in us so that the world may believe that you have sent me. I have given them the glory that you gave me, that they may be one as we are one - I in them and you in me - so that they may be brought to complete unity. Then the world will know that you sent me and have loved them even as you have loved me. **John 17:20-3**

Humanity was made in God's image, as the story at the start of Genesis illustrates, and with that, the need to be in relationship is buried deep within our hearts. We are forever itching to join in with this relational dance with God and with one another. You were designed to dance, whether you are gifted with rhythm or not. Everything is built around the rhythm of relationships.

No person is an island. Everything is connected.

The hunger for connection is inescapable, and therein lies the risk, because to need someone is to put ourselves in someone else's control, and we love to be in control, don't we?

Today, embrace the invitation to step out of the perceived safety of solitude and onto the dance floor of your own life. Surrender control, investigate your design, reach out to a partner, and *dance*.

RN

10. IN HIM ALL THINGS HOLD TOGETHER

He is before all things, and in him all things hold together. **Colossians 1:17**

Having lots of friends doesn't necessarily mean our need for connection is being satisfied. Living in a city of millions of people doesn't mean we're not alone.

People can have millions of followers on social media accounts and still feel lonely. The 'invitation to dance' isn't a competition to see who can get the most friends; it's a proposition to open ourselves up to the contemplative practice of being present in our relationships. It's not about quantity or building more connections; it's about plugging into the One who truly matters, the Friend who has been reaching out to us since 'before all things'. The One who can truly 'hold' us 'together' when we fall apart. Joining the dance is an opportunity to lay down our egos and point our need for acceptance towards the One who accepts all, whose validation means the most.

Joining the dance could actually be as simple as avoiding screens and faces for a couple of hours and going for a walk. Joining the dance could be as simple as a moment of silence or writing a letter to God, the faithful Friend who has been waiting to hear from you since before you were born.

RN

11. FIRM STEPS ON THE DANCE FLOOR

*The LORD makes firm the steps
of the one who delights in him.* **Psalm 37:23**

The music is loud, life is happening, the bossman on the decks is spinning bangers and the room is pumping. 'How do I know whether I'm dancing in time?' I hear you say. 'What rhythm does this God move to?' 'How do I know if I'm in time with everyone else, or is it my time to freestyle?'

Regardless of the soundtrack, we're not alone to figure out the rhythm of the dance, or the steps to take in our lives. In today's reflection, the psalmist says, 'The LORD makes firm the steps...'

Every step we take can be directed by God, if we surrender control and follow the call to live in sacrificial love with our brothers and sisters. We are not Lord of the Dance; we don't have to have it all figured out.

When was the last time you let go of the pressure and embraced spontaneity? When was the last time you stopped pretending you had it all together and took the risk of looking a bit silly? Sometimes we can be so obsessed about getting things 'right' that we forget that when it comes to God's great dance floor - provided our shapes are thrown with love and humility - God takes a huge amount of pleasure in watching us move.

RN

12. NEVER LETTING GO

Though he may stumble, he will not fall,
for the Lord upholds him with his hand. **Psalm 37:24**

God delights in every detail of our lives. If you are prone to panic, to stressing about perfection, to being lost when you don't have all the facts, today's scripture is for you.

God is directing our steps. Not only that, but he also holds the birds of the air in his hands and oversees the growing of the trees and the changes of the seasons like a holy music conductor. We'd be able to witness the splendour in all of this if we were to take our eyes off ourselves and gaze around for even a second. Jesus mentions this in Matthew 13:16 when he says, 'But blessed are your eyes because they see, and your ears because they hear.'

The Spirit surrounds us so closely that every detail of our lives is delighted in by God. Every emotion and every moment are important to God. Every count and every beat, he is smiling and cheering us on. Even if we stumble or fall or fail, God has got us, and will never fail us. So don't worry if this season feels like a hard one for you, if you are struggling to keep pace with your life; God has you by the hand, and he's not letting go of you.

RN

13. MIRROR TALK

The L<small>ORD</small> Almighty has a day in store
for all the proud and lofty,
for all that is exalted
(and they will be humbled). **Isaiah 2:12**

Mirroring is about keeping in step with one another and with creation around us. It's the proximity and vulnerability that is necessary to being authentically seen. To let our guard down in places we feel safe, with people we feel will respect and honour our emotional nakedness, and to allow ourselves to be held in the eyes of the beholder, with no filters, special effects, green screens or camouflage. Core to our role on this planet is to be a loving mirror back, for others to have the opportunity to see themselves through us too.

No one, no matter how much self-reflection or experience we may think we have, is above 'mirror work'. One of the things prohibiting us from the relationships and connections we so yearn for could be our pride. If we compare ourselves to others and think we're more intelligent, attractive, trendy, creative, competent, holy or ... (insert whatever attribute you want here), pride has the power to divide us from God and from other people. It can cause separation and isolation, rather than the unity and connection that God longs for. Life will humble us all; we're better off addressing our pride in private, before it causes us real damage.

Can we spend some time in God's presence today being perfectly seen until his face begins to reflect onto our very own?

RN

14. *SELAH* – DANCING TODAY

What does it mean for you to dance in step with the Spirit?

Are you letting the Spirit lead as you watch the dance unfold, or are you trying to control every move and every step yourself? Consider why you may find it hard to let go and let God! Share your thoughts with God and ask him for his perspective. Why not try journalling his response?

Holy Spirit, I want to be free to dance in abandonment with you – not held back by my fear of loss of control or accompanying worries. Speak to my imagination and show me what it would be like to dance freely with you today, this week and in the months and years ahead. Amen.

15. A VERY PRESENT HELP

God is our refuge and strength,
an ever-present help in trouble.
Therefore we will not fear, though the earth give way
and the mountains fall into the heart of the sea,
though its waters roar and foam
and the mountains quake with their surging. **Psalm 46:1–3**

As I write, I'm aware of how often my soul is fearful. When I'm in a room with very intelligent people, or when I speak publicly, I fear looking stupid. However, recently I've experienced fear like I've never felt it before.

I was at an ATM when a tall man with a knife shouted, 'Give me that money!' I gave him the cash. Adrenaline rushed through my body, my hands were shaking, and, randomly, I soon found myself chasing after *him*, shouting, 'You didn't need to do that! If you'd just asked, I would have given it to you!' This moment reminded me that fear affects our entire bodies.

Maybe we are feeling helpless and overwhelmed by fear as we see the impact of climate change, the lives lost in natural disasters, the increase in crime, the economic crisis. But unlike me at the ATM, you don't need to question the way you are running. The Bible makes it clear that God is the only direction we need to run in; he is our 'refuge and our strength, an ever-present help in trouble'.

Today, let's give our fears over to God, even though we fear the 'earth [will] give way', and allow him to be our safe place and our strength. God cares about our planet, and he cares about us. Ask him how to pray into these big issues of our day, and then act on his guidance and strategies to make this world a safer place.

DB

16. FEAR OF COMMITMENT

Make every effort to live in peace with everyone and to be holy; without holiness no one will see the Lord. See to it that no one falls short of the grace of God and that no bitter root grows up to cause trouble and defile many.
Hebrews 12:14–15

If you listen solely to the media, you will likely think that divorce for married couples is inevitable. In reality, there are still millions and millions of marriages that are healthy, happy and lasting. Sometimes we fear commitment because we don't want to start something that we know might fail.

There is a guy called John M. Gottman who is a renowned researcher in the field of relationships. He said perspective is key for a lasting relationship. He talks about two thought directions. The first is 'positive sentiment override', which is where you continuously assume the best of your partner; you focus on the positive, the good they do rather than the bad. The opposite is called 'negative sentiment override', where everything they do is wrong. Even if they do something right, in your mind they are a write-off; they will mess up sooner or later.

When I look at the way Jesus lived his life on earth, I see the way he focused on the good in people rather than tearing them down with the bad. Jesus gave second chances and believed people could change. He invited the outcasts and the marginalised, the rejects and the despised, from tax collectors to prostitutes. Jesus led with positive sentiment override.

In which of your relationships do you keep focusing on the negative rather than the positive? What relationship are you running away from because you fear it will fail? Ask Jesus for his eyes to see others today.

DB

17. NO WAY JOSÉ

But I tell you, love your enemies and pray for those who persecute you.
Matthew 5:44

Jesus tells us to love our enemies and pray for those who persecute us;
to love those who try to control us, bully and troll us – it sounds pretty
outrageous initially!

In reality, we know that Jesus wants us to live our best lives; lives free from
anger, rage, bitterness and offence. As we have seen already, for us to live this
life we need to be able to forgive others. And here, Jesus gives us another
insight to enable us to do just that: to love our enemies and to pray for those
who persecute us. I have tried this, and though it's not easy, it really works!

Some time ago someone consistently tried to pull me and my wife, Charlie,
down, gossiping and lying about us to many people. We addressed this with
them, but they continued to try to belittle us and turn others against us.
Before long, I began to carry bitterness towards them. But then, after reading
this verse, I began trying to bless them instead.

I felt God challenging me to bless them further. I anonymously sent them a gift
and, as I did, something changed in my heart. I felt peace, a new compassion,
and I was able to give this person, their actions and my concerns over to God.

Blessing enemies is countercultural, but it brings healing and freedom to us.
Sadly, this person continued their destructive behaviour, but my heart stayed
soft towards them and towards God. Hurting people hurt other people, but
forgiven people can forgive others. This is the way of the faithful, not the
fearful, and it's powerful. Who can we begin to bless today?

DB

18. YOU'LL NEVER WALK ALONE

I am with you always, to the very end of the age. **Matthew 28:20**

These days we are more connected than ever before with text messages, WhatsApp, Snapchat, Instagram, BeReal, Facebook, the list goes on. These apps have many positives; however, they can also cause our social fears to increase.

On Snapchat, we see the party that everyone seems to be at that we knew nothing about. On Facebook, everyone else is living the dream, holiday after holiday, celebration after celebration. On Instagram, our close mates are all dating or getting engaged, which just fuels our own insecurity.

It is easy to think that if the external situation changed, so would our internal emotions. If we were invited to the parties, we would feel included; if we had some more holidays, we would feel happier; if we got married, we would feel secure. These things would change how we feel for a moment, but soon we'd start to feel that same sense of lack again.

God never created us to have to live with lack, with loneliness. When we begin to understand that no matter where we go or what we do he is always with us, it gives us an inner confidence that cannot be knocked. I don't mean to quote the strapline of Liverpool FC, but it's true: 'You'll never walk alone',[2] and when we truly get that, everything changes.

DB

---

[2] 'You'll never walk alone' from the Rodgers and Hammerstein musical *Carousel* (1945).

19. FACE IT TOGETHER

I sought the LORD, and he answered me;
he delivered me from all my fears.
Those who look to him are radiant;
their faces are never covered with shame. **Psalm 34:4–5**

Fear of rejection isolates us. It makes us think that if others really knew what we were like, or what we'd done, we would be rejected. It causes us to live our lives behind a mask. We think if we can just get through this, it will all be OK, and no one will know anything about what we are really facing.

The truth is, we heal better together.

Community is where people can listen to us, encourage us and pray for us. The fear of rejection will cause us to distance ourselves from the ones who love us the most, but if we are serious about healing, recovering and overcoming this fear, then opening up is the first step in doing so.

An authentic community encourages us to be our authentic selves. If we can't be ourselves in our circle, then maybe we need a new circle, to find a Jesus-centred community that encourages us to live the lives God created us for.

Today, perhaps you need to prayerfully reflect on the communities you are a part of and the company you keep. Thank God for the good and fruitful and pray for his guidance to navigate any areas that are challenging or that you feel need to change.

DB

20. OPEN THE EYES OF MY HEART

Open the eyes of their hearts, and let the light of Your truth flood in. Shine Your light on the hope You are calling them to embrace. Reveal to them the glorious riches You are preparing as their inheritance. **Ephesians 1:18** (VOICE)

We cannot be seen by others if we are not first willing to see ourselves. People will reflect the openness we present. There are very few mind readers around. Jesus had a phenomenal ability to see people exactly as they were, as God saw them, but we mortals need some help.

'Open the eyes of our hearts' is a declaration of surrender, of surrendering our limited view in order to see how God sees. To paraphrase the contemplative James Finley, your thoughts of you are not you. How you see the world is but a fraction of the beauty that is truly present; it's like we're seeing in poor-resolution quality, and God is inviting us to see in high definition.

Lord, open the eyes of our hearts, to see ourselves, to see each other and to see you. Let the light of your truth flood in and wash away the fear that blinds us from seeing our true beauty. Amen.

RN

21. *SELAH* – RELATIONSHIP REFLECTION

Relationship with God and with others is what we were created for.

What struggles, fears or battles have you kept to yourself and shared with no one? God has provided others to walk through life's struggles and hardships with you so that you do not walk through these things alone. Who has God provided in your life that you could open up to?

Spend some time thinking about the people in your world who encourage you and cheer you on, who accept you, warts and all. Who has God given you to encourage you in your faith? Thank God for these relationships and think about how you can thank and value those involved. Who is God asking you to reach out to with encouragement? Ask God what words you may need to share with these people.

Jesus, thank you that you never leave or abandon me, and thank you for those friends and encouragers you have placed in my life. Bless them and their families. May they give me courage to live wholeheartedly for you. Help me to encourage others so they will take courage and follow you wherever you lead them. Amen.

22. SHAME FREE

Fear not, for you will not be ashamed;
be not confounded, for you will not be disgraced;
for you will forget the shame of your youth,
and the reproach of your widowhood you will remember no more.
Isaiah 54:4 (ESVUK)

As a youth leader for many years, I have been to my fair share of youth camps and conferences. They are always a highlight for me, seeing young people experience new levels of freedom and making lifelong friends along the way.

One thing that remains consistent, regardless of whether I am at a youth gathering in Indonesia, Ireland, South Africa or Scotland, is that the young people arrive carrying huge amounts of guilt and shame. Guilt says to the person, 'You did something bad,' but shame says, 'You are a bad human being.' Guilt makes a person feel regret, but shame makes them feel small and insignificant. Guilt makes a person think about how their actions affected others, whereas shame makes people concerned with how others see them.

When Jesus went to the cross in punishment for our sins, his sacrifice covered all our guilt and shame. Salvation, through Jesus, is a complete work and removes all condemnation that we may be facing or feeling. This leaves us free to celebrate because we have been forgiven for the wrongs we did yesterday, for those we do today and for any we may do tomorrow. There is nothing we can ever think, say or do that can separate us from God's love.

DB

23. NAUGHTY NOAH

When he drank some of its wine, he became drunk and lay uncovered inside his tent. **Genesis 9:21**

Noah built an ark before anyone had seen rain. He led people and animals through the flood and then, when he found ground, he planted a vineyard (as you do). One night, after sampling his Pinot Noir, he'd had too much and passed out naked. One of his sons, Ham, found him in his sorry state and started to tell people and shame Noah. However, Noah had two other sons, Shem and Japheth; they acted differently out of their love for their father. They walked towards their father backwards, so they did not see his nakedness, and proceeded to cover him.

We see a lot of people acting like Ham today. Quick to expose, quick to gossip, quick to point a finger and quick to judge others. The truth is that none of us is perfect, and we will all more than likely have a Noah moment at some point in our life. A moment where we do something that is out of character and causes us embarrassment, guilt or even shame.

When we have those moments, who do we want around us? Someone who will tell everyone or those who will help us with our nakedness and shame? Noah didn't need his failure exposed; he needed restoration. He needed people around him who would help him and sit with him. I have always been against cover-ups to maintain a person's or an organisation's reputation. However, I am all for covering someone with grace and love so they can learn, be restored and move on.

Every day we get a choice. To behave like Ham and shame people, or to live like Shem and Japheth and help to lift shame off them in the first step of restoration.

DB

APRIL

24. CONFRONTING OUR HIDDEN SELVES

And from his fullness we have all received, grace upon grace. **John 1:16** (ESVUK)

Facing our fears means confronting our 'hidden selves' and addressing our 'shadows', as described by psychiatrist Carl Jung – the darker parts of ourselves that we don't like to dwell on as much as the 'lighter' parts. This can be an excruciating but also an enlightening process.

I don't have to scratch far below the surface to see the parts of myself that I'd rather remained out of sight and out of mind. No matter how well we present, we all carry destructive traits that are hard to face. Those parts that drag us into the darkest corners of our hearts and, left unaddressed, have the power to destroy our lives and rob us of our joy. But the power of bringing those hidden parts before God is where we can find freedom from the fear of being fully known and found lacking.

More often than not, the destructive parts of ourselves may at some point in our lives have been useful to us. As warped, weird or toxic as they may have become, at one point they may have filled a need, healed a wound or built an impenetrable defence for us. So, as we look at the ugly parts of ourselves, we must do so lovingly, with forgiveness, grace and compassion. We need to be kind and patient with ourselves and others, else we end up adding guilt and shame to the list of things we're trying to get rid of. Grace upon grace. Compassion on compassion. Healing comes through acknowledging our flaws, bringing them into God's light and then lovingly setting them aside.

RN

25. BEAUTIFUL MESS

The LORD your God is with you,
the Mighty Warrior who saves.
He will take great delight in you;
in his love he will no longer rebuke you,
but will rejoice over you with singing. **Zephaniah 3:17**

To spend time with God is to know him better. How many of us hide ourselves from God because we fear that he is put off, disappointed or let down by our shortcomings. God is not the fire-breathing, lightning-throwing God of War, who shakes his head in disappointment. More importantly, God is not afraid of the beautiful mess that is you.

When we stand face to face with God, there is no shame emanating from his side. One of the scariest thoughts for me is that once I begin to reveal my true self, shedding the layers of appearance away, presenting this 'unfiltered version', exposing the sides of me I deem 'ugly', to the people I love the most, they'll run for the hills.

The scripture in Zephaniah reads, 'He will take great delight in you.' Another word for 'delight' here is 'captivated'; God will be captivated with love at the sight of who you truly are. And the only way that the people closest to you can truly come closer is if you begin to risk giving them a glimpse of who you really are and trust that they, too, will delight in your vulnerability and honesty.

RN

26. QUIET IN LOVE

He will rejoice over you with joy;
He will be quiet in His love [making no mention of your past sins],
He will rejoice over you with shouts of joy. **Zephaniah 3:17 (AMP)**

We can falsely believe that our brokenness is too overpowering, but it's only when we stop suppressing those parts that truly need to be revealed that we become healed and transformed.

I wanted to repeat the scripture from yesterday in a different translation – this time the Amplified Bible – to provide us with a slightly different perspective. This translation reads, 'He will be quiet in His love [making no mention of your past sins].' What a lovely image of God remaining lovingly silent. The silence here is key for me.

When we reveal ourselves fully to God and to those who love like he does, we will not be met with judgement but with silence. By revealing our true selves, the 'good', the 'bad' and the 'ugly', we give people in our lives the opportunity to love all of us. God rejoicing over us is a sign of his acceptance, as he lovingly embraces all that we are. We should not worry about what will be seen when we let the walls down. God has seen it already and, through Jesus, we are already accepted.

RN

27. EVERYONE'S INVITED TO THE PARTY

I will rescue the lame;
I will gather the exiles.
I will give them praise and honour
in every land where they have suffered shame. **Zephaniah 3:19**

When we first start walking – or dancing – more closely with God, our skills may feel reminiscent of an infant attempting their first steps. We are clumsy and awkward, and we stand out like a sore thumb. In these moments, we can begin to spiral downwards and think, are people watching me? Am I supposed to be here? I don't fit in, do I? And if the voices in our head stay locked between our eyes, they can do more damage than any 'hater' we could ever come into contact with.

God through the prophet Zephaniah declares that everyone who thinks they're out of the loop is in his loop. He gathers all who feel different, unworthy, written off, and writes them into the kingdom.

God gathers us and reinstates our peace, celebrating us with praise. It's a shame exchange. You weren't invited because of your gifts, your talents, your attractiveness or your strength; you were invited because God wants you there, and a party without you isn't the party God desires.

RN

28. *SELAH* – FREE FROM SHAME

Are you carrying shame, feeling unworthy, thinking you are beyond redemption?

The good news is that no one is beyond the reach of Jesus' cleansing blood, which takes our crimson-stained lives and makes them white as snow.

Take time to remember the power of the cross with some bread and wine (or grape juice!), and know that all your shame is pinned on that cross with Jesus. Leave it there and walk away with restored dignity and acceptance. Think of a creative way to mark this event and never doubt that 'It is finished' (John 19:30).

Jesus, thank you that you bore all my shame, so I don't have to. Thank you for adopting me and accepting me into your family. Thank you for giving me your righteousness. May I live freely and joyously because of all you've done for me. Amen.

29. BLOOD, SWEAT AND FACING FEARS

Instead, they were longing for a better country - a heavenly one. Therefore God is not ashamed to be called their God, for he has prepared a city for them.
Hebrews 11:16

In the pursuit of living with open eyes and heart, we can't ignore the sacrifice to our self-image, and the humbling of our ego that precedes deep relational mirroring.

There is no easy path. It takes blood, sweat and facing fears. It begins with the desire to change, to acknowledge our sins and to turn back towards God in repentance. Once we do, we find that God has more than enough forgiveness for us, that through the blood of Jesus we are set free.

Sometimes we can know this in theory but find it hard to walk out in practice. Life is happening - and love can soak through every moment, if only we have eyes to see it. The invitation to dance with the Holy Spirit, to soak more deeply in our relationship with God and subsequently our awareness of ourselves allows us to stand before our Maker, naked and unashamed. And today's scripture reminds us that God is not ashamed to be called our God.

How reassuring and comforting it is that God is not ashamed to publicly declare his love for us. Being seen by God transforms our hurt into healing, our shame into peace, our guilt into gladness.

RN

30. 365/360 REFLECTION

If you are reading through these reflections in time with the physical seasons, April will have us springing forwards as new life appears all around us in nature.

This last month has given us opportunity to reflect on some of the unhelpful things that are holding us back from joining in with the dance of the Trinity – Father, Son and Holy Spirit – that we were designed to be a part of. We hope that a renewed desire is birthing and burning within you to surrender your lives afresh to the One who redeems and restores us.

And we are not alone in this dance; God has given us friends and comrades to accompany us in our journey of faith. So, as we set aside another chunk of time to reflect on the month that has gone and the month that lies ahead, ask yourselves these questions:

- Are you all in?
- Is there anything you are holding back?
- Who are those God has given you to walk with, dance with and fight alongside in times of battle?
- Can you name one person you would love to see join in the dance with you?

MAY

1. FEAR OF VULNERABILITY

His pleasure is not in the strength of the horse,
nor his delight in the legs of the warrior;
the LORD delights in those who fear him,
who put their hope in his unfailing love. **Psalm 147:10–11**

When it comes to being vulnerable, to opening up or exposing the chinks in our armour, very few of us are running to the front of the queue. Putting ourselves in a vulnerable position is one of the most terrifying experiences we can face as human beings, because we're going out of our way to put ourselves at risk. Rendering ourselves completely defenceless, laying it all down, in the hope that we're rewarded with healing, with comfort, with safety, with connection.

If anyone finds a tool that makes being vulnerable a simple and painless practice, please tell me all about it. I avoid being vulnerable like an Olympic figure skater avoids falling on the ice. As of yet, I have not come across a cheat-code to vulnerability; the only way is through.

Vulnerability can be defined as exposing ourselves to the possibility of being attacked or harmed in some way. Being vulnerable is therefore an inherently risky business, but the paradox at the heart of vulnerability is that God says our weaknesses can expose more and more of God's strength and therefore should not be avoided. God doesn't need us to be strong; he invites us to be honest. The walls we put up will only deny his loving gaze and keep us trapped in fear.

RN

2. PAIN OF VULNERABILITY

Surely he will save you
from the fowler's snare
and from the deadly pestilence.
He will cover you with his feathers,
and under his wings you will find refuge;
his faithfulness will be your shield and rampart. **Psalm 91:3-4**

The very act of exposing the pain that terrifies us can create an opportunity for God to be present in our suffering. And revealing to others the emotional nakedness we are ashamed of can enable them to be strong on our behalf, to simply be with us in our fragility.

In those precious moments of humility, we unearth the hidden strength within us; the truth is that we have the Holy Spirit dwelling within our very beings to help us endure the impossible.

Moments where we have been vulnerable with others only to have them hurt or reject us can have us recoiling back into our turtle shells, but this scripture is a gentle reminder that God is different.

Under his wings we will find refuge.

Come before God, find a quiet place and present your open heart to him. Brick by brick, with every step of trust, we can build lives that are sanctuaries for him, where we feel safe enough to expose the darkest, most embarrassing and fearful parts of ourselves, all the while knowing the truth that we are never alone, and we can endure the impossible with the Spirit of truth living within us.

RN

3. SECRET PLACES OF LOVE

I call on you, my God, for you will answer me;
turn your ear to me and hear my prayer.
Show me the wonders of your great love... **Psalm 17:6-7**

In a powerful poem the medieval mystic Rumi[3] describes how lovers are able to find secret places in a world full of chaos, where they trade violence for beauty.

We may have walked our lives, measured the walls of existence down to the centimetre and come to the conclusion that there is no love to be found, yet love says there is. As much as our reason or past experiences can have us thinking that secret places inside this violent world don't exist, we must hold on to the truth that they do.

The psalmist, too, calls out in the knowledge of the existence of this secret place; he knows that this secret place is available to all those who seek it: 'I call on you, my God, for you will answer me.'

Being vulnerable can be a struggle, as we seek out spaces where our hearts will be met with love. But search on; we cannot lose hope, despite reason's claims, Love says, 'Here I am.' God will answer our call and 'turn [his] ear' to hear our prayer.

RN

---

[3] Rumi, 'Secret Places', in Coleman Barks, *Rumi: Bridge to the Soul: Journeys into the music and silence of the heart* (New York: HarperOne, 2007), p. 48.

4. BUILDING SANCTUARIES OF TRUST

Keep me as the apple of your eye;
hide me in the shadow of your wings
from the wicked who are out to destroy me,
from my mortal enemies who surround me. **Psalm 17:8-9**

Secret places can be people too.

I experience such safety when I'm having a coffee with a friend and the whole world seems to disappear. When I'm on the phone to a mate and laughing, floating above my problems as they sail on down the river for a moment. When I'm sitting in silence with my kin, with no desire to project anything other than what and who I am.

You may not yet have those people that you can be vulnerable with. All relationships need to be nurtured, trust needs to be earned, sanctuaries need to be built, and that takes time and faith. With every transaction of honesty and exchange in authenticity, we create secret places with people, where healing can take place, where we can be our true selves, where we can be hidden in the shadow of love's wings.

The enemies that prohibit us from creating these places can be the inner voices that convince us that these individuals or secret places don't exist, that there is no place to take refuge. These voices lose their power when we remember that the Spirit of God is in us and those around us, and that because of this we are the very places where the wonders of love can be experienced.

RN

5. FEAR NO EVIL

Even though I walk / through the darkest valley,
I will fear no evil, / for you are with me;
your rod and your staff, / they comfort me.
You prepare a table before me / in the presence of my enemies.
You anoint my head with oil; / my cup overflows.
Surely your goodness and love will follow me / all the days of my life,
and I will dwell in the house of the LORD / for ever. **Psalm 23:4-6**

Today's verses speak about walking through a dark valley, not staying in one!

Sometimes we can get lost in the valley and set up camp there – living in darkness, fear, worry and anxiety. If today we feel lost and don't know how to move forward into the light, let's know that Jesus is with us. In the pain, grief, sorrow and hurt, he has not left us. He understands and wants to lead us through that valley as our Shepherd. Sometimes we get lost there because we forget about God's goodness and mercy following us every day (if it helps to imagine this, Middle Eastern shepherds often lead from behind their flock).

Today we don't need to put a filter on our feelings or pretend that depression, anxiety or fear is not affecting us, but the first step of getting through is to acknowledge the place we are in and listen for God's voice there, right where we are.

Pray for his goodness and mercy to fill you now, and don't be afraid to ask for the support of a good friend or church leader who can pray and walk with you; we were never designed to walk through dark valleys alone, fearing evil. We were designed to walk together, with God as our guide.

DB

6. FRIENDS ARE BORN FOR FIRES

A friend loves at all times,
and a brother is born for a time of adversity. **Proverbs 17:17**

We all need people we can trust to be open with, but sometimes they are hard to come by.

If you're looking around, struggling to find a space to be vulnerable, then maybe the first step is to become the very thing you want to find in someone else.

Now, of course, I'm not suggesting we ignore our own tensions and wrestles. In moments when we've hit the wall and our empathy capacity is at an all-time low, we need to rest and recover. Yet we cannot ignore the power we possess to be the change we wish to see in the world, to be the answer to our prayers for someone else.

Sowing the seeds of vulnerability and honesty in our relationships, communities and workplaces can be the catalyst that ignites environments of kindness, compassion and accountability.

We are hardwired for community and connection, and I dare to dream what our friendship groups, families and partnerships would look like if we were to foster the capacity to look beyond ourselves to our fellow comrades during their times of adversity. These bonds can last a lifetime; such relationships are reflections and echoes of the kingdom of heaven itself.

RN

7. *SELAH* – PAUSE AND LISTEN

We started this week reflecting on the power of vulnerability and finished by looking at how fostering open relationships that point one another to Jesus is central to our walk with Christ.

The world is not looking for fake perfect Christians. The world is searching for authenticity and truth. Is vulnerability something you are comfortable with? If not, what stops this?

There is power in being our vulnerable, authentic selves! Think about those with whom you can be your true self and thank God for them! How can you be more vulnerable and authentic with others?

Jesus, thank you for your openness, honesty, authenticity and vulnerability. You never hid behind a mask to impress people. You were your true self with every person you met so you could connect, engage and reach them with the love of God. Show me how to do the same. Amen.

8. INFLUENCERS

He said, 'Do not fear, greatly beloved, you are safe. Be strong and courageous!'
Daniel 10:19 (NRSVA)

These days, some want the validated 'blue tick' on social media, to be an influencer with a large online following to get sent free stuff to wear and eat on a weekly basis. Don't get me wrong, I'm not against free stuff, and many influencers are inspiring. However, influencers are limited in what they can actually influence.

Generally speaking, influencers influence the external – our appearance, where we go, what we eat. Role models, however, affect the internal – our character, our values and our principles. Some of my role models are my dad, my stepdad and my church leader. They have nothing helpful to say about my hairstyle, but they encourage me to live a grace-filled life with integrity.

I love empowering young people. They don't need influencers in the wild so much as role models in their community, home and church. Daniel in the Old Testament was a role model who demonstrated courage and trust in God, and he influenced many. He became this inspiring person because he had a relationship with his heavenly Father and reflected his characteristics.

We all have people we do life with every day, but who are we a role model to?

DB

9. OFFENCE OR GLORY

A person's wisdom yields patience;
it is to one's glory to overlook an offence. **Proverbs 19:11**

Unless we are cast away on a desert island, we will come into contact with others.

Since no one on the planet is perfect, at some point we will be offended. Someone might intentionally, or unintentionally, hurt us. In that moment, we have a choice.

We can't change the feeling of being offended, but we can decide what to do with it – whether to hold on to it or let it go. If someone is taking advantage, manipulating, bullying, belittling or excluding us, we need to make changes to ensure the abusive behaviour cannot continue. But later, when we feel the anger, rage and unforgiveness start to build, we need to ask God to give us what we need to leave it with him, otherwise the pain and unforgiveness will continually attach us to that person and that event. In many circumstances, it can be really helpful to speak to someone else about this too; often someone older, wiser and detached from the situation at hand.

Offence excludes people from our lives – who do we need to build a bridge with and forgive? There is more freedom for us to experience in our relationships today.

DB

10. ACCUSTOMED

Do not conform to the pattern of this world, but be transformed by the renewing of your mind. **Romans 12:2**

When I was eighteen and living in Sydney, Australia, lads started wearing skinny jeans! It was an odd look – an upside-down pear, a big top and small legs. I vowed I'd never wear skinny jeans! Soon, though, they were everywhere – on TV screens, in magazines, in shops and on every street.

One day, with few alternatives, I walked into a shop, grabbed a pair and tried them on. I looked in the mirror and, to my surprise, I loved them! For the next decade, skinny jeans were part of my life. Because everyone was wearing them, I ended up wearing them.

It's the same with fear, although fear has a negative impact on our lives. When people around us are fearful and anxious, we can copy this and become fearful too. We live at a time in history when it's normal to assume the worst. The media exaggerate facts with fake news and lies. We are in danger of conforming to the pattern of this world if we don't filter the truth from the lies in the presence of God.

God wants to infuse our minds with courage and boldness so that we can come against the prevailing fear and bring hope to our neighbourhoods. How can we carve out some time to look upwards (to God) and outwards (to our neighbours) today?

DB

11. INTIMIDATED

I came to you in weakness with great fear and trembling. My message and my preaching were not with wise and persuasive words, but with a demonstration of the Spirit's power, so that your faith might not rest on human wisdom, but on God's power. **1 Corinthians 2:3-5**

Recently, I was thinking about my own journey with fear over the last year. I've become bolder and more confident, and this brought a smile to my face. That same day I bumped into someone who had unintentionally intimidated me at an event in the past. The person is a creative genius who makes me feel like every word I say has to carry substance and depth. As we chatted, I found my confidence shrinking and it felt like I took five steps back in my battle against fear.

The apostle Paul, a church planter and preacher, gave his all so that people could hear about Jesus and experience true freedom, but he also experienced fear! He was not sure about his communication skills, but his confidence was not in his talent or skill; it was in the Spirit of God.

God does not need us to feel confident in ourselves for his power to move; he needs us to be confident in him. There may be people who intimidate us today or in the future, but let's remember not to let our faith rest in the wisdom of others, but in the power of God. Our weakness is the precondition of God's power.

DB

12. PEOPLE-PLEASER

Am I now trying to win the approval of human beings, or of God? Or am I trying to please people? If I were still trying to please people, I would not be a servant of Christ. **Galatians 1:10**

People-pleasing and serving others can look the same on the outside; the difference is the inner motivation. People-pleasing is what we do in order to feel accepted, fearing rejection otherwise. Serving others is what we do when we know we have been accepted by Jesus. People-pleasing is what we do to get ahead or climb the career ladder. Serving others is what we do when our motivation and heart are to help others succeed and step into their God-given potential. People-pleasing causes us to speak flattering words. Serving makes us speak truthful words of encouragement.

Maybe today we are wondering if we are people-pleasing or serving others?

Let's ask ourselves the tough question: what is our motivation in this situation or relationship? Is it a fear-based response, or a response that is secure in God's love? Is it to build our little kingdom, or to see his kingdom come and his will be done on earth as it is in heaven in our places of influence? Ultimately, is it for my glory, or God's?

Spend some time listing the areas of your life where people-pleasing could be rife; ask God to reveal your inner motivation in these circumstances.

DB

13. SPIRIT-LED OR SENSE-LED

Now the L<small>ORD</small> is the Spirit, and where the Spirit of the L<small>ORD</small> is, there is freedom.
2 Corinthians 3:17

In life we have a choice. We can be led by our senses or led by the Spirit. Many people are led by their senses. Sight, sound, smell, taste and touch! If it looks good, we go towards it. If it looks hard, inconvenient or scary, we move away from it.

God gave us our senses to use, but he wants to lead us by his Spirit.

Our soul reactions can lead us to unhelpful or even sinful actions, but the Spirit always leads us on pathways to freedom. When we feel like taking revenge, the Spirit leads and enables us to forgive. When we feel like gossiping about a person who hurt us, he enables us to bite our tongue and find peace. When we feel like lying to get ahead, and we fear missing out, he leads us to speak the truth and trust him for opportunities and promotions.

I have never regretted listening to the guidance of the Holy Spirit, because on the other side of all our fears is freedom.

Are there some areas you need to pray through with the Holy Spirit, so you make Spirit-led decisions rather than fear-based soul decisions? Spend some time today asking the Holy Spirit to reveal any blind spot or area of your life where you need to step out in faith and trust him.

DB

14. *SELAH* – ALIGNING OUR MOTIVATIONS

Have you fallen into the trap of people-pleasing? Peacekeeping rather than peacemaking?

People-pleasing and serving others have different motives and agendas. Ask God to search your heart, and make a note of any insecurities driving your behaviours.

Give them to God and ask for his truth and healing.

Think about people you can serve who can't do anything for you in return. Ask God for opportunities to bless them this week.

Jesus, I want to be led by your Spirit and not by my insecurities and agendas. I want to be a role model who makes your love visible and influences others to seek you. Help me not to people-please, but to serve others and love them as you do. Amen.

15. THE GIFT OF VULNERABILITY

Give, and it will be given to you. A good measure, pressed down, shaken together and running over, will be poured into your lap. For with the measure you use, it will be measured to you. **Luke 6:38**

I have always heard this scripture spoken of in the context of generosity linked to finance. But it also came to mind recently when I was reflecting on being vulnerable, especially when related to lifting our eyes off our own adversity and creating the space to extend compassion or a listening ear to those around us. 'For with the measure you use, it will be measured to you,' our Lord says, and this is no different whether we are making a transaction with beauty or sharing vulnerability.

We so often wait for doors to open before we open the door for others; instead, we can step forward and create the culture of vulnerability that we are seeking for ourselves. It may be as simple as inviting a friend for a coffee, FaceTiming someone we know is going through a rough patch, or asking a housemate or family member how their day was. These moments can generate the momentum to grow a culture of self-sacrifice. I guarantee you will not be the only person in your sphere of influence looking to lay down their burdens. The bonds made in brokenness are some of the most solid connections we can make along our journey in life. To be a friend to someone else is to sow friendship into our own future, paying it forward for the stormy roads ahead.

RN

16. NOBODY IS PERFECT

If we go around bragging, 'We have no sin,' then we are fooling ourselves and are strangers to the truth. But if we own up to our sins, God shows that He is faithful and just by forgiving us of our sins and purifying us from the pollution of all the bad things we have done. **1 John 1:8–9** (VOICE)

Humans are heartbreakers. There is no escaping that reality. Giving our heart to someone is simultaneously giving them the opportunity to break it, even if they do so unintentionally. If only everyone respected the invisible 'handle with care' sign that comes attached to our emotions, the world would be a glorious place. But we must all admit that we've probably broken a few hearts, or at least caused a hairline fracture to a heart in our time on this planet.

No one is perfect, no one has 'no sin'. So we must extend compassion to ourselves when we let people down, and extend forgiveness when we let ourselves down – as hard as that may be.

As soon as we enter into a tango of vulnerability, no matter how experienced our dance partner is, there is a chance they may step on our toes or miss a beat.

Now that doesn't mean people have a free licence to abuse our love, nor does it mean we must refrain from trusting others with our truths, but we must embrace the reality that even the most caring human we know won't always get it right.

RN

17. YOU ARE NOT INVINCIBLE

In my distress I called to the LORD;
I cried to my God for help.
From his temple he heard my voice;
my cry came before him, into his ears. **Psalm 18:6**

Reality check: you are not indestructible. Of course, many of us know that already, but every so often we need a gentle reminder that we're far more Clark Kent than Superman. As mighty as we may feel, our fragility is exposed in the smallest of ways. For example, remember the last time you stubbed your toe? Or twisted your ankle? Or when you burnt your hand in the oven? Even if you're blessed with sandpaper for skin, having a high pain threshold doesn't make you invincible; the damage is still done, and healing is still required whether you feel it necessary or not.

Bleeding out on the battlefield of life, when we could reach out for help, has more to do with pride than resilience. Leaving ourselves stranded on an island of suffering, rather than calling out in our distress, is self-sabotage. The weight of the world does not rest on our shoulders alone, even for those of us who have become seasoned emotional baggage carriers.

Our cries for distress don't even have to be loud. Sometimes the biggest sign of surrender is standing still, admitting things are hard and whispering, 'I need your help,' to the God who always hears.

RN

18. PART-TIME SUPERHEROES

He reached down from on high and took hold of me;
he drew me out of deep waters.
He rescued me from my powerful enemy,
from my foes, who were too strong for me.
They confronted me in the day of my disaster,
but the LORD was my support.
He brought me out into a spacious place;
he rescued me because he delighted in me. **Psalm 18:16–19**

The role of superhero is not a sustainable one for us to play full-time. We may want to fight our battles alone, conquer the universe, but in actual fact the moment we admit it's too much, the moment we let our guard down and confess we need help, we tag in the most experienced hero in the known universe to take our place. We give permission to be saved by the One who saves.

We have this incredible image in Psalm 18 of the earth trembling, the very foundations and mountains shaking, God parting the heavens, shooting bolts of lightning at the enemy, and taking hold of us. God tears through time and space to rescue us, drawing us out of the deep waters.

Nothing will stand in the way of God tearing through the cosmos to be right beside you in your moment of weakness. But will you admit you need saving?

Are you allowing yourself to be honest with the depths in which you find yourself? Let God be God, let the Spirit save you from the deep; he will do so because he delights in you.

RN

19. HEARTS OF STONE

Above all else, guard your heart,
for everything you do flows from it. **Proverbs 4:23**

Sometimes we're so good at guarding our hearts that we leave no room to experience any sort of love. While wisdom and discernment are valuable tools for navigating this often tricky existence, we cannot lock our hearts away from joy, just to avoid suffering. The word 'guard' in Psalm 4:23 points towards us 'keeping watch, preserving'; there is a fine line between our heart being protected and our heart being a prisoner.

C. S. Lewis reminds us in his book *The Four Loves* that to love means being vulnerable, and the only way to escape being heartbroken is to not give our heart to anyone.[4] But if we do this, our hearts will grow cold and void of love itself. The only other option we have is to be prepared for the awkward mishandling of our emotions by others and for people to let us down. We must try not to let those things pull us apart; instead, we can persevere, we can continue to choose to trust, to forgive and to ask to be forgiven, and in doing so we can draw closer to each other.

This transaction of beauty and honesty is not void of pain, but is a pathway to true restoration and healing, and to relationships that can carry the weight of misunderstandings and disappointments. Vulnerability and love are synonyms - you can't have one without the other.

RN

[4] C. S. Lewis, *The Four Loves* (London: William Collins, 2012).

20. COME

Come, all you who are thirsty,
come to the waters;
and you who have no money,
come, buy and eat!
Come, buy wine and milk
without money and without cost. **Isaiah 55:1–2**

Honest brokenness is more powerful than the illusion of wholeness. We must not be fooled into believing anything other than this truth. 'Fearlessness' in overdrive, to the point where we are pretending to be invincible, works against the deep peace that is experienced when we lay down our weapons and accept our inner experience: that our labour is in vain, and that the bread feeding our egos is stale.

Pretending everything is fine when in reality we're carrying pain has us walking around wearing a mask, fearing that any moment it could slip and reveal to others what we fail to reveal to ourselves. I've done this too many times, gone through my day with a smile on my face, when dropping the facade would have been liberating, because living with the lie was hard work. I don't know about you, but for me, living that way for any length of time is exhausting.

God says, 'Come, all you who are thirsty.'

Come to the waters, with no cost other than admitting you're thirsty. Once we surrender to the truth that we need help and need to drink from the well that never runs dry, then we can truly be replenished, by the Living Water that is God, and by the rivers of water that run through our friends and God's creation.

RN

21. *SELAH* – COME AND DRINK

How we need God!

We need his rescue and salvation, his protection and provision, his guidance and leadership. People can say that only those who are needy seek God, but in truth we all need him. Are you comfortable being dependent on him? Are you happy to admit that to others, with honesty and vulnerability, while sharing the joy of security in him?

Take some time to think about how knowing Jesus has made you discover who you really are – no mask required! Ask God what he delights in about you and jot down those things that come straight to mind!

Jesus, thank you that you know who I am; you know my every thought, desire and action. I can be real with you about my joys and sorrows, successes and failures. You accept me fully and didn't make a mistake when you made me! Help me to be my true self today, and may my openness and vulnerability point people to you. Amen.

MAY

22. OUR FUTURE IN GOD'S HANDS

Therefore do not worry about tomorrow, for tomorrow will worry about itself.
Each day has enough trouble of its own. **Matthew 6:34**

D. L. Moody is quoted as having said, 'Our greatest fear should not be of failure but of succeeding at things in life that don't really matter.'[5] And yet, 'The Good Childhood Report 2020' by The Children's Society said that more than 30% of 10–17-year-olds fear they won't have enough money in the future, and more than 25% worry about future employment.[6]

Children and adults alike are constantly under pressure to live their #bestlives. Many believe this is determined by their income and career.

There's much pressure to be what society describes as 'successful', driven by the fear of rejection or loneliness that we may feel if who we are without praise and accolades is simply not enough.

If we are confident and secure in who we are, we won't spend time and money to fit into a group that only accepts us if we look and dress like them. Real success is found in being the best of ourselves where we are right now – faithful with whatever job, responsibility or income we have and trusting God for our future. Success is what we do every day when we seek to faithfully follow Jesus and do the things he did, and this process of spiritual formation is a journey, not a destination.

DB

[5] Jesse Carey, '12 of DL Moody's Most Profound Quotes about Faith', 5 February 2016, https://relevantmagazine.com/faith/12-dl-moodys-most-profound-quotes-about-faith/ (accessed 20 June 2023).
[6] The Children's Society, 'The Good Childhood Report 2020', www.childrenssociety.org.uk/sites/default/files/2020-11/Good-Childhood-Report-2020.pdf (accessed 17 April 2023).

23. A HOPE AND A FUTURE

'For I know the plans I have for you,' declares the LORD, *'plans to prosper you and not to harm you, plans to give you hope and a future.'* **Jeremiah 29:11**

Earthly fathers want the best for their children. This involves not giving into all their greeds, but helping them with their needs; not always giving them handouts, but hand-ups, so their children can be all they can be.

Father God's plans are to give us all a hope and a future. When Jeremiah the prophet spoke this message from God to his people, they must have been deeply encouraged. However, it took seventy years for this prophecy to become a reality – I wonder how many doubted God's words?

Can we hold fast to the fact that God is always good, and he does want to give us a hope-full future, even when we don't see it immediately? Can we hold on to God's promises, without fearing that he has forgotten or abandoned us, trusting him and his goodness decade after decade?

Faith and trust are not just believing in the sunshine but also trusting God in the middle of the storm, in the longing and waiting for it to pass. Spend some time today declaring the goodness of God and his promises to us! You may want to write down and remember some of his promises for you.

DB

24. PEACE IN HEART

Let the peace of Christ rule in your hearts, since as members of one body you were called to peace. And be thankful. **Colossians 3:15**

I recently read a quote along the lines of, 'Worry doesn't take away tomorrow's troubles - it takes away today's peace.' When we worry, we often think of the past or fear the future - and that stops us being at peace today! The Bible tells us to not worry about tomorrow but to focus on today.

I was asked to speak at the SSE Arena in Wembley, London, for a big Christmas church service. The venue holds ten thousand people and I was asked to speak twice. From the moment I accepted, I was crippled by fear. I had sleepless nights and night terrors. I felt nauseous. Fear was trying to rob me of my peace every day in the lead-up to that big event.

In those moments of worry, I pressed into God for comfort. In those times of prayer, I recovered my peace and courage. When I wasn't praying, I worried about failing and my peace disappeared again. The day arrived and I shared to the best of my ability. I sensed God's presence and his peace, and I knew he'd come through for me.

The moral of my story, as we have touched upon in earlier reflections, is that we can't pray and worry at the same time, so if we want to worry less, we need to pray more!

DB

25. GOOD SHEPHERD

The LORD is my shepherd, I lack nothing.
He makes me lie down in green pastures,
and leads me beside quiet waters,
he refreshes my soul.
He guides me along the right paths
for his name's sake. **Psalm 23:1–3**

I have been involved in pastoral work since I was twenty-one. The word 'pastor' means shepherd – one who cares for, feeds, protects and serves God's flock, pointing people to Jesus so they can become more like him and live the lives he intends for them. Sometimes we put those pastoring us on an unhealthy pedestal, thinking they are the ones in control of our spiritual growth.

God has given gifts to his Church: apostles, prophets, pastors, teachers and evangelists to support and equip us, but there is only one Shepherd who leads our lives, and that is God. If we put our pastor or leader in God's position, we are likely to have dashed expectations and disappointments, owing to their human frailty. When we expect perfection from humans, we become disillusioned, but when we trust and hope in our heavenly Father, he never disappoints. He will lead us and guide us and, in times of struggle, he will encourage, refresh and restore us.

Those who lead us should be good role models, but if a person has a moral failure, it is heartbreaking for them, their family and their community, but no one is left without a Shepherd to guide them and redeem the situation.

Let's pray today for those who pastor us.

DB

26. CLOTHED IN BEAUTY

Consider the ravens: they do not sow or reap, they have no storeroom or barn; yet God feeds them. And how much more valuable you are than birds! Who of you by worrying can add a single hour to your life? Since you cannot do this very little thing, why do you worry about the rest?
Consider how the wild flowers grow. They do not labour or spin. Yet I tell you, not even Solomon in all his splendour was dressed like one of these. If that is how God clothes the grass of the field, which is here today, and tomorrow is thrown into the fire, how much more will he clothe you - you of little faith!
Luke 12:24-8

I love the straight-talking nature of these verses. If God provides for the birds, then how much more will he provide for us, his precious, beloved family?

Luke challenges us to see how much valuable time we waste worrying about our care and provision. He is not saying to lie back and let God do everything. God never supports laziness or presumption! The raven still needs to leave its nest, or its roost, and search for food. When it does, God provides!

In the same way, we too need to leave our comfort zones and be responsible in using the gifts and skills God has given us and put ourselves to work. Work is a gift from God, whether paid or unpaid. However, if we play our part in working, giving and being generous to others, God will supply everything we need. It's called co-labouring with him! Let's remember we are co-labouring with God, carrying his love and kingdom as we go, and trusting him for everything we need today.

DB

27. WHEN WEARY, WE WORRY

Come to me, all you who are weary and burdened, and I will give you rest. Take my yoke upon you and learn from me, for I am gentle and humble in heart, and you will find rest for your souls. **Matthew 11:28-9**

Despite my fear of public speaking, I was asked to speak again – this time live at a conference for 100,000 people – it was my worst nightmare.

I'd been away from home for a week with a packed schedule and hadn't caught a wink of sleep on the thirteen-hour flight back to London. I landed one day before the conference and was feeling burdened and scared. I whinged to my wife, as I often do when feeling fearful, 'I don't want to do this; I'm going to pull out!' She'd never seen me so defeated and asked if I was having a panic attack. I don't think I was far off. We prayed together and gave my burden to God.

I went to bed and woke up the next day feeling different, feeling free. Overnight my view and language had changed; I was now up for the task ahead. Sleep helped, but I know that the Spirit did something supernatural in me too. The heavy burden was lifted, and I was filled with hope and expectation.

I often ask God why he keeps asking me to do things that make me fearful. His reply is always, 'So you learn that I am always with you!' What burden can we give to God today?

DB

28. *SELAH* – BE STILL AND TRUST

We started this week thinking about the future. Are you confident that God has the best for your future, or is fear or worry robbing you from being at peace in the present?

Have you been carrying your burdens alone or giving them to God and asking for his provision?

If God provides for the birds, how much more will he provide for you? Remember and write a list of how he has provided for you so far this year. Consider his goodness and thank him for providing.

Jesus, thank you that you are in my past, present and future. I pray you will provide for my needs and help me to surrender my anxieties about future possibilities and provision. Shift my focus from my worries and help me remember and be thankful for your faithfulness to me over all these years. What you did before, you will do again! Amen.

29. PLEASE DON'T FEED THE FEARS

Come to me, all you who are weary and burdened, and I will give you rest. Take my yoke upon you and learn from me, for I am gentle and humble in heart, and you will find rest for your souls. **Matthew 11:28-9**

When we are sleep deprived, we just need sleep. For some, sleep is tricky because our minds are full and burdened. This is better described as being weary, and today's scripture reminds us that we need to spend time with Jesus, who promises us rest for our souls.

God provided a day of rest for humans - Sabbath - so we would rest from the demands of work and be refreshed in him. It breaks the drivenness and fear of not achieving, and reaffirms that we are God's children, not slaves (as, unlike slaves who never have a day off, we are free to simply be).

Sabbath rest could be spending time in quiet, alone or with friends and family, enjoying hobbies or walks in nature. It can be journalling or creating art, going off grid or having a digital detox.

How do we rest? When we don't rest, our fears and stresses increase. So we don't feed the fears, we must choose ways that work for us to have Sabbath rest. Put it in the calendar. The world encourages us to hustle and hurry hard. Jesus invites us to come to him and rest. This is so we can have our best life, a long life, full of impact and purpose. Rest.

DB

30. FEAR OF BEING IN LEADERSHIP

Where there is no guidance, a people falls,
but in an abundance of counsellors there is safety **Proverbs 11:14** (ESVUK)

In today's climate of 'cancel culture', the fear of leadership is increasing. Many people don't want to take a lead; they don't want a position of responsibility or authority. In many ways, I understand where they are coming from, and on some days carrying the weight of responsibility and authority in my different leadership roles can be challenging. But the question I often have to ask myself is, 'If I don't lead, then who will?' Now, I'm not saying I'm indispensable in my role, but if we all allowed fear to keep us out of roles of responsibility, then there would be no one to steer important teams, charities and organisations.

We have to ask ourselves, if we don't raise our voice to advocate for the voiceless, then who will? If we don't use our God-given skills to positively influence, support and help others, who will do it? If we don't speak about God's goodness, other voices will fill the void: social media, politics and cultural trends that don't care about the future of Christ and his reign will fill the gaps.

Jesus didn't want to endure the shame, torture and separation of the cross, but he did, because his love for people was greater than his fear of suffering and death. In the same way, if our hearts break for people and God is moving in us to act, let's not fear stepping up. If our motivation is love and desire to please and serve God, then he will be faithful to equip and guide us in leading those he has entrusted us with.

DB

31. 365/360 REFLECTION

Jesus was always himself in every situation.

He was emotional, vulnerable, open, honest, compassionate and consistent with everyone he met. He wore no mask and never felt the need to perform or put on a brave face. He was secure in his Father's love and secure in who he was because of that.

Are you confident in being your true self, knowing that God has made us all different and with a unique contribution to make?

Let's pause for five minutes - or perhaps we could challenge ourselves to sit in prayerful silence for longer today - to reflect on our God-given unique attributes and seek to use them for his glory as we move into the month ahead.

JUNE

1. FEAR AND CREATIVITY

He builds his lofty palace in the heavens
and sets its foundation on the earth;
he calls for the waters of the sea
and pours them out over the face of the land –
the Lᴏʀᴅ is his name. **Amos 9:6**

It has been said that all great art comes from suffering, and that the greatest storytellers and innovators who ever lived all had one experience in common: they were tortured souls who used their trauma to impact the world.

Van Gogh, Jimi Hendrix, Oscar Wilde, Amy Winehouse – they all suffered greatly throughout their lives and were able to capture those experiences within great works of beauty born out of pain. But believing that pain is the only route to meaningful creativity can cause us to sabotage our joy, neglect our mental health and pursue paths of destruction in the hope that they will lead to creative fulfilment.

It is true that anguish, death and sadness can be home to moments of divine creativity. But we do not need to be a tortured soul in order to create something of value.

Having inner joy and peace will not extinguish the fire of creativity within you. Your happiness may change the tone of your art but it will not compromise its potency or the importance of the stories you have to share. If the God of love is the creator of all things, surely we should be rolling out his framework for creativity, and not our own?

RN

2. GOD, THE CREATIVE DIRECTOR OF THE UNIVERSE

In the beginning God created the heavens and the earth. **Genesis 1:1**

It is important that this truth sinks in: creativity is not always born out of fear.

If we are to embrace where the true source of all creativity lies, there's no better place to run to than straight to Genesis, the first book in the biblical canon.

God is the architect of all creativity. The beginner of the beginning. The first ever Creative Director, and his lifetime project encapsulates the entire universe and beyond.

God isn't a tortured artist and he didn't create the universe out of desperation, paranoia, jealousy or heartbreak, but rather out of the overflow of love that God is. The universe is a by-product of the Trinitarian relationship between all the Persons of God. We are God's love child.

There was no fear or doubt when God breathed life into our nostrils. Love, in all its complexities, with its infinite depth and resilience, is the greatest creative force in the universe; everything born from that centre point has the chance to stand the test of time.

RN

3. A LITTLE LOWER THAN THE ANGELS

You have made them a little lower than the angels
and crowned them with glory and honour.
You made them rulers over the works of your hands;
you put everything under their feet. **Psalm 8:5-6**

Our brains enjoy boxes. Often when people talk about 'creatives' or 'innovators', our brains make all sorts of associations and stereotypes based on what we've witnessed over the years through the media and other conversations closer to home. We hear the word 'creative' and some of us picture the most 'alternative' person we know. I'm sure you can see them in your mind's eye now, sitting in an artisan coffee shop, scrolling on their cryptocurrency app, about to join another 'online brainstorm'.

Often, we rule ourselves out of creative pursuits because we don't fit a particular type of look, style, age demographic or geographical location.

One of the most powerful ideas in Christianity is that we are all created in the image of God. You are a direct descendant of the creator of all creators. You were born to problem solve and innovate solutions. It's not something you have to become; it's something that you already are.

So let's begin by clearing our mental whiteboards when it comes to what makes a 'creative' and begin questioning: what does creative look like for you?

RN

4. MADE IN THE IMAGE OF GOD

Then God said, 'Let us make mankind in our image, in our likeness, so that they may rule over the fish in the sea and the birds in the sky, over the livestock and all the wild animals, and over all the creatures that move along the ground.'
Genesis 1:26

Moments after God creates the universe, he declares 'Let us make mankind in our image, in our likeness.' To reiterate what we saw in yesterday's reflection, we are descendants of the creator of all creators, but more than this, we are made in God's image; we carry the same DNA as God.

The myth is that there is a certain crop of humans who are creative, who reserve the right to form the future, who are qualified to sculpt their lives and the lives of others, and the rest of us must sit idly by, watching in awe. In actual fact, every human being at their core has the capacity, permission and authority to create. To bring things forth out of the formless void and to bring new life.

It doesn't matter if we're an accountant, a single mum raising three children, or under the perception that we don't have a creative bone in our bodies - we can all create! The definition of innovating is introducing new things, ideas or methods, and we all carry the ability to do this because we are designed in the image of our creative Father in heaven.

We were formed to form new things, not to fear them.

What would we initiate if fear didn't hold us back?

RN

5. BRINGING ORDER TO CHAOS

Now the earth was formless and empty, darkness was over the surface of the deep, and the Spirit of God was hovering over the waters. **Genesis 1:2**

The earth was 'formless and empty', unordered and uninhabited; there was no purpose and no order. Chaos reigned supreme, but what seemed lifeless contained the potential for all things.

How often do we find ourselves in the same space: directionless, seeing no clear path for the future and with no inspiration to push ahead?

These moments can render us defeated, but we have all the potential within us to bring life out of the depths and, together with God, to bring order to our own chaos.

When it comes to creating something new, hardship and chaos have the potential to rob us of our vision and throw us off course. It doesn't matter how good we are; the speed bumps in the road are part and parcel of the human experience, but we must remind ourselves again that God has put the divine power within us to bring order to chaos, as exhibited by God in the very beginning.

RN

6. LET THERE BE LIGHT

And God said, 'Let there be light,' and there was light. God saw that the light was good, and he separated the light from the darkness. God called the light 'day', and the darkness he called 'night'. And there was evening, and there was morning – the first day. **Genesis 1:3–5**

We must mirror our maker, the author of creativity. In Genesis it says that God 'sculpted' this unordered, formless chaos, and the first words that ever echoed throughout eternity were, 'Let there be light.' What a powerful sentence to speak into our own lives. To speak it in the face of injustice. To scream it to the heavens when darkness threatens to rob us of joy in our souls.

God's words separated the light from the dark, gave meaning to the perceived emptiness and brought beauty out of barrenness. As we have seen, we are created in God's image and so we too have the same authority within us to slice through darkness like a hot knife, and to give life to opportunity, love, happiness, truth and restoration, with the help of the Holy Spirit.

We must speak, 'Let there be light,' into the areas of our lives where there seems to be only darkness and, as we see how God sees, we will bring vision where there seems to be no purpose or direction.

Which areas of your life might you need to speak, 'Let there be light,' into today?

RN

7. *SELAH* – LET THE LIGHT IN

God has made us in his image, which includes being creative, like him!

Adam's first task was naming all the creatures God had made – co-labouring in creativity. This week we've reflected on the fact that we are designed to co-labour with God to bring creative solutions to the world's challenges.

Research has shown that the majority of children are born creative geniuses and lose most of their creativity as they become older, influenced no doubt by others and the surrounding culture.[7] Spending time with our Creator Father can inspire us to release creative acts of kindness to others.

Do you believe you are creative and able to make a difference? Spend time with God and ask him where he wants you to begin; what creative act of kindness can you bring to your family, a particular situation, your college or your workplace? Let your childlike self explore and enjoy the journey!

Father, thank you for making me creative like you. Thank you that the Holy Spirit in me is full of creative ideas. Help me co-labour with you in bringing creative ideas and solutions to bless and encourage those in my situations and environments.

[7] 'Study Shows We Are Born Creative Geniuses but the "Education" System Dumbs Us Down', Twenty One Toys, twentyonetoys.com/blogs/teaching-21st-century-skills/creative-genius-divergent-thinking (accessed 18 April 2023).

8. DIVINELY IMPRINTED BY CHRIST

Therefore, since we have such a hope, we are very bold. **2 Corinthians 3:12**

Humanity has been created in the image of God and given the authority to go and create, design, build and innovate. With that knowledge in hand, I find myself asking some questions. If I truly believed that the Spirit who created the dolphins of the sea and the eagles of the sky lives within me and works through me, would my day-to-day look different? Would the vision for my life be so one-dimensional? Would I still be governed by the same inferiority complex?

What would my life, relationships, business projects, music production, scriptwriting, scheduling and even my grocery shopping look like if I believed that I was sculpted in the image of God?

Whether you believe it or not, the truth doesn't change. We have a divine identity through Christ, and we all, every single one of us, have the potential to bring a new perspective to the world.

This is not just limited to our businesses or the arts; this is key to our relationships with all of creation, ourselves and God. This thought could revolutionise how you see yourself, because if you haven't realised it yet, you are uniquely gifted for the works God has for you; you are one of one!

RN

9. DO NOT DISTURB

The Lord will again delight in you... if you obey the Lord your God and keep his commands and decrees that are written in this Book of the Law and turn to the Lord your God with all your heart and with all your soul. **Deuteronomy 30:9–10**

When I need to get important work done, I switch my phone to 'do not disturb' mode so that I can focus and give the work my full attention. I am usually quite disciplined, but it's amazing how disciplined I can be with my work life and not my devotional life. How often do I set my phone to 'do not disturb' mode when I am spending time with God?

Recently, I realised how distracted I can get, ending up with hardly any time with God, even though I claim that he is the most important person in my life – and far more important to me than work.

Turning to God with our heart and soul and helping our relationship grow and deepen takes time. Maybe we fear that we won't get everything done if we spend time with God, but giving time to God will have the opposite effect – we will be more efficient, creative and fruitful if we work from the place of having rested with him, allowing ourselves to be refreshed and refilled by his grace.

I now put my God-time first in my calendar, so it's more important than all my other meetings. A simple discipline to stop the distractions. What can we do to prioritise our time with God?

DB

10. THE SAME SPIRIT LIVES IN ME

And if the Spirit of him who raised Jesus from the dead is living in you, he who raised Christ from the dead will also give life to your mortal bodies because of his Spirit who lives in you. **Romans 8:11**

The claim Paul makes to the church in Rome is wild.

The same Spirit who raised Jesus Christ from the dead lives in me. Repeat that five times right now, and really let it sink into every inch of your mind. This is an absolutely reality-altering revelation, and repeating this statement daily may have to become my new contemplative practice.

Not only are we vessels designed by God, in his likeness, but we also contain the same Spirit who changed the course of human history forever. The same Spirit who was floating above the formless earth at the very beginning of time. The same Spirit who raises the dead back to life, heals the sick and heartbroken, and defies the laws of science over and over again.

When you look in the mirror, do not be blinded by your packaging. Instead, see through the eyes of faith; open your eyes to the boldness, creativity, problem solving and vision casting that you carry.

The anchor that keeps us safe in the storm is the knowledge that we carry the Spirit of God. It's time we began looking at our fears through the lens of the spiritual authority that we carry.

RN

11. LOSING LAZINESS

Lazy hands make for poverty,
but diligent hands bring wealth. **Proverbs 10:4**

I envy (in a healthy way, I promise) musicians who are classically trained, or who have learnt the ins and outs of their instruments so much so that they're able to 'break the rules' and operate with a freedom that can only come out of discipline.

I spend most of my days listening to a 'peaceful piano' playlist that has a host of new-classical artists, gliding up and down the keys of their pianos effortlessly. The compositions on that playlist have the power to transport me from my noisy apartment block into a realm that transcends the confines of the walls, police sirens and run-down carpets that surround me.

Their accomplishment is a mixture of both talent and hard work. For sure, there is undeniably an aspect of natural ability that these composers are blessed with. Nonetheless, a flame in its infancy needs to be fanned and fuelled before it flourishes. These talented individuals could not have escaped the years and years of practice required. We are all made in the image of God, but whatever the gifts God has given us, hard work and devotion are an entry-level requirement across the board if we are to make the most of what we have been given.

Laziness is the enemy of progress, but diligence is a pathway to peace.

RN

12. CREATIVE DISCIPLINE

He who gathers crops in summer is a prudent son,
but he who sleeps during harvest is a disgraceful son. **Proverbs 10:5**

Did you know that you are a priceless piece of marble, uniquely sculpted and infinitely loved by God? Knowing this is fantastic, but embarking on the painstaking process of chiselling away, bit by bit, until shape begins to be revealed can take blood, sweat and tears. Sculpting the marble into something that radiates more of the vision the Sculptor had in mind in the first place can be hard work, but we are not created to go through this refining process alone.

Though we are containers of this unlimited potential, our frustrations can arise when we have all these ideas stored up inside us that have nowhere to go, when we have no agency to do the hard yards it takes to create a masterpiece. We have to work hard to close the gap between what's stored inside our imaginations and making it reality, but this hard work begins with simply spending time with Jesus. As we work and create from the safety of knowing who we are in God and what motivates us to create in the first place, this begins to yield the fruit that can truly change the world.

Creativity and discipline are best friends – even though it's rumoured that they rarely hang out – and this discipline comes with spending time with God. Get your chisel ready; there's work to be done.

RN

13. WHO BEFORE HOW

Before a word is on my tongue
you, LORD, know it completely.
You hem me in behind and before,
and you lay your hand upon me.
Such knowledge is too wonderful for me,
too lofty for me to attain. **Psalm 139:4-6**

Once we truly grasp that we are all inherently creative, we can too quickly move on to the 'What now?' questions; how does this play out in my relationships, my job role, my response to injustice?

We are quick to rush to pragmatism, to making things happen in our own strength. The truth is, we need to dwell in who and whose we are for far longer than we often think before moving to 'How?'

Everything we do will be born out of who we are, and the more we uncover the layers of who we are and explore our inner landscape, the more we can begin to shift our focus to have an impact on the world around us.

Pausing to look within may be excruciating or exhilarating, but it will be ultimately rewarding, because being defined or finding worth outside God is not a firm foundation on which to build. To understand how and who we are, we need to dial in to the One who originated our very design. Let's sit still in stillness and listen to the One who knows our thoughts before we think them. We may be mysteries to ourselves, but we're not a mystery to our God.

RN

14. *SELAH* – GOOD WORKS FOR US

God has good works for us to do; things that will bring us fulfilment and are a blessing to others.

Are you available to receive these opportunities from God? Are you responsive to act upon his nudges when you get them? If not, what might be stopping you? Why not spend some time in prayer, asking God to reveal his love for you and his will for you.

Ask God to remind you of the times you have responded to his leading before. What was the impact, both on you and on those around you? If it was a positive experience, praise God for his kindness and provision. If stepping out bruised you, ask God to heal you and give you courage to go again.

Jesus, help me to see the opportunities you provide for me to do good works, bless others and change the atmosphere around me. Help me to be quick to respond without fear or hesitation. Thank you that you have planned a fulfilling life for me, and seeing you work through me is a great blessing! Amen.

15. SO... WHAT DO YOU DO?

You have searched me, Lord,
and you know me.
You know when I sit and when I rise;
you perceive my thoughts from afar.
You discern my going out and my lying down;
you are familiar with all my ways. **Psalm 139:1–3**

It's likely that each one of us has been to a party where everyone takes turn answering the question, 'What do you do?'

It can often be the first question we're faced with when we meet someone new. This question can essentially mean, 'How do you pay your rent?' So much of our worth, social currency and affirmation is based upon the way in which we contribute to the economy, and it's heartbreaking.

In those 'what do you do?' moments I tend to scramble, trying to think of the most exciting response in order to portray the dynamic and/or interesting human I am. We reduce ourselves to titles and job roles, but how we contribute to the economy, our LinkedIn profile title or our employment does not have the first or final say about who we are; we simply need to ask the One who created us.

Today, remember, our spirit of creativity is not defined by what job we have, but by who we are.

RN

16. REAL GRASS

Keep your lives free from the love of money and be content with what you have,
because God has said, 'Never will I leave you; never will I forsake you.' So we
say with confidence, 'The Lord is my helper; I will not be afraid. What can mere
mortals do to me?' **Hebrews 13:5-6**

Money is talked about a lot in the Bible. It is not that money is good or bad;
rather, it is the heart behind money that Jesus consistently addresses.

One of the keys to overcoming the love of money is to be content with what
we have. To do that it starts with a daily discipline of thanking God for all we
have rather than spending time desiring what we don't have.

My wife and I live in a two-bedroom flat in London with two children and a
small balcony, on which we laid a metre of fake grass just to be able to call it
a 'garden' for the children. We would love a real one, and we don't believe it is
inappropriate for us to ask God for a garden one day. However, what we are not
going to do is spend every day wishing and wanting, groaning and moaning
for something that we don't have. We are going to focus on what we do have.
We have a flat in one of the most creative and inspiring cities in the world. We
have a room for the boys, and we have clean water and heating. We have a
huge green park across the road with real grass, and for that we are grateful.

Why don't you write a list of what you do have and what God has done for
you; be reminded that he will never leave you or forsake you, and out of that
revelation may you experience a new level of contentment.

DB

17. THE TWELVE MISFITS

These are the names of the twelve apostles: first, Simon (who is called Peter)
and his brother Andrew; James son of Zebedee, and his brother John; Philip and
Bartholomew; Thomas and Matthew the tax collector; James son of Alphaeus,
and Thaddaeus; Simon the Zealot and Judas Iscariot, who betrayed him.
Matthew 10:2-4

In his book *The Artisan Soul*, Erwin McManus explores the creative essence
present in all humanity, and the importance of the imagination.[8] One of the
points he touches on is Jesus' recruitment policy.

There are very few roles that have ever been more important or significant
than being chosen as one of the first apostles. Honestly, imagine going for that
interview! Unknown to them, those men and women who followed Jesus Christ
would go on to shape the future of history, inspiring and having an impact on
every sphere of society, so it's quite a shock when we have a quick glance at
their CVs: a tax collector (considered a traitor for making money from Jewish
suffering), fishermen (working class among the working class), sex workers
(Judaism was hot on purity culture, so they would not have been too popular),
freedom fighters (conflict-ready, fanatical), medical experts (potentially
inexorable rationalists), rejects (those whom society deemed unwanted and
unholy). All zero preparation for the task ahead.

If you think you'd be disqualified from being picked to follow Jesus, great.
Shed the shame of being imperfect and welcome to the club.

RN

[8] Erwin Raphael McManus, *The Artisan Soul: Crafting your life into a work of art* (New York:
HarperCollins, 2015).

18. DREAM TEAM INVITATION

'Come, follow me,' Jesus said, 'and I will send you out to fish for people.'
Matthew 4:19

Made in the image of God, the Spirit of God is dwelling inside our one-of-a-kind bodies with all their bespoke characteristics, quirks, beauty and brokenness. God invites us to extend his grace to all the ends of the earth, and to add our handprints to history.

Despite the baggage the apostles brought with them, whether from events that happened to them or insecurity rooted within them, Jesus called them. One by one, name by name, Jesus drew out their potential, and thousands of years later their names are engraved in Scripture.

Jesus saw what they couldn't see for themselves.

Left to their own devices, they would never have actualised such depth of purpose. To quote Erwin McManus in his book *The Artisan Soul* again, 'the movement Jesus started was a movement of dreamers and visionaries, not of academics and theologians'.[9]

You have, without even knowing, fulfilled one of the key requirements necessary to be involved in the greatest story ever told, to be included in the most creative project ever to take place, to be added to Jesus' dream team and sculpt the future you desire: you are alive.

The next step is to jump in with both feet.

RN

[9] McManus, *The Artisan Soul*, p. 101.

19. SHAPED BY WHAT WE SEE

Now the LORD is the Spirit, and where the Spirit of the LORD is, there is freedom. And we all, who with unveiled faces contemplate the LORD's glory, are being transformed into his image with ever-increasing glory, which comes from the LORD, who is the Spirit. **2 Corinthians 3:17-18**

When we spend time with God, we begin to reflect God's kindness, goodness, patience and holiness, and we begin to radiate that very love into all the relationships of our lives. Our careers, our romantic relationships, how we engage with food, health, money, family: everything is rooted in operating out of a healthy sense of self found only in Jesus Christ. Without it, we're merely putting sticking plasters on broken limbs, trying to find wholeness and completion in people, places and titles that have very little to do with our deepest core design.

The unveiling is just the start, and the transformation can take a lifetime, but as we begin to shed the skin of who our culture tells us we need to be, as we begin to take off the expectations of family and friends, as we begin to tune out the myths that we've convinced ourselves are truths, we can begin to walk in who we were truly created to be. We reflect what we look upon.

RN

20. PROUD TO WEAR YOUR SKIN

And we all, who with unveiled faces contemplate the Lord's glory, are being transformed into his image with ever-increasing glory, which comes from the Lord, who is the Spirit. **2 Corinthians 3:18**

Boldness. A definition I enjoy of this word is to have an appearance that is strong, vibrant or clear. Boldness is the result of knowing who we truly are.

The more we strip away the layers, the toxic thoughts of ourselves, the labels that have been put on us by culture, family and foes, our vision becomes clearer and clearer. We build a strong, vibrant appearance, rooted in our true identity, and begin to reflect the God who created us. Bold to be different in the face of adversity, bold to stand for justice in times of inequality, bold to speak love in the face of hate, and even bold to look at our own brokenness with compassion, knowing that God is made even more perfect in our fragility.

Paul encapsulates this process in 2 Corinthians, this ongoing transformation into God's image, with ever-increasing glory. It's never ending. Once the momentum starts, it's pulling in one direction.

Today, can you be bolder than you were yesterday? Not aggressive in your expression of self, not self-centred or egotistical, but proud to wear your skin, knowing the Spirit sits within your soul.

RN

21. *SELAH* – YOU ARE QUALIFIED

This week's reflections have shown us that none of us is disqualified from being a follower of Jesus, a kingdom advancer, or from having a faithful impact in our spheres of influence.

It doesn't matter about our past, our background, what we've done or haven't done; we all have equal potential to be world-changers through the Holy Spirit living in us.

Do you realise you are a world-changer – one person at a time? Ask God who he has on his heart for you to build a relationship with, to serve and to bless. That person in turn may go on to do great things for God, all because you brought Jesus to them.

Jesus, thank you for giving me not only salvation, but also meaning and purpose in my life. Thank you that you have made me a world-changer, one person or situation at a time. Show me my person this week and the ways I can show value and worth to them. Amen.

22. MOSES, AKA USAIN BOLT

When he went out the next day, behold, two Hebrews were struggling together. And he said to the man in the wrong, 'Why do you strike your companion?' He answered, 'Who made you a prince and a judge over us? Do you mean to kill me as you killed the Egyptian?' Then Moses was afraid, and thought, 'Surely the thing is known.' **Exodus 2:13-14 (ESVUK)**

Meet Moses. He is an Israelite who has been raised as an Egyptian, and his identity is all over the shop. He doesn't know who he is or where he belongs and, in a moment of rage, ends up killing an Egyptian man. He thought it would be kept on the quiet, but people talk, and Moses fears for his life. He flees to a hideout in a place called Midian. Fear is now the compass directing his life.

Everything he was familiar with, everyone he grew up with, everything he has ever achieved is now gone. He has nothing but God. But, as we are going to discover, that is all we need.

Often our fears will cause us to run into a space we had not planned to go. A relationship that should have been avoided, a career that has left us full of doubt. However, just because we are in an unknown place, it doesn't mean God can't use us there.

No matter where fear pushes us, it is never out of God's reach. Maybe today you are wondering how you got yourself into a certain situation. Know that God is with you yesterday, today and forever.

DB

23. MOSES, AKA FREEDOM FIGHTER

Then he said, 'I am the God of your father, the God of Abraham, the God of Isaac and the God of Jacob.' At this, Moses hid his face, because he was afraid to look at God.
The Lḭḭ said, 'I have indeed seen the misery of my people in Egypt. I have heard them crying out because of their slave drivers, and I am concerned about their suffering.' **Exodus 3:6–7**

Moses is out in the desert and a bush lights up on fire and starts talking to him. I think I, too, would hide my face in fear if that happened to me. God tells Moses that he has heard the cries from the Israelites who are in slavery and goes on to say that it is Moses himself who is going to do something about it: 'You are going to set my people free.'

God never has and never will be OK with slavery, and he still hears our cries for the people stuck in slavery today. My wife, Charlie, is the European Director for an anti-human trafficking organisation, called A21, which exists to abolish slavery in our lifetime. Often, we fear that our impact or influence can have little effect, so we end up doing nothing, but all God needs is one person to overcome their fear and go where he is calling them to go.

Is God speaking to you today like he did to Moses? Not as a burning bush, but is your heart burning to make a difference where there is injustice in the world? Don't let fear hold you back. Pray prayers of desperation, make that call to find out what is being done about the injustice on your heart, do the research, give to that charity that is making a difference or start a charity to bring freedom and rescue to the area you are passionate about. Ask God today to give you the best next step.

DB

24. MOSES, AKA THE MAN OF EXCUSES

But Moses said to the Lord, 'Oh, my Lord, I am not eloquent, either in the past or since you have spoken to your servant, but I am slow of speech and of tongue.' Then the Lord said to him, 'Who has made man's mouth?' **Exodus 4:10-11 (esvuk)**

God is sending Moses on a mission to rescue the Israelites from slavery, and Moses has the audacity to ask God (the *creator* of the heavens and the earth) to send someone else.

Fear is gripping Moses as he ponders walking up to Pharaoh and asking for the slaves to be released. God in his graciousness responds to Moses by asking, 'Well, who made your mouth?'

What God is saying is, 'I know who you are and what you can and cannot do. I am not setting you up for an epic failure that will end in public humiliation and death. I am your Father who created you, therefore I will give you everything you need to succeed in the task I have given to you.'

So often, like Moses, we too doubt that God would want to use us or can use us. We make excuses to get out of doing things that will bless others. Ultimately, when we say no to God because of our own insecurity or fear, we are robbing someone else of the blessing that is attached to it. Excuses are a great indicator of what we fear doing. What have you let fear talk you out of this week?

If you feel a stirring in your soul as you read today's scripture and know that you have been making excuses or avoiding doing something that God has asked you to do, know that God is quick to forgive when we confess our shortcomings to him. His grace is more than sufficient, and he longs to speak words of truth and encouragement over you today.

DB

25. MOSES – RETURN TO SENDER

*Moses returned to the L*ORD *and said, 'Why, L*ORD*, why have you brought trouble on this people? Is this why you sent me? Ever since I went to Pharaoh to speak in your name, he has brought trouble on this people, and you have not rescued your people at all.'* **Exodus 5:22–3**

Moses went to Pharaoh and told him to set the Israelites free. Pharaoh pretty much laughed in his face, said no and gave the Israelites even more work to do – but the story doesn't stop there.

The Israelites are angry with Moses and Moses is angry with God. Moses is crying out to God, effectively saying, 'I did this for you, like you said, so why aren't they free? Where are you?'

Often in moments like this, when we step out of our comfort zone to do something God has asked of us and we don't see the result immediately, we can respond like Moses does. We start to fear the worst outcome and to believe that God can't or won't do what he said he would.

Where have you given up? Who have you given up on? Maybe you told someone about your faith and now everyone treats you differently at work? Maybe you helped someone financially and now you're waiting for God to provide for you so can pay your bills?

If you are asking where God is, like Moses, be encouraged that God has not gone anywhere, and his plans for your freedom have not changed. God never said the journey would always be easy, nor did he say it will be fear free, but he did say, 'I will be with you throughout it all.'

DB

JUNE

26. MOSES – PUSHY PARENTS

During the night Pharaoh summoned Moses and Aaron and said, 'Up! Leave my people, you and the Israelites! Go, worship the Lord as you have requested.'
Exodus 12:31

In today's scripture, the wait is finally over. Pharaoh has said that the slaves are now free.

My wife and I enjoy watching the opening weeks of *The X Factor* and *Britain's Got Talent*. We are more interested in watching the people who can't sing but think they can than those with beautiful voices. There was a girl who sang her heart out and wasn't what you would call technically gifted (quite a nice way of putting it!). You could see the judges trying to hold it together as one by one they left the room to laugh. The poor girl went outside where her mum was and told her what happened. The mum then burst through the doors and said something to the effect of, 'My daughter has the voice of an angel. Why did she not get through to the next round?' The judges stopped laughing and one looked directly at the mum and said, 'You are responsible for the embarrassment she is feeling right now. You have told her she can do something which she is not talented or gifted for. If you really loved her, you would tell her the truth.'

The good news for us is that our heavenly Father could not be further from this pushy parent. He does not ask us to do something that he will not equip us for.

God does not set us up to fail. When he asks us to do something, he is not asking us to do it in our own strength but in his strength. He is not asking us to go alone; he is inviting us to go on an epic adventure with him.

DB

27. MOSES, THE FEARLESS

And Moses said to the people, 'Fear not, stand firm, and see the salvation of the Lord, which he will work for you today. For the Egyptians whom you see today, you shall never see again. The Lord will fight for you, and you have only to be silent.'
Exodus 14:13–14 (ESVUK)

Moses leads the people out of slavery, and they hit the Red Sea. They can't see a way through, and the people are scared. They start calling out to Moses, 'Why did you bring us here? To die?'

Moses' response reveals a lot regarding who he has become. By this point in his journey, Moses has learnt to face fear head on. From the trembling man living in Midian begging God to send someone else, he is now speaking with Spirit-filled authority and clarity. He says, 'Fear not,' and, 'Stand firm.' The Lord will fight for [us], and [we] have only to be silent.'

Did we just read that right? Silent?

Spending time with God in silence is a weapon God has given us to face fear. If you have never tried it, find a quiet space, shut your eyes and utter some simple words to show your openness to God. Say, 'Come Holy Spirit, come and deliver me from my fears.' Do this every day for a month, and try to increase the amount of time you spend in silence over further days, weeks and months.

Increasing your time in silence with God will increase your confidence to stand firm, even when it looks like you have a Red Sea in front of you and your enemy behind you. It is in the silent place in the middle of the storm that God speaks. God tells Moses to lift his staff over the Red Sea, and the water parts in two, allowing the Israelites walk through to their freedom.

DB

28. *SELAH* – BE STILL AND GO

Do you identify with Moses at all? Confused in identity, fearful of speaking up, impulsive at times? This was Moses when God first chose to use him to liberate a nation. God's hand on his life took Moses from being an insecure, confused man to being one of the greatest leaders of all time.

God has chosen you to bring freedom to others. Like Moses, all you need to achieve this is a humble dependence on God, trusting him to equip you for what might seem to you an impossible task. Never think that you're not up to the standard required, because God can transform any willing person into a mighty leader in their situation – even if they try to make excuses at first.

God, I praise you because you are God of the impossible, and I thank you for making me part of your big story! I ask you to enable me to bring freedom to those I meet in my daily life. I make myself available to you and depend on you to lead and equip me for your purposes. Amen.

29. LOVE OVERRIDES FEAR

Do not be afraid; keep on speaking, do not be silent. **Acts 18:9**

There was a house on fire, and as the Fire Brigade arrived they saw huge orange flames pouring out of the windows. The sound of a baby crying pierced through the noise of the burning building.

Out of nowhere, a woman ran through the crowd towards the front door. The fireman told her she couldn't go in, but she pushed him off and sprinted up the stairs. She got to the baby and leaped out of the window into the safety cushion laid out by the firemen. That lady was the baby's mum. The moment she realised that her baby was in that building, fear may have been present, but love took over. Love caused the mum to do what others feared to do.

There will be many times in our lives when we need to speak up for the voiceless and make a stand against injustice. We can fear that those times will hurt us or even get us cancelled on some level.

There are many people who will try to shut us down just for speaking the name of Jesus. When the fear of these people causes us to be silent, let's allow our love for people to override our fear so that we say what needs to be said, so that God's will be done and his kingdom will come.

DB

30. 365/360 REFLECTION

Looking back on this past month, we have seen that the creator of the universe trusts us to work with him in making all things new and is inviting us to co-labour with him in the good works he has planned for us to do - not in our own strength, but through his power working within us.

Whether you feel like it or not, he is inviting you. With all your individual gifts, character traits, hang-ups and excuses - he doesn't want a replacement and he will wait patiently for your 'yes'.

As with other months, today's devotional is an opportunity to pause and take stock of the days that have gone and the days that lie ahead. We encourage you to set a timer on your phone or, better still, switch off your phone for a while all together and reflect on the following questions with God:

- Are you living with a sense of God-given meaning and purpose in your life?
- Are you confident and willing to be involved with his plans?
- What good works has he planned for you to fulfil in the coming month?

Don't be afraid to start small - even seemingly small tasks, like showing kindness to a stranger or smiling at someone on the bus, can have a huge impact for the kingdom of God.

JULY

1. FEAR OF CHAOS

In this world you will have trouble. But take heart! I have overcome the world.
John 16:33

Chaos, disorder, dysfunction: whatever you call it, we've all experienced it. Inside our minds the sirens are ringing, and there's a red neon sign with the word 'danger' burned into the back of our foreheads. We've all faced metaphorical hurricanes that have swept us off our feet; moments in our lives when we're unable to distinguish what's up from down, losing our centre of gravity as everything is thrown into disarray.

Whether it's a church scandal that has rocked a local community, a completely unexpected breakdown in a relationship, political dysfunction on the highest level that divides a country or a personal battle you feel you keep on losing, sometimes our lives are on fire through no fault of our own. The first question in these times of instability can be, 'What did I do to cause this?' – feeling that we are to blame for the mayhem. But the truth is, sometimes we have done nothing at all.

We are not always to blame for disorder in our lives; chaos is inescapable, another cog in the wheel of reality. So rather than panic when the alarm goes off, or feel guilt when the 'danger' sign is on, let's begin to build a 'fire exit strategy' for ourselves so that our souls are prepared for dealing with the next fire, rather than being surprised by the unavoidable.

A 'fire exit strategy' may simply be the commitment to stop in times of chaos and acknowledge that God is in control, memorising today's scripture and speaking it over ourselves in times of need.

RN

2. IT RAINS ON THE 'GOOD' AND THE 'BAD'

He causes his sun to rise on the evil and the good, and sends rain on the righteous and the unrighteous. **Matthew 5:45**

Everyone will encounter rain and sunshine. Similarly, chaos is inevitable in our lives. There is no escaping it, and hardship is not a sign that we're not loved, or that we are doing something wrong.

Chaos is not evidence that you're a bad person. Moments of change are written into our lives.

While we have the power to create problems for ourselves, we must first find the grace to accept that the chaos that we are confronted by is not because God is angry with us. It's just proof that we're alive. The sun shines and the rain pours on the good and bad alike; no one escapes the seasons and storms of life, and our journey in life will not be measured by whether we face chaos or not, but rather how we respond when faced with those very storms.

Can you think of a storm you are facing now? How have you responded? Ask God to reveal to you his thoughts on this response, knowing that he is quick to forgive and longs to encourage us.

RN

3. GOD IS NOT AFRAID OF CHAOS

The earth was formless and void or a waste and emptiness, and darkness was upon the face of the deep [primeval ocean that covered the unformed earth]. The Spirit of God was moving (hovering, brooding) over the face of the waters. And God said, 'Let there be light'; and there was light. **Genesis 1:2–3 (AMP)**

Storms, floods, fires, health scares, job redundancies and heartbreaks happen. No matter how well we've lined all our ducks in a row, at some point chaos is going to come knocking at our door. But when it does, we must hold firm to our identity: no matter how big the storm is, we are children of God who have been designed to speak order, peace and life in the face of chaos.

It is important to remind ourselves afresh: God is not afraid of our chaos. God existed before all created things, and since the very beginning of time God has been speaking order to chaos. God brings 'goodness' out of formlessness and creates beauty out of materials we would consider waste.

Since the opening lines of Genesis when 'the earth was formless and empty, darkness was over the surface of the deep... the Spirit of God was hovering over the waters'. God speaks order. God drags creation out of nothingness, bringing meaning to the meaningless.

As we've seen already, God's first words in Scripture, are, 'Let there be light,' and out of those words all creation flourished, in ways we could never have imagined, forecasted or dreamed.

RN

4. SIFTING THROUGH THE CHAOS

God saw that the light was good (pleasing, useful) and He affirmed and
sustained it; and God separated the light [distinguishing it] from the darkness.
Genesis 1:4 (AMP)

God spoke to the deep and brought forth life. Can we be so bold, so brave,
so prepared for chaos that when faced with darkness we too look for light,
look for good, look for God? Even when there is nothing good to find in the
situation. Even if it's through tears. Even if we have no strength left. Even if we
have to muster the courage to scream, 'God is faithful,' at the top of our lungs
because the pain, the chaos and the noise around us are so loud.

What will be our response to the trouble in our lives?

Darkness and light cannot exist without one another. So instead of hiding
from the darkness, from trouble, we must learn to redeem it by looking for
the light. We must accept the chaos with both hands, and yet sift through it,
searching for the good that can be unearthed. Because when we do, we imitate
our Creator, following in the footsteps of the One who is able to make flowers
bloom in the desert, and the One who has the power to make all things new.

Where can you see the light in your life today?

RN

5. CREATED TO RESHAPE

*So God created man in His own image, in the image and likeness of God He
created him; male and female He created them.* **Genesis 1:27 (AMP)**

Now you may be thinking, 'Who am I? I have no right to stand in the face
of trouble and say, "Be still".' You may be mortal, but do not discredit or
undervalue the power that is stored within you.

The reason why we should be so bold as to walk in the footsteps of God and
to speak light into the darkness that knocks on our doors is because, as we've
said before, we are created in God's image.

The result of this reality is that we have the same capacity to bring order to
chaos that God possesses. Just after God brings order to the formlessness
that came before, he creates humanity: 'Let us make mankind in our image, in
our likeness, so that they may rule over the fish in the sea and the birds in the
sky, over the livestock and all the wild animals.'

We have been designed in the image of a God who can reshape reality to bring
life, no matter how desolate the environment may be. No other creature in
the known universe has the consciousness to partner with God in shaping our
destinies like humans can.

RN

6. THE POWER TO ENDURE

I can do all this through him who gives me strength. **Philippians 4:13**

Our self-talk can define our spiritual walk. Sometimes drama in our lives has us forgetting who we are and what we have the capacity to face. The odds can seem so stacked against us that it feels like we're facing Mount Everest. Yet buried within our souls is the ability to bring beauty, peace and hope to any situation, no matter the stakes. It's what you were created to do, and who you truly are.

In order to operate in this God-given identity, we have to be mindful of how we speak about ourselves and others. You are not a loser, although you may lose sometimes. You are not a failure, even if your hopes or aspirations fall by the wayside. Your life isn't a waste, and darkness will not prevail. You are not pathetic, even though right now you may feel weak.

Those little voices grow into screams if left unchecked and become 'truths' because they are cemented in our minds. Our opinion of ourselves is not the truth; it's just another opinion. Our weakness doesn't define us; with the power of God's love on our side, we can endure all things.

We are conquerors, because our God has conquered.

RN

7. *SELAH* – GOD IS IN CONTROL

We have seen over the last week how, though we are designed in God's image and so have power to create, we cannot control the situations we face. Sometimes there will be chaos in our lives, and it's what we do in these times and where we turn to for comfort that matters most.

Take some time to pause today and ask yourself:

- What are the chaotic areas of your life?
- Where does it feel like chaos is reigning?
- What parts of your life feel out of control?

Acknowledge these areas before God and ask him to fill you with his peace which surpasses all understanding (Philippians 4:6).

Lord, you hold all things in your hand, and all things are under your control. Since the beginning of time, you have brought order to chaos and you have commanded light out of darkness. Teach me how to bring order and to speak light to the chaos that surrounds me. Amen.

8. SPIRITUAL MILLIONAIRES

For those who are led by the Spirit of God are the children of God. The Spirit you received does not make you slaves, so that you live in fear again; rather, the Spirit you received brought about your adoption to sonship. And by him we cry, 'Abba, Father.' **Romans 8:14-15**

We have the potential to be spiritual millionaires.

We are birthed and adopted into God's family, with the ability to speak, mould and shape chaos into order, but if we don't believe we have the capability to face hardship, it's like walking around with a poverty mentality even if we have millions in the bank.

We are children of God, which sounds odd the first time we hear it, because we already have earthly parents, but we were created by God out of his abundance, his grace and his love.

We are caught in the overflow of God's mercy, and therefore can cry out, calling him, '*Abba*, Father.' Not only Lord, or Saviour; not only Almighty God and King, but also Dad, Mother, Friend. We are invited to reach up to a God who wants intimacy, not distance, and relationship alongside our reverence. God promises to never leave us nor forsake us (Deuteronomy 31:6), to walk by our sides through the fire in our lives; to guide our every step, and to sit with us in the dead of night.

RN

9. CHILL OUT

That day when evening came, he said to his disciples, 'Let us go over to the other side.' Leaving the crowd behind, they took him along, just as he was, in the boat. There were also other boats with him. A furious squall came up, and the waves broke over the boat, so that it was nearly swamped. Jesus was in the stern, sleeping on a cushion. The disciples woke him and said to him, 'Teacher, don't you care if we drown?' **Mark 4:35–8**

How do we become the kind of person who is the epitome of chill despite the whole world being on fire? Irrespective of how far that reality may be removed from my life right now, that is my dream. And, in pursuit of peace, who better to study than Jesus Christ himself?

In Mark 4, Jesus and his band of followers came face to face with a real storm, so extreme that the boat they were travelling in nearly capsized. The ferocity was unrelenting, but when the disciples went to find Jesus, he was sleeping on a cushion.

Jesus, awoken by the panicked apostles, 'rebuked the wind and said to the waves, "Quiet! Be still!" Then the wind died down and it was completely calm' (Mark 4:39). Jesus wasn't asleep to distract himself from the storm; he wasn't hiding; he was totally at peace. The disciples thought Jesus' action showed he didn't care about them, but this couldn't be further from the truth. Jesus was sleeping because he'd already taken care of them. He knew they were safe.

God isn't sleeping on you. He's not ignoring your cries. Don't mistake his silence for abandonment. He's in control of the very thing that terrifies you.

RN

10. THE LIFE OF NAOMI - PART 1

In the days when the judges ruled, there was a famine in the land. So a man from Bethlehem in Judah, together with his wife and two sons, went to live for a while in the country of Moab. The man's name was Elimelek, his wife's name was Naomi, and the names of his two sons were Mahlon and Kilion. They were Ephrathites from Bethlehem, Judah. And they went to Moab and lived there.
Ruth 1:1–2

Naomi has it all planned out. She and her husband, Elimelek, are going to move to the country of Moab and begin a new chapter.

The future is looking bright; they've escaped famine in their home town, and together with their young sons, they take the leap of faith to leave behind what they know and venture into the unknown. But just as they begin this journey, heartbreak awaits them...

Naomi's husband unexpectedly dies.

Despite this emotional uppercut, Naomi continues to move forward, and she gathers the courage to continue. All is not lost, her two sons are by her side, and together they can grieve, heal and then continue to build on what Naomi and Elimelek started – a new life together in a new land.

Part 1 of Naomi's story reminds me of the resilience required to continue going on, even after a setback. When we set out to start a new chapter, we have all the hope and expectation imaginable, and major disruptions can send us into a spiral. As my mother always says, 'Delays are not denials, and joy can be tasted on the other side of adversity.'

RN

11. THE LIFE OF NAOMI - PART 2

Now Elimelek, Naomi's husband, died, and she was left with her two sons. They married Moabite women, one named Orpah and the other Ruth. After they had lived there about ten years, both Mahlon and Kilion also died, and Naomi was left without her two sons and her husband. **Ruth 1:3-5**

The amount of visceral pain experienced in these three verses is tragic. Naomi has lost her husband, but she has not given up. This vision, the hope for the future, is now anchored on the families her sons are beginning to build, and the good times begin to return as they both find wives and get married! Things are looking up. For ten years, despite the pain and grief, they rebuild, they heal and they begin to taste the joys of life once more. Then disaster strikes again...

Both of Naomi's sons die unexpectedly. The dream is once and for all shattered. She is thrown into a tailspin once again. How can this be happening when God is in control?

I cannot even begin to imagine what Naomi must be experiencing in that moment. To be fair, I cannot begin to imagine what you might have experienced or still be experiencing today, either.

You may have lost a loved one or had dream after dream fall through your fingertips. Whether you have picked yourself up from the ground only to be knocked down again, or whether you're not sure whether you can keep trusting God in the midst of it, be assured that wherever you find yourself today, God can handle your heartbreak - and, importantly, the story doesn't stop there.

RN

12. THE LIFE OF NAOMI – PART 3

Then the women said to Naomi, 'Blessed is the LORD who has not left you without a redeemer (grandson, as heir) today, and may his name become famous in Israel. May he also be to you one who restores life and sustains your old age; for your daughter-in-law, who loves you and is better to you than seven sons, has given birth to him.'
Then Naomi took the child and placed him in her lap, and she became his nurse.
Ruth 4:14–16 (AMP)

Naomi's tragic story doesn't end there. One of her sons' wives, Ruth, returns home with her to Bethlehem and embarks on her own journey, finding love and eventually providing Naomi with a grandson. Naomi and Ruth's unlikely relationship, based on Ruth's faithfulness to Naomi in her time of despair, gives way to a restoration that Naomi must have thought impossible.

Face to face with the pain of loss, in the midst of her suffering, it was impossible for Naomi to foresee the moment in Ruth 4:16, where she is bouncing her grandson on her lap, filled with joy. Now, that moment doesn't make up for the loss she's experienced, but that taste of joy is all the sweeter on the other side of the heartbreak. Joy can be experienced in the midst of pain, but here it bubbles over and this happy moment almost seems like a reward for her resilience.

Naomi was desperate, to the point where she believed God had forsaken her, but he hadn't. God can help us experience joy in sorrow, and he longs to bring goodness out of our pain.

RN

13. THE LIFE OF NAOMI - PART 4

The neighbor women gave him a name, saying, 'A son (grandson) has been born to Naomi.' They named him Obed (worshiper). He is the father of Jesse, the father of David [the ancestor of Jesus Christ]. **Ruth 4:17** (AMP)

Naomi had no idea that her unexpected trainwreck would set her down a path that entered her into the genealogy of King David, one of the most significant figures in the Jewish tradition. Nor did Naomi know that the loss of her husband and sons would bring her back home, where her story would be written into the biblical narrative as a distant relative of Jesus Christ.

All that Naomi had lost was returned to her in a different way; the legacy she had wanted to establish was restored tenfold. Who would have thought? It was not her plan, but God had a plan to restore her dream in a new way, through Ruth, even when it seemed like all hope was lost.

If you are facing insurmountable odds, take courage from Naomi's story and know that you are not alone; your story is not yet over. You may be standing at the gravesite of dreams, mourning the loss of a loved one or nursing unimaginable heartbreak, but God is with you.

God's love still reigns; he is able to turn things around and bring good out of them. Even at the gravesite of your dreams, you too can taste joy again, in ways you could never have seen coming.

RN

14. *SELAH* – SITTING IN THE PAIN

Naomi's path began with despair and ended with jubilation. It began with utter chaos and ended with new life. Today, hold on to the thought that your story is not finished yet; you may just be in the space between the miraculous things God is going to do with your life.

Do you have a safe place where you can process your pain today?

Why not grab a journal or scribble within the pages of this book the areas of your life where you long to see God's goodness break through? Spend some time in prayer, asking God to reveal to you where and how he is already working. You may want to invite a friend into some of the pain you are experiencing; ask this person to speak God's truth over you when you can't see it yourself.

God, grant me the patience to endure this season. As I hold on to the hope that you walk beside me, I pray for endurance to remain on the path that you are leading me down, knowing you are here every step of the way. Amen.

15. BURYING OUR HEADS IN THE SAND

He got up, rebuked the wind and said to the waves, 'Quiet! Be still!' Then the wind died down and it was completely calm.
He said to his disciples, 'Why are you so afraid? Do you still have no faith?'.
They were terrified and asked each other, 'Who is this? Even the wind and the waves obey him!' **Mark 4:39-41**

Sometimes we cope by closing our eyes, burying our heads in the sand or distracting ourselves, but pretending our fears don't exist isn't the answer. In this scripture, we see Jesus trusting the Creator of the crashing winds. He trusted that the volatile waves, the bellowing thunder and heavy rain that could have terrified him would in fact carry him safely to the other side.

No matter how scary the journey seemed, no matter how bleak the outlook was or how hard the boat rocked back and forth, Jesus was resting in God's goodness and faithfulness. Jesus calmed the storm not for his own sake, but for the sake of the disciples because they were not ready to ride out the storm, to exercise that depth of trust.

Maybe we, too, aren't at the depth in our trust of God that we can sleep through our storms. But perhaps today we can begin to slow down to see that the very thing we are scared of bows before God. No matter how powerful the winds seem, God calls them to 'Be still.'

RN

16. WALK ON THE WATER

'Lord, if it's you,' Peter replied, 'tell me to come to you on the water.'
'Come,' he said.
Then Peter got down out of the boat, walked on the water and came towards
Jesus. **Matthew 14:28-9**

No matter the chaos you are confronted with in your life, whether it's a broken relationship, the loss of a job, failing an exam, struggling with poor mental health, a terminal diagnosis; whatever it is, Jesus says, 'Come,' and ushers us to fix our eyes on him and move forwards.

Christ is not scared of the environment, emotions, individuals, organisations, institutions, addictive patterns or scale of the storm. Christ sees straight through them all and invites us to walk in trust to follow his footsteps on the ocean.

Now that seems a bit bonkers, I'm sure Peter thought the same too, and your situation may look just as unbelievable. Yet Jesus said, 'Come,' because he knew that as long as Peter kept his eyes on him and not on the crashing waves around him, he would be empowered to walk on the water.

You, too, are being invited to walk forward, to take your first step out of the boat and onto the ocean that seems as though it will swallow you up. Let's remember today that this ocean obeys the same God that is inviting you forward, and that same Spirit lives in you; he's not going to let you drown.

RN

17. JESUS, THE VULNERABLE ONE

Jesus went out as usual to the Mount of Olives, and his disciples followed him. On reaching the place, he said to them, 'Pray that you will not fall into temptation.' He withdrew about a stone's throw beyond them, knelt down and prayed, 'Father, if you are willing, take this cup from me; yet not my will, but yours be done.'
Luke 22:39–42

Vulnerability is at the heart of the Christian tradition and has been modelled by God himself, no more explicitly than in the life, death and resurrection of Jesus Christ. Yes, there are lots of moments within the Scriptures of power and strength, of the Almighty God conquering his enemies, but we are also shown the Suffering Servant through the person of Christ.

In the Gospels, a humble, fiercely empathetic and open-hearted Saviour demonstrates time and time again what it means to wear your heart on your sleeve to the bitter end. Though fully God, he was also fully human: he laughed, he cried, he got hungry, he got sleepy; the list goes on.

In Luke, on the Mount of Olives, Jesus was distraught, in anguish – face down, crying out to God for the cup of death to pass from him. We see Christ acknowledging his inner experience, not ignoring what he was feeling in that moment or covering it up with false bravado.

The disciples are close by, but he is not ashamed to get down on his knees, open his heart and admit, 'Father, I need your help.' What a blueprint from God for us when we, too, feel distraught, distressed, out on a limb or out of control. Even the strongest, most powerful, Almighty Spirit knows the importance of being honest with himself and with God.

RN

216

18. JESUS IN THE GARDEN

An angel from heaven appeared to him and strengthened him. And being in anguish, he prayed more earnestly, and his sweat was like drops of blood falling to the ground. **Luke 22:43–4**

In the Garden of Gethsemane, Jesus was a fearless leader, coming before God unfiltered and unashamed, accepting that his soul was thirsty and he needed water.

In his moment of vulnerability, Jesus wasn't afraid that God would be disappointed in him or think him weak. He didn't fear that God would hold this display of weakness against him in the future. God doesn't hold a grudge and isn't in the business of emotional blackmail. Jesus ran straight to God with his pain, holding nothing back, and he knew he could trust God with his innermost torment. God responded by sending an angel from heaven to comfort Jesus in his time of need, walking through the shadow of death with him and letting him know that he was not alone.

We are welcomed by God to create these secret spaces in our own lives, to lay down the mask, and there is no better place to start than with God. God will never hold our vulnerabilities and fears against us. He will never betray our trust, and if we're walking around with the weight of the world on our shoulders, remember God's power is made perfect in our weakness (2 Corinthians 12:9).

Today, like every day, the door is always open to exchange our pain for his comfort and peace.

RN

19. GOD OUR SHIELD

After this, the word of the LORD came to Abram in a vision:
'Do not be afraid, Abram.
I am your shield,
your very great reward.' **Genesis 15:1**

Abram was afraid and God told him not to be fearful. God met Abram in his battle with fear and said he was his shield, which means protector.

Abram had no heir and feared his family line would die out. God told him that he would have a child. Abram was hopeful, but as years passed, so did the weight and clarity of the promise from God. Abram took the matter into his own hands and married his servant Hagar and had a baby called Ishmael. Eventually, Abram's first wife, Sarai, now renamed Sarah, became pregnant and gave birth to Isaac.

God did exactly what he said he would do. Like Abram, when we don't see things coming to pass in our own timing, we can get discouraged, seek to take control and try to make things happen in our own way. Fear drives this response, but we need to soak ourselves in the truth of Scripture to the point where we learn from Abram's mistakes and instead trust God's promises to us.

Are we waiting on a promise of God to be fulfilled? Let's trust him to bring his promises to completion at the right time and not be tempted to take matters into our own hands or to try to make things happen in our own strength. Remember, he is our shield, and he is faithful.

DB

20. GOD IS WITH US

Then she went and sat down opposite him a good way off, about the distance of a bowshot, for she said, 'Let me not look on the death of the child.' And as she sat opposite him, she lifted up her voice and wept. And God heard the voice of the boy, and the angel of God called to Hagar from heaven and said to her, 'What troubles you, Hagar? Fear not, for God has heard the voice of the boy where he is. Up! Lift up the boy, and hold him fast with your hand, for I will make him into a great nation.' Then God opened her eyes, and she saw a well of water. And she went and filled the skin with water and gave the boy a drink. And God was with the boy, and he grew up. He lived in the wilderness and became an expert with the bow. **Genesis 21:16–20 (ESVUK)**

In today's scripture we read a small part of the great unfolding narrative that leads to God asking Abraham to sacrifice his son Isaac in obedience to him, as a foretaste of what God will ultimately do with his own son, Jesus Christ, the once-and-for-all sacrifice for our sins. In this part of the story, Sarah could see that Hagar and Ishmael would bring trouble to Isaac, God's promised child, and so she asked Abraham (previously Abram) to get rid of them. And he did, kicking Hagar and Ishmael out of the house. Wandering homeless in the heat, they ran out of food and water, and Hagar feared they would die. She cried out to God for her child's life.

God met her in her desperation, reassured her she need not fear death or the future, and provided for her and her child in their present need.

Like Hagar, we can take assurance that when people make decisions that negatively affect us, God will still be faithful. Today, can we ask God to remind us afresh that he doesn't leave us or forsake us and that he has a hopeful future for us too?

DB

21. *SELAH* – STOP AND LISTEN

Let's take the time to pause today and remember the foundational truth we've spent much of this past week ruminating over: God is our strength and our shield.

Even when we find ourselves in the wilderness of our lives, God hears our cries and tends to our deepest needs, right where we are.

Today, take a moment to still yourself and meditate on God's goodness. How have you seen his strength play out in your life and the lives of others? Where has he shown himself to be a 'shield'?

God hears the cries of all of his children, but do we hear the cries of those in need around us? If we are God's hands and feet as he seeks to build his kingdom here on earth, how can we use our words and our actions to share God's strength and shield with others today?

Heavenly Father, I need your help. As I cry out to you this day, I know you hear me, I know you see me and I know you love me. May your hand be over me and all your children. And as I look to the world around me, I see that so many people are struggling. Please show me how to love them well and share something of you and your goodness and your glory with them. Amen.

22. PEOPLE OF PEACE

The Lᴏʀᴅ spoke to Moses, saying, 'Speak to Aaron and his sons, saying, Thus you
shall bless the people of Israel: you shall say to them,
The Lᴏʀᴅ bless you and keep you;
The Lᴏʀᴅ make his face to shine upon you and be gracious to you;
The Lᴏʀᴅ lift up his countenance upon you and give you peace.'
Numbers 6:22–6 (ᴇsᴠᴜᴋ)

In today's passage, God gives an encouragement to Aaron and his sons,
through Moses.

One of the ways we can give courage to others is to encourage them. I am not
talking about flattery, which too often has a personal agenda lingering behind
it. I'm talking about spending some time with God and asking him for a word
for someone, something of encouragement that he would like to share with
another person as we operate as God's hands and feet here on earth.

There have been times I have been helped when I've received a voice note or
a text message from someone with a word of encouragement they received
for me while spending time in prayer. Sometimes, we might receive something
for someone but forget or simply don't bother to pass it on. Every time we fail
to pass on an encouragement through words, email, text, voice note or carrier
pigeon, we are depriving that person of a blessing to strengthen them and
help them trust God instead of fear whatever circumstances might be affecting
their sense of peace.

Spend some time in prayer today, asking God who he wants to encourage
through your words or actions. Does he have a picture or particular scripture
he wants us to share with someone?

DB

23. I SPY

At the end of forty days, they returned from spying out the land... And they told him, 'We came to the land to which you sent us. It flows with milk and honey, and this is its fruit. However, the people who dwell in the land are strong, and the cities are fortified and very large... But Caleb quietened the people before Moses and said, 'Let us go up at once and occupy it, for we are well able to overcome it.' **Numbers 13:25, 27-8, 30 (ESVUK)**

Moses has led the Israelites out of Egypt, through the wilderness on the way to the Promised Land. Here we find him having sent twelve spies to suss out the land. As they return, they provide Moses with their findings. In their reports, ten of the spies focus on the things that have caused them to fear and so their faith is dwindling.

Two of the spies, however, focus on the faith they have to overcome the challenges they face. These faith-filled spies are Joshua and Caleb, two names that are still popular with new parents today – and with good reason. These two names represent those who don't bow to the negative majority, but rather focus on the God who leads them and equips them with everything they need.

Where the majority of spies see themselves as grasshoppers before giants, Joshua and Caleb know they have a giant in God and are able to do all things through him who strengthens them.

Let's pray to be like Joshua and Caleb, seeing situations through eyes of faith, trusting in a mighty God who ensures our victory no matter the odds.

DB

24. GIANT AFTER GIANT

Og king of Bashan and his whole army marched out to meet them in battle at Edrei.
The LORD said to Moses, 'Do not be afraid of him, for I have delivered him into your hands, along with his whole army and his land.' **Numbers 21:33-4**

Moses had seen God give his people victory over the powerful Pharaoh (the king of Egypt), but here he was facing another giant, and despite everything that had gone before, Moses found himself feeling fearful again. I'm not sure if you can relate to such faith-forgetfulness, but I know I can!

Though remembering what God has done in the past is encouraged throughout Scripture and would have been embedded into Moses' culture at the time, God is not too proud to remind us again and again of his enduring faithfulness. Here, we see him reminding Moses afresh: do not be afraid.

The words 'do not be afraid' are littered throughout the Bible, and the key as we grow as disciples is to both learn from and lean on God and his word more and more and on ourselves and others less.

Moses was feeling powerless and inferior to the king of Bashan. Former first lady Eleanor Roosevelt is said to have once famously stated, 'No one can make you feel inferior without your consent.' If there is someone who is intimidating us and making us feel inferior, we can draw near to God and his word and hear what he says about us. Then we have a decision to make - to agree with his word or the word of another or ourselves.

Ask God what he thinks and says about you, and walk in this truth throughout the day!

DB

25. FEAR OF SUFFERING

But even if you should suffer for what is right, you are blessed. 'Do not fear their threats; do not be frightened.' **1 Peter 3:14**

It's human nature to try to avoid suffering. We never choose suffering, but we do choose to do God's will, whatever that looks like, and sometimes that will cause us to experience harm.

Jesus suffered, not for anything he did wrong, but because he chose God's will over his own. So, how do we deal with the fear of suffering?

Sometimes we need to put a decision in place before anything knocks us, to help us face the fear and be ready. For example, if I am walking home one night and someone pulls a knife on me to steal my phone, I've already decided that I will give it to them. No material possession is worth me risking my life, my wife being without a husband and my children being without a dad. But in many circumstances, we can't prepare for suffering, and it isn't helpful to think of every possible scenario we might face. But we can be assured that when the time comes, God will give us the grace and courage we need.

Suffering is not meant to be endured alone. When we suffer, we need to invite God into the situation, as he is the One with the power to change it and change us for the better through it. We also need to invite family or friends to walk with us through these times. Who can you be honest with today about the things you are facing?

DB

26. FEAR OF HUMILIATION

He is before all things, and in him all things hold together. **Colossians 1:17**

I once spoke at a church in Copenhagen. While talking, I moved around on the stage and I ended up tripping over a guitar pedal and falling flat on the floor. I laughed it off and told everyone in the congregation to keep it between us. Afterwards, the church leader showed me his Instagram. Not only did it have the video of my epic fall displayed in full force on the screen, but it had also been edited with music and animation running across the video for extra effect!

I was so embarrassed. I wanted to call my wife and explain what had happened before she saw it online, but in the moment – facing the fear and humiliation – I decided to meet the challenge face on. I put the video up on my own Instagram. Maybe it was God nudging me to do it, but in any case, the moment I did, the fear of humiliation left me. I actually found I could laugh about it!

Maybe we fear saying or doing something because of fear of embarrassment or humiliation. Maybe we have done something and feel embarrassed about it right now? Let's take this to God and ask him what to do about the negative feelings we are experiencing. He can give us a strategy to overcome it, leaving us free to take up the new opportunities he has for us.

DB

27. STRANGER THINGS

For I was hungry and you gave me something to eat, I was thirsty and you gave me something to drink, I was a stranger and you invited me in. **Matthew 25:35**

As I was writing this reflection, the news of thousands of lives lost in an earthquake in Turkey popped up on my news app. Alongside this, the war between Ukraine and Russia was ongoing, and millions of refugees around the world were trying to find a home. What the news app didn't report was that in every situation there were local Christians welcoming, serving and caring for people.

When we encounter Jesus, our hearts break for what breaks his.

Sometimes the fear of others stops us helping people who aren't like us. It's important that we don't just welcome and love people who look, sound and behave like us, but that we show care and hospitality to all. Hospitality in the original Greek is *philoxenia*, with *philo* meaning love and *xenia* meaning stranger. So it literally means to love or befriend strangers.

Where are you at right now when it comes to befriending strangers? Loving people who are like us, or open to loving those who think and act differently? It may be uncomfortable at times, but the joy that will come from welcoming those who have not been welcomed by others is worth the discomfort. Who is God asking us to welcome and offer hospitality to this week?

DB

28. *SELAH* – SAVED TO SERVE

Jesus came to serve, and we too must adopt that servant heart.

We don't have to look far on our chosen news app or in the local paper to witness the suffering taking place all around the world, and it is all too easy to see suffering closer to home when we step out of our homes and into our villages, towns and cities. Wherever you find yourself today, take the opportunity to share love with someone who may not be experiencing it.

Take some time out today to pause and reflect on the following questions with God, asking him to show you the adventures in kindness and hospitality he is inviting you into:

- How can I demonstrate God's love in my locality?
- Are there charities and initiatives I can get involved in that are aligned with God's passions?
- How can I be the small change I would long to see in the world around me?

Jesus, your arms were forever open to the widow, to the orphan, to the ones in need and to the strangers. Help me see the world through your eyes. Give me the courage to be the change, to stand for injustice, to petition for peace and to serve your people. Amen.

29. FEAR OF SADNESS

A time to tear down and a time to build,
a time to weep and a time to laugh,
a time to mourn and a time to dance... **Ecclesiastes 3:3-4**

I don't know about you, but I find this scripture encourages me to slow down and take a deep sigh: there is a time for everything – and thank God for that!

Our culture says life is about always being happy, and if we aren't then there's probably something wrong with us. With this narrative running around our minds, it's easy to see why so many of us live in fear of experiencing times of sadness.

Sadness is not a feeling any of us like, but if we love others, we will experience it, because to love anything is to be vulnerable. In loving others there is a chance we will have sad days when our loved ones are in pain, when our loved ones hurt us or we hurt them, or when we see suffering in the world. Sadness is part of life, and we need to own our feelings rather than fear or deny them. Sometimes we think we've switched off our feelings, but in reality, we've just buried that sadness somewhere else, and if we're not careful we can see it seeping out as it affects us in other ways.

Today's verses show that times of sadness come, just like times of laughter will, which means our lowest lows will pass, as will our highest highs. Life has mountaintops and valleys, and God is with us in them all. Be real with him today, knowing that we don't need to put on a brave face, for he knows everything. He wants to meet us in our season of weeping or laughing, mourning or dancing, to encourage us that all will be well, so we just need to keep going.

DB

30. EVEN WHEN IT HURTS

Not only so, but we also glory in our sufferings, because we know that suffering produces perseverance; perseverance, character; and character, hope. And hope does not put us to shame, because God's love has been poured out into our hearts through the Holy Spirit, who has been given to us. **Romans 5:3-5**

The great theologian A. W. Tozer once reflected, 'What comes into our mind when we think about God is the most important thing about us.'[10] How do we see God? As a loving Father, a strict teacher or a distant stranger? How we see God will dramatically affect how we read today's verses, which say suffering can lead to hope.

Hope is the fuel that enables us to live the life God created us to live. God is a loving Father and does not make us suffer, but he does allow suffering and promises to be with us in it.

When I think back to the times of suffering I have endured, I know they have caused me to persevere, which has developed character, which in turn has led me to write these devotionals to encourage hope. I know God did not make my parents divorce, or make my wife suffer from epilepsy, or put me in a difficult and soul-destroying work environment. However, he has worked every situation for good, and I have encountered him with me in my darkest moments.

As you read and reflect on today's passage, be encouraged that your heavenly Father loves you, is with you and will lead you through seasons of suffering so that hope arises for you and in you.

DB

[10] A. W. Tozer, *The Knowledge of the Holy* (New York: HarperCollins, 1978), p. 1.

31. 365/360 REFLECTION

As we pause to look back on the month we have just lived through, I am sure you can see different seasons and patterns emerging. Life tends to go through cycles of order, chaos and reorder. Regardless of which of these seasons we most resonate with right now, as we have read in the previous passages, God isn't afraid of or defeated by the obstacles we face or bring to him.

Our lives will not be exempt from changes - and change is often uncomfortable - but God's faithfulness is unchanging, and he is present within every situation, moment and emotion.

As we look ahead to a brand new month, pause and check in with yourself and with God. Where are you physically, emotionally and spiritually? Where are you in relationship to him? Have you invited God into your chaos? Or do you fear your mess is too messy for God to speak into?

Now, begin to set your intentions for investing in your relationship with God throughout the season ahead. Are there times in your day or week when you can set aside quiet time to build communication and become more in tune with the Holy Spirit who lives within you?

AUGUST

1. WORSHIP

Praise the LORD.
Praise the LORD from the heavens;
praise him in the heights above.
Praise him, all his angels;
praise him, all his heavenly hosts.
Praise him, sun and moon;
praise him, all you shining stars. **Psalm 148:1–3**

Worship goes beyond scheduled moments in a Sunday church service or listening to God-inspired music alone.

Music, the literal lifting of hands and the coming together to engage in times of communal worship in physical time and space are powerful. I myself have experienced the love of God in ways unimaginable when engaged in sung worship, but worship is so much more than music.

Worship cannot be limited to a meeting, to songs or to specific rituals, just like nature cannot be limited to a greenhouse. A greenhouse is a space we can visit for a concentrated experience, but with open eyes and with intentional practice we can come to realise that there are opportunities to observe nature all around us.

The sun, the moon, the stars and the waters deep, by the fullness of their design, are in constant praise of God. We, too, are invited to understand worship as not just a practice, but a way of being, one that brings honour to God and brings rest to our souls.

RN

234

2. A LIVING SACRIFICE

Therefore, I urge you, brothers and sisters, in view of God's mercy, to offer your bodies as a living sacrifice, holy and pleasing to God - this is your true and proper worship. **Romans 12:1**

The apostle Paul challenges us to understand that worship is not just for a moment, but true and proper worship that is pleasing to God is surrendering our whole bodies as living sacrifices. Not just our flesh and our bones, but our whole essence, actions, words, relationships and thoughts.

Our whole bodies can be consumed with worry, wholly constructed around the avoidance of fear, but Paul indicates another option: to engineer our lives with a reverence for God at the core. To have a continual communication channel open with the Creator of the universe.

Paul demonstrates the kind of worship that is pleasing to God: a posture of praise and thanksgiving in response to God's never-ending grace and kindness, which becomes the very centre of who we are.

How we live our Mondays to Sundays all contributes to feeding and nurturing our peace or fuelling our fears. If worship is one of the greatest tools for us to enter into God's presence, for us to attain a heavenly perspective on our circumstances and for us to access God's wisdom and comfort, then one hour a week really isn't enough, is it?

RN

3. OUR WHOLE LIVES ARE WORSHIP

Love the LORD your God with all your heart and with all your soul and with all your strength. **Deuteronomy 6:5**

If the thoughts, events and experiences that oppose my peace and fuel my fears are working overtime, then what does it look like for my life to be rooted in worship? Does it mean I have to pray continually throughout the day, mumbling throughout every train ride? Or endlessly play worship songs in every environment I find myself in to soak myself with the presence of God?

For me, offering my whole body, mind and soul – all that I am – as a living sacrifice of worship has to go beyond daily moments of contemplation. Living a life of worship means grounding the core of my being, orienting all my activities, towards the establishment of God's love. It's how we answer the phone, how we reply to emails, how we treat our partner, how we prepare our meals and how we think about our bodies. True and proper worship should affect how we engage with God's creation, acknowledging that God made everything to glorify himself.

It's challenging myself to ask moment by moment, is this action rooted in love or pride? Does this decision build the empire of Me, or build the kingdom of heaven? If I'm engaging in beautiful moments of reflection with God, if I'm studying God's word and getting to know God's character, am I allowing those moments to shape my day-to-day life? And if not, then what's the point?

RN

4. FILTER OF LOVE

Finally, brothers and sisters, whatever is true, whatever is noble, whatever is right, whatever is pure, whatever is lovely, whatever is admirable - if anything is excellent or praiseworthy - think about such things. **Philippians 4:8**

For those who love the traditional educational system, the apostle Paul provides us with a helpful flow diagram (or a filter, for those who prefer that analogy) in today's scripture.

If God is inviting me to build my life on the cornerstone of worship, then I have to be intentional with every step I take. If I want to have a life built on love and not fear, I must build a habit of picking love in the moments that may seem insignificant.

A life of worship is the accumulation of potentially 35,000 decisions we make on average each day.[11] Now, most of those decisions are subconscious, but in the pursuit of peace we have to begin being intentional with the decisions we are aware of.

We need to choose truth, authenticity, kindness, over and over, until this becomes like second nature to us. These daily choices allow us to grow our roots deeper into whole-life worship, and the fruit of those daily decisions will be lives that lead us more and more towards our connection with God.

RN

[11] Eva M. Krockow PhD, 'How Many Decisions Do We Make Each Day?', *Psychology Today*, 27 September 2018, https://www.psychologytoday.com/us/blog/stretching-theory/201809/how-many-decisions-do-we-make-each-day (accessed 18 April 2023).

5. SUNDAY IS THE TIP OF THE ICEBERG

You will keep in perfect peace
those whose minds are steadfast,
because they trust in you. Isaiah 26:3

Worship isn't only something we do. We must make the shift in our minds for it also to become a fundamental part of 'who we are'.

Our whole lives can be an act of worship, even brushing our teeth. There is a difference between engaging in worship as a recreational activity and allowing worship to shape our identity. If we rely too much on mountaintop moments of Sunday worship to steer our lives, then, when confronted with fear, we'll continue to look for quick-fix moments of high adrenaline and dopamine rushes to help alleviate the pain. Swinging from crash to crash, addicted to chasing the high, is not what we were created for.

What would it look like if our lives were overflowing with peace? Completely saturated in worship before God, who brings fullness of joy and peace, perseverance and justice wherever he walks. Can we humans break free of our dependence on quick fixes, and instead be dedicated enough to build storehouses of daily experiences with God?

There is nothing like the opportunity to sing with our brothers and sisters of the faith in congregational settings, but those moments alone will not sustain us for a lifetime. Our souls will always crave more, and the great thing is that when we build the entirety of our lives on God, we soon realise that his presence is endless.

RN

6. HANDMADE

Yet you, Lord, are our Father.
We are the clay, you are the potter;
we are all the work of your hand. **Isaiah 64:8**

Today, let our prayer in the face of our fear be: 'Lord, help me be a worshipper, not just in actions or deeds, not just in words or songs, but in all that I am. Oh, God, mould me into an instrument of your praise.'

The Bible tells us that we are like clay and God is like a potter. The process of being moulded into the Christlike image that God intends us to be is given the theological term 'progressive sanctification'. The fact it is called 'progressive' shows us that there are no shortcuts or life hacks when it comes to becoming a vessel of worship; spiritual formation necessarily takes a lifetime.

Let me save you from the future guilt – or at least name it right here: you are not going to get it right every time. But just because there is a flaw in the creation doesn't mean the potter throws everything out. If we consistently show up, he will keep working on us.

We are all works of God's hands; to be moulded by him is to continue to position ourselves in front of him, in all that we do – whether it's taking a walk in the park or resisting a craving. Despite our wrestling, the potter never leaves. Despite how hard we are to mould, the potter never deserts us.

RN

7. *SELAH* – A DAY OF WORSHIP

As we have considered in this section, many of us are used to worshipping in community as a congregation but less comfortable doing so privately. Even then, we can think that leading a life of worship means putting on one or two worship songs in the morning and singing our hearts out.

The apostle Paul speaks of the type of worship that underscores and infiltrates our whole bodies and entire lives, but soaking in worship music or with the Bible is a brilliant place to begin.

Today, take a moment to worship on your own – whatever that looks like for you. It may be listening to worship music, sitting in silence or getting out into nature. Ask God to help you live your entire day from this posture of adoration to him. What would worshipping him in what you say today look like? How about what you do? Or eat? Or wear? Or think? Through the great redeeming work of the Holy Spirit, he can make our entire lives a sacrifice to him.

Lord God, our Father. We are the clay and you are the potter; we are all the work of your hand. Mould me into a vessel for your worship. Shape me into an instrument of your praise. Amen.

8. WHAT ARE WE WORSHIPPING?

Dear children, keep yourselves from idols. 1 John 5:21

Whether we are aware of it or not, we live our lives in worship to something.

There are people, activities or companies that we can put on a pedestal so high that we end up serving them as if they were gods. Celebrity culture, for example, elevates human beings to the status that should only be reserved for God.

No human can handle the pressure of being a supreme being, and we can see the evidence of this as the pressure breaks people over and over again. If we're not careful, we can live in submission to ideologies, to habits, to traditions that bear no image of God in the slightest, and remind us of everything we lack rather than the infinite love we were made by.

The choice presented throughout Scripture is a simple one in theory, even if it is complex to navigate daily. We can choose to worship – to give all our adoration and attention – to the things of God, who has the capacity to quench our thirst for affirmation. Or we can choose to give our worship to 'things' that were never built to love us in the ways our souls need.

What do you find yourself 'worshipping' today? How can you direct those desires towards God?

RN

9. SOCIAL MEDIA 'GOD'

Do not turn to idols or make metal gods for yourselves. I am the Lord your God.
Leviticus 19:4

Why do we spend so much time scrolling or swiping screens with the expectation of satisfaction?

This question is not a war on social media; I enjoy the 'gram' as much as the next person. But any object of our worship that isn't God will eventually leave us wanting, unfulfilled and disappointed.

Personally, I spent so long hoping that the music industry would give me the feeling of safety, stability and affirmation that I craved deep within my bones. But record labels, recording studio songwriting sessions and live gig experiences could never truly satisfy me. That's not to say those moments were bad, or evil – not in the slightest; there were moments where I glimpsed heaven and they enriched my life. But they could never fulfil my desire for intimacy and connection.

Idols will never reciprocate the love poured into them.

Rather than looking to those objects to find God, we should look to God and then discern which of the things in our lives bring us towards intimacy with him, and which are only distractions.

RN

10. IN THE SPIRIT AND IN TRUTH

Yet a time is coming and has now come when the true worshippers will worship the Father in the Spirit and in truth, for they are the kind of worshippers the Father seeks. **John 4:23**

Jesus was a pretty cool guy. Not cool in terms of owning clothes from Dover Street Market, or knowing the hippest spots in the city, but because he constantly pointed people to a future that they couldn't yet perceive. Some two thousand years later we are still grappling to understand his teachings.

In today's verse, Jesus describes the type of worshipper the Father is seeking: people who worship the Father in the Spirit and in truth.

The Father is not expecting us to punch in a timesheet when it comes to worship, or to see being in his presence as a means of getting what we need. But God is seeking people who humbly dedicate their daily walks to the establishment of sacrificial love. Can we be those people? I'll leave you with *The Message* interpretation of this passage, as it's a lovely expansion of this piece of Jesus genius!

> It's who you are and the way you live that count before God. Your worship must engage your spirit in the pursuit of truth. That's the kind of people the Father is out looking for: those who are simply and honestly *themselves* before him in their worship. God is sheer being itself – Spirit. Those who worship him must do it out of their very being, their spirits, their true selves, in adoration.
> (John 4:23-4 MSG)

RN

11. THE SOUNDS OF WORSHIP

Shout for joy to the Lord, all the earth.
Worship the Lord with gladness;
come before him with joyful songs.
Know that the Lord is God.
It is he who made us, and we are his;
we are his people, the sheep of his pasture. **Psalm 100:1–3**

Music can provide the backbone of cries to God and can facilitate a cathartic release when we lend our voices to sing out melodies to the heavens. The way music helps transport us to the upper realms of our consciousness, while unlocking our deepest emotions, is for me unrivalled.

In my darkest moments, when my heart has been overwhelmed, pressing pause and finding a space to surrender and to engage in moments of worship has been the life jacket I've needed. Whether it be on the Tube, waiting for the bus, alone in my room or part of a larger gathering, simply saying, 'Thank you, God,' through song has been the key to unlocking perspective and peace.

Songs, poems and psalms have given me the words I couldn't find on my own, and by stepping into focused moments of reflection I've found the space to lift the weight of the world off my shoulders, knowing God wants to hold all of my cares in his hands.

Why not lose yourself for a moment today? In the symphony of sounds, see for yourself the power worshipping God has to lift our spirits.

RN

12. PSALMS, THE ANCIENT PLAYLIST FOR WORSHIP

*But I pray to you, L*ORD*,*
in the time of your favour;
in your great love, O God,
answer me with your sure salvation.
Rescue me from the mire,
do not let me sink;
deliver me from those who hate me,
from the deep waters. **Psalm 69:13–14**

The book of Psalms is an ancient Spotify playlist of songs, gathered over centuries by communities hungry to know and honour God, those desperate to understand the suffering of life and impassioned to experience salvation from the deep waters we often find ourselves in. What fascinates me the most about these psalms is that, in so many of them, the author is expressing grave fears and doubts.

When writing a collection of songs about God, you'd think they'd have left out all the suffering, but instead the authors are completely transparent about where they're at. In Psalm 69:1-2, the psalmist sings out, 'Save me, O God, for the waters have come to my neck. I sink in the miry depths, where there is no foothold.' Things are not going their way in the slightest, yet as we continue through the psalm, a determined hope emerges, and God's faithfulness is eventually celebrated.

Worship isn't just about coming to God on our good days; it's about being honest on our worst days too, knowing that God can handle it. We have full permission to ugly-cry before God.

RN

13. THE WAR WITHIN

Hear my prayer, O God;
listen to the words of my mouth.
Arrogant foes are attacking me;
ruthless people are trying to kill me –
people without regard for God.
Surely God is my help;
the Lord is the one who sustains me. **Psalm 54:2–4**

Not many of us are surrounded by physical enemies as King David was when he wrote this psalm, but we all face opposition of some kind in our day-to-day lives, and for many, this opposition sits right between our ears: in our very own minds. For many of us, our thoughts can be more dangerous than any physical opposition we face.

Sometimes, my 'arrogant foes' are my own negative thinking patterns, or destructive habits that are the enemy of my progress, more so than the external pressures I face, whether that be a person at work who I feel is acting against me or the adult responsibilities that are mounting more quickly than I know how to handle them.

'You are your own worst enemy' is an iconic sentiment that can be found in some iteration in all cultures because it's so true of humanity. Worship has the power to turn us back into our own friend. In worship, we turn all our attention to God and what he is doing, and before long we begin to reflect his nature and, importantly, his thoughts – about him, ourselves and those around us.

RN

14. *SELAH* – WORSHIPPERS WELCOME

This week we have seen how we all worship something or someone, but sometimes we don't even realise that objects or people in our lives have taken the place of God. God is the one we were made to worship, and no other things, people or desires will ever take his rightful place.

Pause today and list the things that you want, love and desire. Have any of them become an idol? Do any of these get in the way of your connection with the Creator? The first step in ordering our desires under God is to acknowledge all that we currently hold dear.

Once we have acknowledged what we worship, let's invite God to help us reorder these desires. Maybe there's something we need to step away or back from? Perhaps there's an activity or spiritual discipline that God wants us to press into more?

Oh, God, I give thanks to you and praise your name. There is none above you. I lift your name above all other names and set you in your rightful place – over and above all other loves. I was designed to worship you, and I ask that you help my life reflect this in all that I do. Amen.

15. WORSHIP OFFERINGS

I will sacrifice a freewill offering to you;
I will praise your name, LORD, for it is good.
You have delivered me from all my troubles,
and my eyes have looked in triumph on my foes. **Psalm 54:6-7**

We all face opposition in some shape or form, and feeling like we have to take it on alone can be daunting. Yes, sometimes in life we have to be the only body in the room fighting for a cause, but the truth is, wherever we are, we have a Spiritual Entourage who surrounds us.

In the heat of the moment, we can forget this truth and allow our minds to play tricks on us, falling victim to the tornado of terror that builds within our souls. But, friend, we are not alone.

Moments of dedicated worship can stir our trust and build the confidence required to go the distance no matter the odds, but something might need to be sacrificed at our end. We have to stop running away from the fears that challenge us, we need to speak to those voices that spread doubt and anxiety, we must challenge the pridefulness that blinds us to our shortcomings and we must call out the desires that overpower our discipline. God can do all things, but we can also do our part. Even though the days of sacrificing goats and birds are gone, the thoughts that can drag us into despair are offerings just as worthy to present when in search of peace; God is desperate to make that trade.

RN

AUGUST

16. EVERYONE'S HAD A BAD DAY

Hasten, O God, to save me;
come quickly, Lᴏʀᴅ, to help me. **Psalm 70:1**

Today, you have permission to not be OK.

Maybe your bad day was yesterday, or you had a 'day six' a couple of weeks ago (a term my flatmates and I coined after a moment I had during the pandemic lockdown when I dramatically declared that I was over it all!). Millions before you and billions after you have shared in the experience of bad days, months and sometimes even years.

The good news is that we don't have to sanitise our lives before calling on God.

In Psalm 70, no punches are pulled and no lies are told; the psalmist isn't hiding from God any of his heartbreak or disappointment, and we should approach God in the same vein. The psalmist's vulnerability is the starting point for an honest conversation with God; there is no hiding behind strength or status. This psalm speaks humbly on themes poverty and desperation, of suffering and pain, and gives language to some of the things we may be experiencing today.

When we engage in intentional moments of worship, do we ignore the fear we carry and pretend that everything is going well? Absolutely not! If we can't be real before God, then where else can we run? By choosing to worship in our distress, to revere God despite our folly and guilt, we are strengthened through our conversations with God. Don't be shy; let it all out.

RN

17. WORSHIP IS A WEAPON

For from him and through him and for him are all things.
To him be the glory forever! Amen. **Romans 11:36**

When I first encountered Jesus and became a Christian, I remember purposely getting to church late because I knew the first twenty minutes of the service was always just singing. I didn't mind a song here and there, but for someone who can't sing in tune, I didn't see the point of miming for half of the service while everyone else took part in what I thought back then was some sort of Christian karaoke. That was, until I started to read my Bible more and actually discovered what worship is.

The word 'worship' means to give adoration, devotion or glory to someone or something. I realised that worship isn't about the music style; it is about our lifestyle. Worship is a powerful weapon.

Worship is designed by God so that we can become more like him. If he is courageous, then worship leaves us more courageous. Whatever we worship, that thing or person is shaping the person we are becoming.

What I have realised is that when we worship things other than Jesus, those things can end up taking something from us, depleting us of joy and sometimes even destroying us completely. When we worship Jesus, he builds us, restores us, heals us and makes us whole. I ask myself why I would worship people who can sometimes let me down when I can worship the One who will never let me down, never overlook me, never forget me.

DB

18. WORSHIP BRACELET

Be strong and courageous... for the LORD your God will be with you wherever you go. **Joshua 1:9**

When I became a Christian, aged eighteen, while backpacking in Australia, a friend gave me a red bracelet with 'WWJD' on it, which stood for 'What Would Jesus Do?' I didn't realise it at the time, but looking back, that little bracelet had a big impact on my life.

This simple reminder – WWJD – helped me to live a lifestyle of worship wherever I was and whatever I did. Worship isn't limited to a building or location, for wherever you are God is with you. You can worship God any time and anywhere, and you don't even have to sing a note.

Worship is making daily decisions that give God glory. That's what Jesus did – he made decisions that glorified the Father. Jesus turned some H_2O into a fine vintage wine at a wedding, and he gave his life on a cross for humanity. Every day is an opportunity for us to worship God, and those daily opportunities are decisions to give God glory or deprive God of glory. When God asks us to do something and fear stops us from doing it, we just deprive God of glory and deprive ourselves of entering into his purpose and experiencing his blessing.

Each day we get to be generous or stingy, encouraging or discouraging, forgiving or vengeful, gossiping or grace-giving. Ask yourself the question, 'What Would Jesus Do?' today.

DB

19. FEAR OF BEING FOUND OUT

Their destiny is destruction, their god is their stomach, and their glory is in their shame. Their mind is set on earthly things. **Philippians 3:19**

God expects us to surrender our lives so that he can move in our hearts and make us whole.

For some, the thought of giving things up isn't something we want to do just yet. My encouragement today is that that's OK. Our loving heavenly Father doesn't want us to give up something out of some religious requirement. God wants us to fall so in love with him that we don't need those other things we have been clinging so tightly to.

For others, it is a secret addiction or habit that is hard to give up and which you know is having a negative impact on your life. You are not on your own. Many of us have or have had private issues that have held us back from a life of freedom. So what do we do to overcome it? Worship!

In today's verse, Paul is writing to the Philippian church about people for whom food is their god; it's what they worship. We know that if gluttony is our God, we sacrifice our health. Our blood-sugar level, cholesterol level and general well-being are affected if food is the god of our life.

We all sacrifice for what we worship, which means today no one has a sex problem, a drug problem or a gambling problem – it is a worship problem. What we need to do is switch the order and put Jesus back as Lord of our life.

DB

20. TRANSFORMERS

Do not conform to the pattern of this world, but be transformed by the renewing of your mind. Then you will be able to test and approve what God's will is – his good, pleasing and perfect will. **Romans 12:2**

So what happens when we worship? We are transformed; we become more like Jesus.

This isn't something I am just saying; this is something I have seen. I have been on countless youth camps and conferences, and when the young people arrive they can be angry, aggressive, selfish and sometimes bang out of order. As leaders, we would love them regardless as we tried to make the space as safe and welcoming as possible for them.

On the last day we would give the microphone to the young people and listen to the stories of what God had done in their lives. We could see the transformations that had taken place. Change occurred not because of the speakers but because of the Spirit. Not because of the gifted worship team but because young people worshipped Jesus and allowed his will to be done and his kingdom to come in their lives.

Parents would send letters, emails and text messages about the changes that had taken place in their teenagers' lives. This wasn't behaviour modification that lasted a day or so. This was young people experiencing Jesus, worshipping him, giving him their fears for the future and regrets of the past. This is what happens when we worship. If we want to be transformed and become more like him, we simply need to spend more time with him. As the cheesy strapline goes, it was never meant to be DIY (Do It Yourself) but rather CIY (Christ In You).

DB

21. *SELAH* – WORSHIP IS A WEAPON

This week we have seen that worship is a weapon, a hotline that connects us to God. Today, do not hold back from stepping into God's presence, no matter what baggage you bring with you. God wants to see it all. Take the time to pause now and simply be, asking the Spirit to fill you.

Is there anything that is standing in the way of you worshipping God today? Perhaps a feeling, an emotion, an event or a worry? As you pray and worship, leave this distraction at the foot of the cross. Jesus can take care of anything we cast on him. He is trustworthy and worthy of praise.

I will praise your name, Lord, for you are good. Though the storms may rage on, I will fix my eyes on you, the focus of my adoration and the only one I worship. Amen.

22. POWER OF PRAISE – PART 1

Once again Leah became pregnant and gave birth to another son. She named him Judah, for she said, 'Now I will praise [yadah] the Lord!' **Genesis 29:35 (NLT)**

Teachers give their students praise for good work. We praise our chosen sports team when they bring home a victory. We praise God. But what is the power and importance of praise, especially in our battle with fear?

In today's passage we read of a woman, Leah, who had a sister called Rachel. The Bible tells us that Rachel was beautiful and Leah was dull-eyed (Genesis 29:17). A single lad, Jacob, met and wanted to marry Rachel, but the father-in-law put Leah into the wedding outfit, covering her from head to toe, and tricked Jacob into marrying Leah instead of Rachel.

Jacob was furious and so the father-in-law let him marry Rachel too. Leah now feared for her future, facing potential rejection and loneliness. But God saw her and blessed her and Jacob with children. With each child she wanted her husband to find her worthy, but when she had her fourth baby she called him Judah (Hebrew *jadah*, meaning 'praise and thanks to God for what we have received') and she said, 'Now, I will praise the Lord!' She turned her focus to God as the source of all the love and approval she could ever need.

Leah was never rejected and unloved by God, even if her husband loved another. Her dependence, praise and thanksgiving of God ensured her future blessing. Imagine if we were to wake up tomorrow with only the things we praised and thanked God for today – would that change the way we praise?

DB

23. POWER OF PRAISE - PART 2

I am under vows to you, my God;
I will present my thank-offerings [towdah] to you. **Psalm 56:12**

There are two times to praise God - when we feel like it and when we don't!

Today we look at the importance of *towdah*, a sacrifice of thanks. This means praising and thanking God even when we don't feel full of praise and thanks. When we fail the exam and fear for our future. When our partner breaks up with us and we fear being alone. When we lose our job and fear financial hardship. When a pandemic breaks out, taking thousands of lives, and we fear death or loss. In these times, we praise God with *towdah* praise!

Praising God despite our circumstances is a powerful way to face fear.

As we praise, we put our faith in God rather than giving our attention to fuelling our fears. We declare that he is in control, not us. We say he is bigger than the situation or circumstances. He is all powerful and we trust him. We might not feel like praising in the moment, but praise was never meant to be about our momentary feelings; it's about lifting up a faithful, powerful God who never changes in his love for us or his desire to help us!

DB

24. POWER OF PRAISE – PART 3

Come, let us bow down in worship,
*Let us kneel [barak] before the L*ORD *our Maker.* **Psalm 95:6**

Barak means to kneel in praise.

Barak praise comes from having a posture or lifestyle of kneeling before God in holy reverence. It's a lifestyle of humility and service to God and to those around us. This type of praise sees the focus shift on to God and others, reducing our levels of fear because we are no longer only self-focused. Studies confirm that when we do things for others, depression and anxiety are often reduced.

Martin Luther King Jr was someone who knew the power of *barak* praise. In a speech made shortly before he died, he said, 'Everybody can be great, because anyone can serve. You don't have to have a college degree to serve . . . You don't have to know the second theory of thermodynamics in physics to serve. You only need a heart full of grace, a soul generated by love.'[12] Let's spend some time in *barak* praise and ask for opportunities to serve others today for the glory of God!

DB

---

[12] Martin Luther King Jr, 'Drum Major Instinct' sermon, Atlanta, 4 February 1968.

25. FEAR OF LOSING POSITION

How good and pleasant it is
when God's people live together in unity! **Psalm 133:1**

As fear has increased in society, so has separation. Fear pushes us away from people, sometimes including those who love and care for us the most.

Fear of losing position, possessions, prominence and power causes division. If fear is the great divider, faith is the great unifier.

The word 'division' comes from the Latin *di-vision*, meaning 'two visions'. When people have two different visions of the future it would be easy to think that they can't do life together. However, faith encourages us to look beyond human vision to God's vision. His vision is for all humanity to know the love of a heavenly Father, and out of that relationship to live a life of purpose and meaning to the full.

When we put God's vision first, it unites billions of Christians all round the world. People with different heritages, cultures, educations, perspectives, experiences, styles and strategies all united by kingdom culture. Let's take a moment to pray for Christians around the world, especially those in the persecuted church. We all battle fear, so let us take a moment to unite against it as the global body of Christ, cheering one another on in the face of darkness. Through prayer, we can bring light.

DB

26. GHOSTBUSTERS

*When the disciples saw him walking on the lake, they were terrified. 'It's a ghost,'
they said, and cried out in fear.*
But Jesus immediately said to them: 'Take courage! It is I. Don't be afraid.'
Matthew 14:26-7

The disciples were in a boat when a storm hit.

With every wave, the fear of death kicked in. Jesus walked out on the water to
reassure them, but they weren't relieved; they thought he was a ghost! Fear
had risen to new levels as they cried out for the ghostbusters to come and
save them. Immediately Jesus encouraged them to take heart and not give
way to fear, because he was with them.

The disciples were ordinary, everyday people like you and me, who found
themselves in a storm, a situation they couldn't get themselves out of. In these
moments of fear and worry, when we call out to Jesus, we can trust him to be
with us, bringing peace and courage to us.

Today, we might be in a stormy situation or a calm one. We might be on a
mountaintop or in a dark valley, but no matter where we are or what we are
experiencing, Jesus is with us. He encourages us not to give up and to take
heart, to focus on who he is and not solely on what's happening, to trust and
not be afraid because he has power over every storm.

What are you facing today? Does the task ahead feel impossible? Spend time
giving this worry to God, and maybe invite a trusted friend to pray with you or
for you too.

DB

27. WALK ON WATER

'Lord, if it's you,' Peter replied, 'tell me to come to you on the water.'
'Come,' he said.
Then Peter got down out of the boat, walked on the water and came towards
Jesus. But when he saw the wind, he was afraid and, beginning to sink, cried out,
'Lord, save me!'
Immediately Jesus reached out his hand and caught him. 'You of little faith,' he
said, 'why did you doubt?' **Matthew 14:28–31**

When the disciples heard Jesus encouraging them that he was with them in
the storm, Peter trusted Jesus so much that he actually walked on water. What
amazing faith he must have had to step out of the boat!

But then, as he stepped out onto the water, Peter took his focus off Jesus
and moved it back on to the storm, and he soon became overwhelmed by the
wind and waves once more. His fear levels went up and his faith levels went
drastically down, and he soon sank under the waves.

We can think Peter failed, but actually he succeeded in many ways; he walked
on water – something none of the other disciples experienced. Peter called to
Jesus to save him, and Jesus pulled him out, reminding him not to doubt his
power to conquer any storm.

I have been working on my fight or flight response when I'm in a stormy
situation and I feel the fear! I've decided to fight the fear by running to Jesus,
giving him the hard situation I'm facing to use it for his glory. Let's keep
stepping out of the boat, eyes on Jesus, trusting him to keep us afloat!

DB

28. *SELAH* – TRANSFORMING

Praise has the power to transform us, and subsequently our perspective on our day-to-day lives.

Today, reflect on how God extends his hand over the water, inviting us to take the steps to trust him, keeping our eyes fixed on him as we walk closer and closer towards him.

Is there a situation you are facing right now where your vision keeps veering towards the waves rather than worship? How can you intentionally carve out time to worship God today?

Oh, God, I offer a sacrifice of thanks for your help, for leading me onto the water, for taking my hand and drawing me towards yourself. Continue to lead and guide me this week. Amen.

29. TO GOD BE THE GLORY

And when they climbed into the boat, the wind died down. Then those who were
in the boat worshipped him, saying, 'Truly you are the Son of God.'
Matthew 14:32–3

The disciples in the storm ended their experience worshipping Jesus. The outcome was not to focus on Peter who walked on water, but to understand more fully how amazing Jesus was.

Through this stormy experience, their relationship with Jesus went to new, deeper levels, and they gave him all the adoration and glory in return. Our loving heavenly Father does not bring storms to shake us up and cause fear, but he calms them to show us he is always with us.

Whatever difficult situations or circumstances we find ourselves in, my heart and hope are that they will lead us to a place of greater closeness to Jesus, that every storm will become a place of spiritual encounter that leaves us with less doubt and more hope and confidence in him. Less fear and more faith; less anxiety about the future because we are more anchored in the One who is in control of it.

Like the disciples, we can cry out to Jesus and invite him to come to us in the storm, bringing us through it stronger and more steadfast in faith and worship.

DB

30. FEAR OF TELLING OTHERS

For God so loved the world that he gave his one and only Son, that whoever believes in him shall not perish but have eternal life. **John 3:16**

Our culture doesn't welcome sharing faith, and being labelled 'Bible-basher' or 'God squad' have made many of us fearful to share with others.

I believe relationship and trust are key to sharing faith, so when I meet people for the first time, I don't start the conversation with; 'Hi, I'm Dan and I'm a Christian!' I ask questions and find out about them first. Why should I expect people to care about what I believe or do if I don't care about what they are about as well? People don't care how much we know until they know how much we care.

That said, sharing our faith through words and actions is the kindest and most loving thing we can do for someone. I am so grateful that, when I was eighteen, someone did that for me.

Today's verse is a clear message that we need to pass on to others. It's an invitation from God to everyone, inviting them into life in its fullness, forever. If our relationship with Jesus has changed our lives, let's not allow fear to stop us sharing our story with others when God opens up an opportunity to do so, whether that be in what we say or what we do for those around us.

Sharing our faith doesn't need to be overly complicated. Just start building genuine relationships with others and show them God's love first-hand. Who can we begin building with today?

DB

31. 365/360 REFLECTION

Looking back on this month, we have taken a deeper dive into the art and heart of worship and have seen how, when our eyes are truly fixed on God, the waves can simply wane around us.

Pause now, find a safe and comfy space and set your timer to allow for a good chunk of silence, and invite the Holy Spirit to meet you in it. How are you feeling today? How have the past reflections challenged your notion of worship, if at all? What parts of your life might God be calling you to sacrifice into his loving hands again?

Now turn your attention to the month ahead. What activities or experiences allow you to focus your eyes on God and not your fear? How might you build a rhythm of these into the coming days?

SEPTEMBER

1. FEAR OF CONVICTIONS

And let us run with perseverance the race marked out for us, fixing our eyes on Jesus, the pioneer and perfecter of faith. **Hebrews 12:1–2**

'Conviction' can sound like a very intense word, but in actual fact we all have convictions. A conviction is simply a firmly held belief or opinion.

From a very young age, I felt the personal conviction to remain celibate until I got married, which in the twenty-first century is not the most popular or widely held belief. Now, I am not here to virtue signal or force this opinion on anyone, but I have learnt a thing or two about overcoming the fear of rejection in response to standing by my own convictions.

Growing up, I had no idea how challenging a decision to remain celibate until marriage would prove to become in later years. Not having sex when you're fifteen is far easier than when you're twenty-five (in my experience), and especially when it comes to navigating university Freshers Week, adolescent relationships and adulthood conversations where celibacy is considered a mythical lifestyle reserved for monks.

The truth is that not everyone is going to have the same convictions as we do, and whether our belief is about politics, sustainability or physical intimacy, establishing our 'why' is of paramount importance in a world full of opinions, because – as the old adage goes – if you stand for nothing, you'll fall for anything.

2. INTIMACY – PART 1

When I was a child, I talked like a child, I thought like a child, I reasoned like a child. When I became a man, I put the ways of childhood behind me.
1 Corinthians 13:11

There is a kaleidoscope of understandings when it comes to sexual intimacy in the modern world. As I continued to navigate adulthood, I carried the fear that my convictions would ostracise me from the modern dating scene. Who on earth would want to be with me? Surely, I wouldn't find another human with such strong beliefs? Wrongfully, I believed that I wasn't built for dating in the twenty-first century, that I was destined to roam this planet in search of reciprocated love forever.

In the face of that loneliness and rejection, I began to debate whether I should compromise in order to be more in line with my environment. The question spiral began: if this belief was to deny me love, then could it truly be rooted in truth? Would I ever find someone on the same wavelength? Was I following this path purely out of fear, because of religion, because of my parents? All the Sunday School lessons and Christian youth conferences couldn't stand against the reality and depths of the questions I was wrestling with.

At some point, we must mature past, 'I believe this because I was told,' or, 'My family/community thinks this way, therefore I do too.' We are no longer children, and our convictions won't stand up to challenges if our beliefs are rooted in someone else's revelation.

RN

3. INTIMACY – PART 2

Blessed is the one who perseveres under trial because, having stood the test, that person will receive the crown of life that the LORD has promised to those who love him. **James 1:12**

I remained celibate until marriage, and I got married at the age of thirty-one, so you can imagine this lifestyle choice led to various raised eyebrows and questions on my journey within the music industry, while living in the madness of London.

Many a group conversation spiralled into a 'NO WAY' conversation, followed by a hundred questions, disbelief and fun (for them) about this lifestyle choice. The questions I faced from others who didn't share the same view led me on a beautifully long road into a deeper understanding of my decisions. Being asked 'Why?' so many times forced me to truly understand my answers.

I retreated into an internal dialogue with God, with my loved ones and with Scripture, and I came to a deeper peace in the path I had chosen. That doesn't always happen; sometimes we descend into an awakening that stands against the conviction, and the belief, rightfully, loses its weight.

At the other end of that exploration came a boldness and confidence to communicate my convictions with love and clarity. Digging deeper into my 'why' led to a deeper empathy in listening openly to others' experiences, even if they didn't hold the same opinion. Ultimately, as I shed my immaturity and my lack of understanding, I gained a firmer foundation in my faith-filled decisions.

RN

4. STANDING ON OUR OWN TWO FEET

Let your eyes look straight ahead;
fix your gaze directly before you.
Give careful thought to the paths for your feet
and be steadfast in all your ways.
Do not turn to the right or to the left;
keep your foot from evil. **Proverbs 4:25-7**

Our moral standpoints, theological understandings and personal convictions
will be challenged and scrutinised, and rightly so in some respects.

In a world that is in constant search for the truth, the beliefs we deem true will
be put to the test. We can become so occupied with what others are doing that
we can end up losing our way and ignoring the quiet voice of God inside us
leading us down our own lane.

If our convictions are borrowed, naively believed or half-heartedly followed,
when we're faced with a storm, a temptation or even sometimes a simple
question from others, we will be rocked. If we are not careful, we can feel the
pressure to swerve to the right or to the left of our path, to bend towards the
majority or ignore the minority, to follow the crowd because the noise is so loud.

Let your eyes look inwards and forwards. The truth lies within the form of
the Spirit of God, and as intentional listeners, we can become more in tune
with what the Spirit is telling us to build our lives on. The Spirit will remind us
what's been planted in our hearts and will enable those seeds to flourish, no
matter the weather.

RN

5. CONFIDENT IN CHRIST

But blessed is the one who trusts in the L{\sc ord},
whose confidence is in him. **Jeremiah 17:7**

As I write, I am sitting in an airport in Houston, USA.

Everyone around me seems full of confidence compared to people in the UK. People speak loudly and clearly, many walk with a strut. Confidence looks good on people. However, the truth is, the volume of our voice or the way we walk doesn't really indicate how confident we truly are. So where does authentic confidence come from? Are we born with it?

I believe confidence is not a matter of nature but nurture. We can grow to be confident in who we are and learn how to make bold decisions through walking with God and leaning into him!

The more we learn to trust him, the more confident we will become. He can enable us to be bold when we feel like being timid, to be brave and stand up for our convictions when we feel like hiding away, and to be courageous when we want to shrink back. Sometimes it can be hard to discern God's voice if we are not spending regular time reading God's word. The Bible is a gift to us in that the truths written in its pages stand the test of time and never, ever change.

Spend some time with the Bible open, asking God to highlight words and scriptures and promises he wants you to trust in, and watch yourself walk with your head held higher today.

DB

6. THE PRICE OF OUR SOULS

*For what will it profit a man if he gains the whole world [wealth, fame, success],
but forfeits his soul? Or what will a man give in exchange for his soul?*
Matthew 16:26 (AMP)

Inner peace rarely comes attached to material objects, a life of luxury or
everyone seeing eye to eye with us. No, God's ways often run against culture's
definitions of the 'good life'. If you need more evidence, just read Matthew 5.

When our convictions go against the flow we find ourselves in, whether that
be our friendship groups, communities or wider culture, we will be looked at
as odd. We will get backlash, and people may not understand our 'why', but in
spite of that, the comfort of compliance is nothing compared to the peace that
results in obeying God's truth – even if it means temporary discomfort and
friction.

What will it profit you to gain all the riches, fame, success, pleasure, popularity,
if you lose your soul? You may 'lose' by the metrics of Instagram or modern
culture, but your reward will be greater. Your reward will be a life lived in the
flow of the Holy Spirit and in honesty with yourself and before God. Is being
part of the crowd really worth losing who you are at your core?

RN

7. *SELAH* – CONSISTENT CONVICTIONS

Staying true to our convictions isn't an easy task, and it is made more difficult when the foundation we're standing on isn't as solid as we once thought. Are there verses or scriptures you could meditate on today that remind you of the foundations you are building on in God?

What are some of the strong convictions you have? And what has shaped those beliefs? What promises in God's word help give fuel to the thing you are fighting for? You may want to spend some time prayerfully journalling through these in a notebook or in the margins of this book.

Lord God, you said that the one who trusts in you is blessed, and so I place my confidence in you now. Guide my path, stir my heart, give me courage, so I will not swerve to the right or to the left. Please turn my foot away from evil and keep me on the paths you want me to wander down. Amen.

8. STRENGTHS AND WEAKNESSES

He said to me, 'My grace is sufficient for you, for my power is made perfect in weakness.' Therefore I will boast all the more gladly about my weaknesses, so that Christ's power may rest on me. **2 Corinthians 12:9**

When we think of the word 'power', what comes to mind? Positional power within an organisation or government? Physical power like athletes have? Dino Power, or like the Mighty Morphin Power Rangers (RIP Tommy!)? Maybe that last one is just me.

Many people seek the power the world can give, but that power can be used to control and abuse people, to take advantage of others for selfish gain. These days, abuse of power is being called out more and more and people are searching for examples of good authority and power.

Our best example is the person of Jesus, who used God's power to serve and sacrifice for others. Our culture focuses on our strengths and encourages us to hide our weaknesses. Society teaches us that if we want 'success' or 'power', we need to highlight our performance and achievements, posting our 'best life' on social media to impress others. People fear being open and vulnerable in case they are seen as weak and not coping or thriving in life.

Today's verse says that God's grace is enough for us, and his power is perfected in our weakness. Therefore, we are encouraged to own our weakness so that the power of God can shine through us! Being honest about our weaknesses also invites others to be open about theirs, ultimately leading to greater connections with others. Will we boast about our strengths or our weaknesses today?

DB

9. TO ASCEND, WE MUST FIRST DESCEND

Therefore it says,

'WHEN HE ASCENDED ON HIGH,

HE LED CAPTIVITY CAPTIVE,

AND HE BESTOWED GIFTS ON MEN.'

(Now this expression, *'He ascended,' what does it mean except that He also had* previously *descended [from the heights of heaven] into the lower parts of the earth? He who descended is the* very *same as He who also has ascended high above all the heavens, that He [His presence] might fill all things [that is, the whole universe]).* **Ephesians 4:8–10 (AMP)**

We cannot shelter ourselves from the tests, trials and tribulations of life, but we can prepare our hearts by meditating, daily devotion to prayer, understanding Scripture and building a depth in our spirits that will help us ride the storms when they come.

Paul, in his letter to the Ephesians, speaks of how Jesus both ascended to heaven and descended to live in the dirt and dust of earth alongside us: 'He who descended is the very one who ascended higher than all the heavens, in order to fill the whole universe' (Ephesians 4:10), and this journey is one we, too, have to embark on in our own walks.

The journey of descent into our humanness, into our beliefs, into how we have constructed our realities, into how we've been conditioned by family, friends, culture and our faith itself is a lifelong task. At the same time, we journey towards heaven, with the Holy Spirit drawing out the holiness within us. Holding our humanness and our heavenliness in tension is something we can only do with God's grace.

RN

10. GROWING IN CONFIDENCE

They will be like a tree planted by the water
that sends out its roots by the stream.
It does not fear when heat comes;
its leaves are always green.
It has no worries in a year of drought
and never fails to bear fruit. **Jeremiah 17:8**

If we want to grow our confidence, we need to look at where we place it. Some put it in their money and possessions, some in their status and others in their physical strength. Placing our confidence in these things can give us boldness in the moment, but not in the long term. A recession could hit, a war could start, our social media status could be cancelled, or we could become physically ill. If we desire confidence that is secure and unshifting, we need to put our confidence in something, or Someone, unchanging and lasting – Jesus, and him alone.

If we put our faith in Jesus, it means that whether we are on the mountaintop or walking through a dark valley, we can be confident in his faithfulness to us. We will not crumble with fear when times of pressure come and, regardless of what hardship is predicted in our world today, we can still be fruitful.

What scripture can you speak over yourself today that will help remind you of the confidence that you have in Christ? Perhaps you can read a larger chunk of the book of Jeremiah and see that God has always been faithful to his people and longs to be in close relationship with them.

DB

11. REBUILDING WITH LOVE

Then we will no longer be infants, tossed back and forth by the waves, and blown here and there by every wind of teaching and by the cunning and craftiness of people in their deceitful scheming. Instead, speaking the truth in love, we will grow to become in every respect the mature body of him who is the head, that is, Christ.
Ephesians 4:14-15

The goal when coming to understand our beliefs and opinions is not just to tear them apart, but to lovingly uproot ways of thinking that can lead us off the track that a selfless love has in store for us.

The hope is that, through the process, we are able to reroute ourselves away from lives controlled by anxiety, shame and guilt and towards integrity, resilience, compassion and empathy.

Integrity is the reward for digging deeper, laying foundations closer and closer to the truth of Jesus at the centre of it all. As we draw nearer to God in prayer and worship, his vision for us and the path he wants us to take, how to spend our time and who to spend it with become clearer. Maybe not the whole route our lives will take, but at least the next step.

A by-product of this soul searching, this foundation laying, is that we are not 'tossed back and forth by the waves, and blown here and there by every wind of teaching and by the cunning and craftiness of people'. Our journeys of descent into greater depths in our spiritual lives, of pulling apart things that we think have been holding us together but are actually holding us back from God, can lead us to stability in the One who cannot be moved. What do you feel God might want to knock down and rebuild in your heart or life?

RN

12. AUTHENTICALLY ATTRACTIVE

But the fruit of the Spirit is love, joy, peace, forbearance, kindness, goodness,
faithfulness, gentleness and self-control. Against such things there is no law.
Galatians 5:22–3

In the Bible, spiritual 'fruit' is the visible evidence that God is moving in our
life. We can't force fruit or produce fruit ourselves; fruit grows over time.
The tree is planted, has access to water and sun, then fruit starts to grow. In
the same way, for spiritual fruit to grow we don't need to try to improve our
behaviour; we just need to spend time with Jesus.

Fear of being excluded or rejected from community can cause us to wear a
mask and try to say and do all the right things at church, but this is surface-
level stuff, behaviour modification for one day of the week. Jesus is about real
transformation; not a one-off event, but a journey.

When I see a person displaying spiritual fruit, it is attractive. When I see people
showing love, peace and self-control, I see people drawn to them like bees
to honey.

To be authentically attractive has nothing to do with how good we are but
how good Jesus is looking in our life. The fruit of the Spirit helps us and helps
others to face fear. Why not create some time today to simply sit and spend
time with Jesus?

DB

13. GOD'S LOVING KINDNESS

How precious is Your lovingkindness, O God!
The children of men take refuge in the shadow of Your wings. **Psalm 36:7** (AMP)

I'm not sure if you've ever seen the 1998 cult classic film, *The Truman Show*?

The film centres on an insurance salesman who discovers his whole life is actually a reality TV show. Watching it was one of the most jarring experiences of my life. I spent the following weeks brushing my teeth, looking in my bathroom mirror, suspicious that a secret camera was filming me and live-streaming out to the whole world. On my route to secondary school, as a keen skipper in my youth (you may laugh, but skipping is the perfect mode of transport - not quite running but faster than walking), I would freeze in panic, as I remembered that I was being watched by millions, and falling over would lead to universal ridicule.

How often do we live in fear that we're being watched by a judging God who wants to ridicule us and expose our weakness, to our detriment?

Today's verse reminds me that God is not waiting for you and me to mess up so he can stream our humiliation out to all the nations. The heart of God is rooted in loving kindness, and he is casting his eye upon us to catch us when we stumble, to point us in the right direction and to hide us under the shadow of his wings. So, rest assured, you can brush your teeth in peace tonight.

RN

14. *SELAH* – FRUIT: VISIBLE EVIDENCE OF GOD AT WORK

We all have strengths and weakness, and the variety of personalities we possess means some things are easier for some than for others. How can you be a conduit of God's loving kindness today, in your workplace, with your family or with a stranger you interact with?

Galatians 5:22-3 lists the fruit of the Spirit as 'love, joy, peace, forbearance, kindness, goodness, faithfulness, gentleness and self-control'. What fruit of the Spirit could you develop and exercise throughout your day?

Holy Spirit, I pray you bring forth your kindness in me. Drown me in your peace, stir me with your self-control, teach me how to be gentle and awaken me to your love, so that I may walk in line with your ways. Amen.

15. GROWING UP

Like newborn babies [you should] long for the pure milk of the word, so that by it you may be nurtured and grow in respect to salvation [its ultimate fulfilment], if in fact you have [already] tasted the goodness and gracious kindness of the Lord.
1 Peter 2:2-3 (AMP)

Carrying childlike faith into adult-shaped situations can prove problematic.

While Sunday School lessons and songs lay a firm foundation for children, these things alone were not created to stand up against the realities of heartbreak, addiction, rejection and anxiety that can be experienced in adulthood. 'He's got the whole world in his hands' and other classroom bangers such as these are true, but as we gain more life experience we are invited to read Scripture in more depth, applying these truths to our everyday lives.

Part of the fear we can encounter around our beliefs and convictions is based on a lack of preparation for the present. It's feeling out of our depth when face to face with reality, whether it be a decision in our work lives, a personal crossroads or a spiritual battle that we didn't see coming. It feels like we've turned up to a professional construction site with a winning smile and a box full of Lego®, hoping that everything's going to be alright.

We long for pure milk and are urged to grow beyond the Sunday School understanding of God and our place in his plans for the universe. We've been reading a snippet of Scripture a day up until now - how can you begin to use these verses as a springboard for longer and deeper readings throughout the coming days and weeks?

RN

16. THE MIND OF A BEGINNER

And Jesus grew in wisdom and stature, and in favour with God and man.
Luke 2:52

The New Testament provides us with an extremely small window into Jesus Christ's adolescence.

In saying that he 'grew in wisdom and in stature', the Bible gives us a brief insight into the fact that even Christ himself had to endure a process of growing, of not knowing and of gaining wisdom. The fortitude we long for is gained through humility, through maturity and in gaining favour with God and others around us – it provides us with great encouragement to know that Jesus had to go through this too.

We must draw on the wisdom within and around us, building our beliefs on firm foundations that can take the weight of our experiences. Not only on how we feel, not only on what culture tells us is 'right', but on the balance of God's word and wisdom from the ones who have gone before us.

If we position ourselves as students, we will never mistake ourselves for the Master. If we accept that we have a lot to learn, we'll never be naive enough to think we've got it all figured out.

When presented with an event or situation that seems to be inviting us to new depths, are we prepared to engage with God in a new way?

RN

17. CHRIST, THE CONTROVERSIAL ONE

I have given them your word and the world has hated them, for they are not of the world any more than I am of the world. **John 17:14**

In his prayer to God for his disciples, Jesus said that the world 'has hated them' because they are 'not of the world' and do not belong to the world. When I read these words, I don't hear a declaration of war with everyone who doesn't believe; rather, I hear the truth that our collective and individual egos shriek at the sight of self-denial and sacrificial love. The hate of the world is fuelled by the selfish parts of humanity trying to survive, and Christ calls us to die to those selfish parts buried within ourselves.

Christ's controversial message is to embrace and love all things that oppose us, especially our enemies. I see these words from Christ as an affirmation of our true identity, creations of the Creator, and Jesus prophesies this future tension of emotional and spiritual homelessness that we might feel in a place that doesn't live out of this divine centre. It explains why sometimes we feel like we have no anchor, and we don't know our right from our left.

Christ's words are not permission to treat everyone like an enemy, but to understand why we feel the strain when trying to follow his teachings. The establishment of God's never-ending love is in direct opposition to jealousy, envy, lust, gossip, greed, hatred, injustice – and with so many systems built on these ideologies, it's understandable that living in this world can be so darn hard. But take courage, Christ has overcome the world!

RN

18. NUMBER EIGHT

People look at the outward appearance, but the Lord looks at the heart.
1 Samuel 16:7

Samuel was a prophet, which means he heard directly from God with clarity and told the people the words God gave him. God told Samuel to go to the house of Jesse to anoint one of his sons as the new king of Israel. Jesse had eight sons but only presented seven of them to Samuel. The seven sons were tall, buff, strong and Thor-like - perfect king material, you would have thought!

However, God wanted someone with character and heart rather than height or might.

God would not let Samuel anoint any of the seven, so Samuel asked Jesse if he had more sons. He said there was a younger son, David, who was looking after the sheep. The moment David was brought to him, God told Samuel, 'Rise and anoint him; this is the one' (1 Samuel 16:12). David's dad had not even considered him an option, thinking he was the *haquatton* [Hebrew for the runt of the litter]. But what man writes off, God raises up!

We must not compare ourselves to others, or fear being unseen or unnoticed. The most important promotions and anointings come from God. Today, he is not looking at our qualifications, popularity or looks - he's looking to see a heart like his own.

DB

19. RESIDENT EVIL

For our struggle is not against flesh and blood, but against the rulers, against the authorities, against the powers of this dark world and against the spiritual forces of evil in the heavenly realms. **Ephesians 6:12**

We can believe that everything bad and fearful in our world is the result of humans. That fear can make us bitter and vengeful. But there is a bigger force at work, and our struggle and battle are not against people, but against the powers of darkness influencing this world.

We are not to fear this evil but to come against it in the greater power of the Holy Spirit, who equips us to forgive rather than take revenge; to show grace and love to the ungracious and unlovable.

When we do this, the kingdom of light advances and the kingdom of darkness decreases. Are we aware of evil in the world? How can we come against it in the power of the Spirit? Who can we show grace, kindness and forgiveness to in our world, who doesn't deserve it any more than we deserve the love and forgiveness of Jesus? By living like this, we win the battle against evil.

DB

20. CREATING A HOME FOR ALL

My prayer is not that you take them out of the world but that you protect them from the evil one. They are not of the world, even as I am not of it. Sanctify them by the truth; your word is truth. As you sent me into the world, I have sent them into the world. **John 17:15–18**

Jesus says that the reason we don't feel at home sometimes, the reason that 'the world' doesn't truly understand us, is because our true home is when we are in communion with our God alone.

We are truly at home, at peace, when we live out of the overflow of the Spirit of God within us, acknowledging the Spirit within each other and respecting the Christ who is present in all of God's creation. Through him, we can live in harmony, in mutual loving exchange with the earth, with our brothers and sisters who are also walking the planet, and with ourselves.

We don't have to be at war with people who don't follow the same path we do; we are called to love them, to create space for them to feel at home with us, to listen and to extend grace and compassion. To behold a reflection of God that they may never have seen before.

A deep sense of belonging is unlocked when we are connected to those around us. Seeing our enemies, those who don't share our beliefs or convictions through the eyes of God, is to acknowledge the image of God within them and to connect to something deeper than what we see.

RN

21. *SELAH* – SOW THAT SEED

We have been called to be in the world but not be consumed by ideologies or patterns that draw us away from God. We are not absolved from the wrestle and fight with our desires, so today we pause to pray for perseverance and strength as we break chains and claim ownership of our lives again.

Are there patterns of behaviour, habits or addictions that are keeping you trapped in a dependency? Spend some time asking God to reveal these to you and to heal you from these today?

Lord, you look at the heart, and while my flesh is weak, I know your love never fails, and your unmerited grace covers all my mistakes. Let your kingdom of light extend into my life, and may all the areas of my being be submitted to you. Help me to show more of you to others. Amen.

22. LOVING THE 'OPPOSITION'

You have heard that it was said, 'Love your neighbour and hate your enemy.' But I tell you, love your enemies and pray for those who persecute you, that you may be children of your Father in heaven. He causes his sun to rise on the evil and the good, and sends rain on the righteous and the unrighteous.
Matthew 5:43–5

The fear of being rejected can have us doing the oddest of things. When we decide to stick to our convictions, there can be pushback, and that opposition can push us to aggressively try to convince others to believe what we believe. When that doesn't work, we instead opt to ring-fence ourselves with people on our frequency, cutting ourselves off from the world and from the potential of being rejected. These echo chambers feel glorious because everyone thinks the same, but the kingdom of heaven doesn't look like everyone agreeing with one another; it looks like every nation and every tongue coming together to worship the only thing that truly matters: God, our heavenly Father.

In this lifetime, we have to step out and learn to live and love the 'other' and the 'opposition'.

Jesus said the world is exactly where he wanted us to be, so we must learn to live in harmony, to live in love and to pray for those who oppose us. Love our enemies, which means we all must extend God's favour and grace, mercy and kindness, patience and understanding, and sacrificial kindness to those who persecute us. Wild idea, I know, but it's not mine; these are the words of Christ.

We can extend that love far more easily when we ourselves have experienced it, and we can give that love with more confidence when we know it is not in our strength but God working through us.

RN

23. STAY HYDRATED

You, God, are my God, / earnestly I seek you;
I thirst for you. / my whole being longs for you,
in a dry and parched land / where there is no water. **Psalm 63:1**

There is nothing like drinking after feeling dehydrated.

Our physical bodies are made up of around 60% water;[13] we are built to need water running through our systems, and it's no different when it comes to our spiritual life. Our souls need water too, and vulnerability is admitting it's time to come to the well of God. Vulnerability is a gift, rooted in the act of surrender, and surrender is not as much a 'giving up' moment as it is a 'giving to God' one.

It's not a losing position, even though our pride will try to convince us that it is. We must begin the work of transforming our minds to realise that strength comes in knowing we are not strong enough to save ourselves, and that we were all built to have living water flowing through our Spirit.

To deny that we're ever thirsty or hungry for love is to ignore one of the deepest truths and one of our most fundamental needs. By reaching out and surrendering, like the psalmist, we give our emotions the honour they deserve. When we accept the invitation to open up, to return to the waters and to drink, we begin the long journey towards restoration.

RN

[13] Claire Sissons, 'What is the average percentage of water in the human body?', *Medical News Today*, 27 May 2020, www.medicalnewstoday.com/articles/what-percentage-of-the-human-body-is-water (accessed 19 April 2023).

24. VALUE OTHERS ABOVE YOURSELF

Therefore if you have any encouragement from being united with Christ, if any comfort from his love, if any common sharing in the Spirit, if any tenderness and compassion, then make my joy complete by being like-minded, having the same love, being one in spirit and of one mind. Do nothing out of selfish ambition or vain conceit. Rather, in humility value others above yourselves, not looking to your own interests but each of you to the interests of the others.
Philippians 2:1–4

I'm not sure when you're reading these devotionals – whether you've adopted them as your morning practice or whether they're read en route to work, during your lunch break or last thing before you fall asleep. Regardless of where and when you read them, it is my prayer that you leave enough time around your readings to fully let the words of Scripture sink in.

Face to face with Scripture, with God, with our experiences and with our communities, we must force ourselves to build lives that showcase God's unrelenting love, God's compassion, God's kindness and God's forgiveness in action through us. Our convictions, whatever they are, must ultimately lead to us creating more of the kingdom of heaven on earth, instead of helping us build empires where a few are elevated at the expense of others.

In order to cultivate that kingdom orientation in our own hearts, it is not enough to simply read a few words each morning and then forget about them as we go about our day. No, we must spend time meditating on them, questioning them – even disagreeing with them, provided we allow God into the wrestle. How are you going to make time to chew on these verses today?

RN

25. DISMAYED BY DIRT

So do not fear, for I am with you;
do not be dismayed, for I am your God.
I will strengthen you and help you;
I will uphold you with my righteous right hand. **Isaiah 41:10**

Just as a seed has to press in and push through the dirt to bloom and flower, we as humans have to press in to God and push through the negative voices and fears if we are to mature and blossom.

If we want to flower and bloom in a way that blesses not only ourselves but also others, we must make the difficult decision to persevere and face our fears, rather than run away from them.

Being honest, saying 'no' to sharing our story seems the easiest option, to back out of praying out loud for someone, to never stand up for the one being bullied or gossiped about, to compromise our character so we fit in with our colleagues. These 'easier choices' won't enable us to grow into the person God has called us to be, and they won't bring God glory.

If we are feeling dismayed because we have given in to fear and we've just blended in with everyone else in order to belong, today God reminds us that he is with us and will strengthen and uphold us as we step out for him and have the courage of our convictions.

Is there an area where you feel you may have 'fallen down'? Where do you need God's 'righteous right hand' to hold you up? Invite him into this today.

DB

26. WHERE IS OUR CONFIDENCE? - PART 1

Now faith is confidence in what we hope for and assurance about what we do not see. This is what the ancients were commended for.
By faith we understand that the universe was formed at God's command, so that what is seen was not made out of what was visible. **Hebrews 11:1-3**

Is our faith in Jesus or in other things?

It's easy to place our security in our own strength, talents, possessions, appearance, career, salary, relationship status, a strong economy, a good government, a decent prime minister or president, our partner or even our church leaders. Putting our faith in things other than Jesus actually leaves us feeling quite fearful because we know that all these other things can change in a moment, but he never changes.

God is always loving, faithful and true. Jesus intended us to live life to the full, secure in him. Without Jesus we may get to live a comfortable life, but we were created for so much more!

When we live our lives with radical trust and faith, we can expect Jesus to do something radical through us, and what a difference we could make when he does.

What would it look like to put a bit more faith in Jesus and a bit less faith in the security the world promises but cannot deliver? Many people cling tightly to their security blanket and loosely to faith, but what would it look like for us to cling to Jesus tightly and hold everything else loosely? How can we give Jesus our full trust and reliance today? You may want to write down just one idea.

DB

27. WHERE IS OUR CONFIDENCE? – PART 2

Now faith is confidence in what we hope for and assurance about what we do not see. This is what the ancients were commended for.
By faith we understand that the universe was formed at God's command, so that what is seen was not made out of what was visible. **Hebrews 11:1–3**

One of the questions I get asked a lot is, 'How can I believe in something or someone I cannot see?' We can fear being taken for a ride.

I reply, 'How can you believe in radio waves?' and they answer, 'Because I can hear the music when they get picked up by the radio.'

In the same way, when I was eighteen and asking questions about faith, one thing I couldn't deny was the impact other people's faith had on their lives. There was a transformation in their well-being (mentally, physically and spiritually), in their relationships and in their lifestyle choices and outcomes that couldn't be explained any other way. I couldn't see Jesus in person, but I could see the impact of his presence in them. In the same way that we can't see radio waves but we can hear the beauty of music, we can't see Jesus but we can know the beauty of his presence within us.

Today, let's take time to consider the difference Jesus has made to our well-being, relationships, lifestyle choices and outcomes, and let's be thankful for all the ways he has moved in our lives. May our lives make Jesus' love and grace visible to those around us.

DB

28. *SELAH* - CHEWING ON TRUTH

As mentioned earlier, it is not enough to simply read a few words each morning and then forget about them as we go about our days. We must spend time meditating on them, questioning them. Today, rewind and find a verse from the past seven days to sit with. Read the words once and see what stands out. Read them again, more slowly this time, and ask God what he'd like to reveal to you.

You may want to memorise these words so that you can refer to them throughout the day when you feel something other than God pulling at your thoughts. Use this verse to recentre on him.

God, I may not see you, but I know you are here. My trust is in the architect of my soul, the creator of all things - how wonderful to know that you care for the stars and planets, but you also care for me. I will not fear, for you are with me; I will not be dismayed, for you are my God. Amen.

29. THE SLIMY PIT

I waited patiently for the LORD;
he turned to me and heard my cry.
He lifted me out of the slimy pit,
out of the mud and mire;
he set my feet on a rock
and gave me a firm place to stand. **Psalm 40:1-2**

In the book *Generation Alpha* (about those born after 2010), Collett Smart, a child psychologist, said:

> When children are anxious or depressed, one of the things we might do is ask them who they can help, [taking the focus off themselves and onto somebody else]. It's not to minimise their pain, but to put it in perspective. Their own problems tend to fade into the background for a little while, while reaching out to somebody else.[14]

I believe Collett's advice is for all ages, and it echoes God's heart that in serving him and helping others we can find greater freedom, meaning, purpose and fulfilment. God is not angry or disappointed in us if we struggle with depression or anxiety. He is our loving heavenly Father who wants to be with us, and who wants to heal us and lift our spirits.

How can we encourage ourselves or others struggling with depression to face the fear? Let's focus on one kind thing we can do for someone in need today.

DB

[14] Mark McCrindle and Ashley Fell with Sam Buckerfield, *Generation Alpha: Understanding our children and helping them thrive* (London: Headline, 2021), p. 104.

30. 365/360 REFLECTION

Looking back at this month, we've reflected on standing up for what we believe in. Though the fear of rejection can lead us to inauthentic lives in service to the culture around us, God is inviting us to put all our confidence in him.

'Blessed is the one who trusts in the LORD, whose confidence is in him,' says Jeremiah 17:7. As we pause to reflect on another month gone by, can you see areas in your life where you are growing in confidence in God? How about where you need more of the Spirit's shaping work within you?

Why not spend some time today writing down your own core values and convictions. Can you find a corresponding Bible verse or biblical truth to root these views in so that when the challenges come, you can hold fast to what you believe in? If there is no biblical truth behind these statements of belief, you may want to invite God to show you why you are holding on to these so tightly. Perhaps you might want to reach out to a wise and trusted friend to chat about this too?

OCTOBER

1. RELATIONSHIP WRECK - PART 1

Samson went down to Timnah and saw there a young Philistine woman. When he returned, he said to his father and mother, 'I have seen a Philistine woman in Timnah; now get her for me as my wife.' **Judges 14:1-2**

Samson, a Nazirite man set apart for God, had supernatural strength through his uncut hair. He was also terrible at finding a decent partner.

In today's scripture, we see Samson choosing his wife based on appearance alone. For those fearing being alone and not finding a decent partner, we can learn from Samson's life and actions that choosing a partner based on their objective beauty and looks does not create a healthy relationship. Many people believe that you can have love at first sight, but I believe you can have 'like' or even 'lust' at first sight, but not real love.

The Bible shows us that real love is a different thing entirely. 1 Corinthians 13:4-7 tells us that love is patient, kind, doesn't envy, isn't proud and doesn't dishonour others. Love always hopes, protects, perseveres and never fails. Lasting love like this is not based on the external but on the internal qualities of a person - something that it takes some time to find out! This love is discovered through friendship and closeness and maintained through our choice to love every day.

Samson lost his wife as she betrayed him, running off with his best man. If we want to find a partner with whom to do life together with God, rather than just to change our relationship status, let's refuse to choose this person based on looks alone, but rather let's pursue someone who loves God and who demonstrates the true definition of love we see in Scripture through their character and their actions.

DB

2. RELATIONSHIP WRECK - PART 2

Some time later, he fell in love with a woman in the Valley of Sorek whose name was Delilah. The rulers of the Philistines went to her and said, 'See if you can lure him into showing you the secret of his great strength and how we can overpower him so that we may tie him up and subdue him. Each one of us will give you eleven hundred shekels of silver.'
So Delilah said to Samson, 'Tell me the secret of your great strength.'
Judges 16:4-6

Samson fell for Delilah, another Philistine woman, again drawn in by her beauty. She seduced him and wore him down until he revealed the secret of his strength. She betrayed Samson to the Philistines and told them how to weaken him. They came for him, shaved his head and blinded him.

Trust is something that many of us want in a relationship, but there is much disloyalty out there and we can fear being betrayed as Samson was. How can we deal with this fear and mistrust?

When it comes to cultivating trust, many of us need to understand that we can't change other people; we can only change ourselves and how we respond to the actions of others. It is also important to treat our partner as we want to be treated. If we want a loyal partner, we need to be loyal and trustworthy.

We also see in today's short passage that Samson seemed to lack faithful friends. If I was his mate, I would have said, 'This girl isn't looking to build up your strengths; she's trying to tear you down by exposing your weaknesses.' Let's make sure we are trustworthy and loyal to our friends and families.

Who do we trust to speak the truth in love to us? Thank God for them! Who can we speak love and truth to in return? Ask God to highlight them to you today.

DB

3. RELATIONSHIP WRECK – PART 3

*Then Samson prayed to the L*ORD*, 'Sovereign L*ORD*, remember me. Please, God, strengthen me just once more, and let me with one blow get revenge on the Philistines for my two eyes!'* **Judges 16:28**

Samson denied his calling as a man of God and joined himself to women who were enemies of God. He was unwise and lustful, and what trouble it brought him!

His choices left him hurt, betrayed, imprisoned and blind, full of bitterness and desire for vengeance. Retaliation fuelled by hurt and fear never brings restoration and healing. Samson managed to put things right with God and he brought down his enemies, but he died in the process.

As we have touched upon in previous reflections, hurting people hurt others and themselves. Bitterness eats away at souls and keeps us connected to those who hurt us.

Freedom comes when we find in God healing and the power to forgive. If we are carrying hurt from betrayal, let's take our pain to God and ask him to stop bitterness becoming rooted in our lives and affecting all our relationships.

God's healing can restore us and release us from fear of being betrayed again, and it keeps us free from lies that tell us we deserve such treatment and enables us to make wise relationship choices in the future!

DB

4. RELATIONSHIP WRECK – PART 4

For the Spirit God gave us does not make us timid, but gives us power, love and self-discipline. **2 Timothy 1:7**

Forgiving others frees us from bitterness, fear and victimhood.

Some may feel that what happened to them is too hard, or even impossible, to forgive. And it is, in our own strength; only time with the Holy Spirit and the active choice to forgive again and again and again can soften our hearts.

We may also think that if we forgive, we will become more open to getting hurt again, or that the one who hurt us will get away with their actions. We may see unforgiveness as self-protective. But this coping mechanism is not freedom and can emotionally tie us to those who hurt us.

God knows the bind that unforgiveness can have on us and wants us to bring our pain and brokenness to him. He wants his love and truth to heal us from the lies we believed in the pain, setting us free to confidently be ourselves, full of power and love and self-discipline (rather than being controlled by our fear, pain and reactions).

As God's truth sets us free, our supernatural healing enables us to release those who hurt us into his hands to help or judge as he sees fit, and we can move forward free from the weight of unforgiveness.

Are there people who have hurt us that we need to speak to God about? Let's acknowledge their wrongdoing and our pain to him and ask what he wants us to know about it or about them.

DB

5. RELATIONSHIP WRECK – PART 5

Peace I leave with you; my peace I give you. I do not give to you as the world gives. Do not let your hearts be troubled and do not be afraid. **John 14:27**

In this life, many people will hurt us, but we will also hurt other people.

No one is perfect; we all have things that trigger negative thoughts or responses, and we all have unique perspectives that sometimes colour how we see the world around us.

Poor communication and actions can trigger us to retaliate in unhelpful ways, or things can be misunderstood, causing damage. We need to keep short accounts, putting things right and apologising to others quickly, but sometimes fear stops us doing that. Fear says, 'If we apologise, others won't respect us and will see us as weak.' Fear says, 'Apologise and that person will walk all over us.' The truth is, if we apologise, people will respect us for being real, open and honest; it means that we are OK with vulnerability and mistakes, which brings a level of trust, strength, collaboration and togetherness which would not happen otherwise.

Jesus, the Prince of Peace, calls us to be not peacekeepers but peacemakers. This means sorting things out and releasing each other from offence.

Ask the Holy Spirit if there is anyone you need to apologise to, and ask for the right moment to sort things out. Whether the person accepts your apology or not, you are released to experience greater freedom in Jesus as his peace brings you to peace.

DB

6. RELATIONSHIP WRECK – PART 6

For by grace you have been saved through faith. And this is not your own doing; it is the gift of God, not a result of works, so that no one may boast. For we are his workmanship, created in Christ Jesus for good works, which God prepared beforehand, that we should walk in them. **Ephesians 2:8–10 (ESVUK)**

I love to build Lego® with my son, Knox. As we were building a Batman base, Niko, my youngest, came in and destroyed it. Knox was devastated; he had put so much love and care into it, and to see it come tumbling down was hard to handle.

It made me think how God must feel every time we destroy his creation, both people and planet, when we respond out of fear and hatred rather than faith and love.

In today's passage, we are described as God's workmanship, created to do good works. God lovingly created every human, yet throughout history we see humans damaging and destroying God's workmanship with their power and control moves to get ahead and climb the ladder.

As children of God, we can do things differently; we can pray and make sure we are responsive to the opportunities God gives us for doing good. God has prepared and equipped us for this. We can give grace to others because God gave us grace as a gift. This gift was not based on our behaviour but on us being his workmanship, his creation, his children. Who can we show grace to today?

DB

7. *SELAH* – WE ARE THE PEACEMAKERS

We are called to be peacemakers, reconcilers, agents of restoration, like our Father in heaven.

As we reflect on our relationships, is there anything that stands out to you? Are there people to be thankful for? People you may need to apologise to or forgive? Is there a coffee catch-up or dinner date that you need to get in the diary which could begin to bridge the gap between you and start the process of healing for relationship hurts gone by?

Spend some time today asking God to put his finger on the relationships he wants you to invest in.

God, you did not give me a spirit of fear, and I will not route my life in walking fearfully in my relationships. Lead me to extend the forgiveness you have extended to me, teach me to love like you, and help me practise the peace you exhibited while you walked among us. Amen.

8. FEAR OF DEATH – PART 1

If we live, we live for the Lord; and if we die, we die for the Lord. So, whether we live or die, we belong to the Lord. **Romans 14:8**

The Pulitzer Prize-winning book, *The Denial of Death* by Ernest Becker, goes into detail about different physiological and anthropological understandings of death, and the fear surrounding it.[15]

There is a multitude of origin stories for the fear of death and how much of an impact it can have on our day-to-day lives. Some thinkers believe the fear of death underpins all of our insecurities and basic anxieties, and others believe that through healthy socialisation from childhood we can build healthy understandings around mortality, and not be completely gripped by our finitude.

Irrespective of the origin, or which side of the psychological fence you sit on, one of the overarching realities is that the fear of death, whether ignored, repressed, embraced or exaggerated, is at the core of the human experience – and our fear of it perhaps points to the fact that death was never supposed to be part of God's plan. And yet it is something we need to deal with this side of eternity. Death is a topic we must stare in the face, and as Christians we can be confident in the knowledge that – thanks to Jesus – death is not the end of the story.

RN

[15] Ernest Becker, *The Denial of Death* (London: Souvenir Press, 2014).

9. FEAR OF DEATH – PART 2

For this very reason, Christ died and returned to life so that he might be the Lord of both the dead and the living. **Romans 14:9**

Death is an inevitable part of our reality, whether it's the death of someone we love or the loss of a friend or family member; even the loss of a dream can be followed with a period of mourning.

I've always wrestled with how something so commonplace, so integrated into life itself, can have such a negative hold on us. It can be a topic we avoid so much that it nearly always takes us by surprise in events or conversation.

It is a paradox that we must come to terms with. We are of infinite value, we possess the power to shape the world, we contain the very Spirit of the living God who brought all things into being, but in the same breath we are contained within finite vessels this side of heaven. No matter how big our businesses get, how large our families grow, how deep we push our feet into the sands of time, our lives on this planet are not permanent.

The tide will eventually come in, and another chapter will begin.

We can never truly prepare ourselves for an event we have never before experienced, but I believe that staring this paradox in the face and not hiding death in a back cupboard in our minds will mean that we, like Christ, can conquer death, instead of living lives conquered by it.

RN

10. THE MIRACLE OF LIFE

*Be careful, or your hearts will be weighed down with carousing, drunkenness
and the anxieties of life, and that day will close on you suddenly like a trap.*
Luke 21:34

The experience of death can be a sudden wake-up call to the fact that we are
not in total control.

We, as human beings, unlike any other creature or animal in existence, have
the power to understand time in a unique way. No other animal in the world
has the cognitive function to contemplate their own mortality like human
beings do, to bargain with tomorrow by sacrificing today, to grasp the totality
of death and appreciate the miracle of life.

With that power comes a great weight, a weight we don't have to carry alone
but often try to anyway. In order to escape the finite nature of our realities,
we build, we create, we consciously or subconsciously over-invest into the
lives we lead to escape the fear of death. We buy property, forge career paths,
carry last names from generation to generation, all in the hope of achieving
immortality. As beautiful, as magical, as important or impactful as our lives
might be, they too must come to an end one day. We can run, but none of us
can hide away from the reality of death here on this earth, but as we will see
in the following reflections, death is never the end of the story.

RN

11. HEART OF GRATITUDE

He reveals deep and hidden things;
he knows what lies in darkness,
and light dwells with him. **Daniel 2:22**

Our full and fast-paced lives can sometimes be calculated distractions from reality.

You may not have met me, but trust me when I say that I am a human who is all for optimism and good vibes. However, sometimes these 'good vibes' can be a front for what is really going on, and permanent residence in the 'shallow end' of life means that we can be completely knocked for six when moments of harsh reality arrive at our doors.

The danger of living a distracted life with our heads floating in the clouds is that we can miss the wonders of the here and now. Ironically, embracing the reality of death this side of heaven can allow us to see the beauty of this life in even sharper focus.

Moments and seconds are all the more precious, every drop of this gift we have been given can be honoured and experienced. Yes, that will often come with heartbreak, but it can also, in time, unlock joy of infinite measure. Hearts of gratitude are completely aware of the miracle of life and of the reality of death. They also have an awareness that every gift comes from God, and he can call us to return to our heavenly homes whenever he sees fit. It's our job to be thankful for the journey.

RN

12. THE MIRACLE OF LIFE

There is a time for everything,
and a season for every activity under the heavens:
a time to be born and a time to die. **Ecclesiastes 3:1-2**

At every funeral service I've been to, Ecclesiastes 3 has been read aloud at some point in the service. 'There is a season... for everything and a time for every delight' (AMP). There is a season to be born, to experience joy, for laughter with friends and for experiencing moments of happiness we never thought possible. There are also times to grieve with family and for weeping alone in our bedroom over a loved one or a lost one. One day, there will come a time to die. Though we as Christians do not believe in reincarnation, there is a natural flow of life, death and rebirth that we can see play out in the great biblical narrative and, indeed, in our lives.

Moment by moment we are engaged in this flow - life, death and resurrection - led by God, and to fight against this cycle is to fight against the natural order of things. As hard as we try, we cannot within our finite bodies live forever, and though we have the power to momentarily bring heaven to earth through doing the things that Jesus did and ushering in the miraculous, no one can escape the so-called circle of life. As we embrace the rhythms of this circle, we are awoken to the true beauty of what we are a part of.

RN

13. THE MAGIC IN THE MUNDANE

Do not boast about tomorrow,
for you do not know what a day may bring. **Proverbs 27:1**

Moments are fleeting. Everything, except for the eternal things of God, come to an end. Time, and its limited nature, is what makes life this side of eternity all the more precious, and we need to rise to the gift of life rather than shrink into the fear of death.

Going to the local pub with friends, throwing off the cares of the week gone by, breaking your ribs laughing so hard until the sun rises: such moments are precious because the sun eventually steals the night away. Knowing that everything is temporary should remind us to live in a constant state of gratitude for the present moment we get to experience with God. For what is here and now. For the memories that we have been blessed to accumulate, and to truly appreciate the people we may not see again this side of eternity. There is a time for everything, so let's be present enough in our lives to embrace every second that we can, because there always comes a time to let go. But let's also use these moments - the magic and the mundane - to point others to the eternal life that is yet to come.

One day, the Bible promises, God will bring a new heaven and a new earth, where there will be no more pain or suffering and we can dwell with God forever (Revelation 21:1-4). As much as we should embrace this life as the gift it is, we must ask God to help us enjoy and endure our days in light of his plans for eternity.

RN

14. *SELAH* – WITH HIM IN GLORY

Jesus said, 'Blessed are those who mourn, for they will be comforted' (Matthew 5:4), so just as we look for comfort, we can also be the ones giving comfort to those around us when they are experiencing loss.

We can point them to the reality of heaven, but in order to do this we need to have eyes to see this reality ourselves. Sometimes our busy lives can be a distraction from the eternity with Jesus to which all Christians are travelling. Do you struggle with slowing down and being present?

Today, take a moment to slow down and check in with yourself. How do you feel about loss? Is there any unresolved grief that you need to take to the foot of the cross? Is there anyone around you who needs to know the promise of heaven in their time of hurting?

Ask God to show you how to bring his kingdom to earth today.

Whether we live or die, we belong to you, Lord. We take this moment to thank you for the miracle of life, and to mourn those who have walked into eternity. We pray for comfort for those who mourn all over the world, and ask that you extend your love to your broken-hearted children, calling them ever closer to you and reminding them of the reality of heaven. Amen.

15. FOR SUCH A TIME

For if you remain silent at this time, relief and deliverance for the Jews will arise from another place, but you and your father's family will perish. And who knows but that you have come to your royal position for such a time as this?
Esther 4:14

Esther was a woman who had been given a seat at the king's table; she had the king's ear, his favour and a position of potential influence. With this power at her disposal, Esther had a choice to make. She could keep quiet about her identity as an Israelite and let her people perish, or she could try to speak to the king and ask for their freedom.

For some of us, speaking up about our own identity doesn't seem so scary; others will completely get why Esther might have had to think long and hard about this decision. To put Esther's particular choice in context, no one would ever approach the king uninvited because they could lose their life in the process! If the king did not accept or favour them or their request, it was game over.

Esther asked her people to pray and fast for her and the situation they were facing before she went to the king, because she knew she needed God's intervention. With the strength and courage that comes from prayer, she faced her fear and spoke to the king. As a result, the plot of an evil manipulator, Haman, was exposed and her people were set free.

Freedom is always on the other side of our fear. The question is, will we face our fear or be held captive by it? The secret is to prepare ourselves for moments of courage by spending time with God - praying and fasting like Esther's people did - and going forward with confidence in him and any strategy he gives us.

DB

16. OUR GOD, KING OF THE SWELLING SEA

You rule over the surging sea;
when its waves mount up, you still them. **Psalm 89:9**

I remember when a childhood friend of mine tragically died in a car accident. Nothing could have prepared me for the pain that hit me that morning as I was told the news. It was like getting a hot sledgehammer smashed into the centre of my chest. Without warning, my soul was reduced to rubble. I was completely broken in half. How do we even begin to put the pieces back together?

I cannot truly put into words what that experience was like: the shock, the confusion, the gut-wrenching feelings of anger - towards God, towards anyone who could have prevented it. Why? What? How? The questions were endless and the answers were few. I was caught in a whirlwind of emotions, suspended in utter chaos. In the midst of the storm, when the waves had risen so high they blocked out the sun, I lost all grounding. I struggled to cling to something, anything.

Looking back, I can see that God was still in the centre of my circumstances, even though at the time I couldn't have felt more alone. God rules the swelling seas and stands beside us, holding us in the undercurrent. It may feel like the pain will never end, but trust me, God will still the sea.

RN

17. LET THE WAVE CRASH IN

You are God's chosen people. You are holy and dearly loved. So put on tender
mercy and kindness as if they were your clothes. Don't be proud. Be gentle and
patient. **Colossians 3:12 (NIRV)**

The same day we received the news of my childhood friend's tragic accident,
our friendship group gathered together. The Nti house was always a
community centre of sorts, so friends from around the area congregated.
People came from all over. Some knew the boys involved in the accident;
others just wanted to support us in our suffering. Together, we wept, we
laughed, we reminisced and we prayed. We sat in the moment and held the
chaos the only way we knew how – together.

We let the wave crash in. We created space for all the different emotions that
we were all feeling to be honoured, and to be presented in all their mess and
with no condemnation. We created a sacred space to feel the depth of that
moment, that grief, together.

In times of despair, finding a sanctuary in which we can be truly honest with
our feelings can provide much-needed oxygen for a body in desperate need
of air. To sit with others or with God and simply be still, breathe deeply, letting
the waves crash in, can be the first step towards healing.

What feelings – or waves – do you need to let in today, knowing God holds you
through it all?

RN

18. THE PROCESS OF GRIEF

The LORD himself goes before you and will be with you; he will never leave you nor forsake you. Do not be afraid; do not be discouraged. **Deuteronomy 31:8**

People grieve in a multitude of ways. In her book *On Death and Dying*, Elisabeth Kübler-Ross identified five stages of grief: denial, anger, bargaining, depression and acceptance.[16]

Space needs to be created to journey through all of these moments in the grieving process. We are all complex and completely different in the way in which we process experiences; some want to shout from the rooftops, some want to curl up and ignore the outside world.

The journey towards healing can begin once we have opened ourselves to the truth that something is in fact gone, whether that be a dream or a person, and we can't rush through the process.

Do not be afraid as you walk through, or as you take others by the hand through their own despair, because God promised that 'he will never leave you nor forsake you'. The Lord knew what was going to happen before it happened, and he has gone before you to clear a way towards peace, towards the wholeness we think is unattainable, towards the happiness we believe will never be experienced again. He is leading you by the hand.

RN

---

[16] Elisabeth Kübler-Ross, *On Death and Dying: What the dying have to teach doctors, nurses, clergy and their own families* (New York: Scribner, 2019).

19. FEAR IS A COMPASS

But Jonah ran away from the Lᴏʀᴅ... So he went down to the port of Joppa. There he found a ship that was going to Tarshish. He paid the fare and went on board... He was running away from the Lᴏʀᴅ. **Jonah 1:3 ɴɪʀᴠ**

Fear is a compass: how we respond to it is a choice we all have. When a deadly shark, snake or spider is coming for you and fear is telling you to run... RUN! No point facing fear here and losing your life; this book is not about disregarding survival instincts that have served us for thousands of years.

However, there are other times when social fears, such as the fear of failure, fear of rejection, fear of ridicule and fear of humiliation, will stop us from doing what God is asking us to do. In today's scripture, God asks Jonah to deliver a message, and he ran as far away as he could. Fear was his compass, which ended up getting him caught in the belly of a fish. When God asks us to do something, it is for our good and his glory. If fear is directing you away from what God is asking you to do, allow the Holy Spirit to be your compass, your navigator, your guide.

> Give me your lantern and compass, give me a map, So I can find my way to the sacred mountain, to the place of your presence.
> (Psalm 43:3 ᴍsɢ)

DB

20. FEAR OF NOT MAKING A DIFFERENCE

Do to others as you want them to do to you. **Luke 6:31** NIRV

We live in an age where, if you can dream it, you can do it. We are surrounded by start-ups, and are constantly reminded of people's successes on social media. It doesn't take long before we start to look at our own lives and feel as though we are not doing anything of significance and not making a difference. Fear sets in, causing us to think our life is meaningless. However, the truth couldn't be more different. Every day can have meaning and purpose because every day we can make a difference.

I have a lot of admiration for my dad. He has given many voluntary hours over his years managing football teams. He would always get Luke 6:31 printed on the kit: 'Do to others as you want them to do to you.' He said this is the best way to play.

Living by this scripture daily might not make it as a viral video or be the headlines in the paper, or even be written in the history books. But this lifestyle does make a difference. All we need to do is notice the people around us and, regardless of how they treat us, treat them the way Jesus would, the way we would like to be treated. This way of living life is significant; it brings purpose and meaning. It shapes society and changes culture.

DB

21. *SELAH* – WALK, DON'T RUN

We've spent time this week reflecting on the process of losing loved ones and loved things. We cannot rush through the stages of grief, and everybody experiences grief in different ways.

It is vital to remind ourselves that God is walking through every stage, experiencing every twinge of pain, holding us in the moments when we feel like we can't take it any more.

Today, we invite you to sit with God, taking time to process your present reality. Where are you in your mind, your body, your soul? Is there any unresolved heartbreak or grief anchoring you to pain you could leave in the past? Are you at peace or are you experiencing pain? Perhaps you are experiencing pain and peace at exactly the same time?

Ask God to fill you with his peace, joy and wisdom as you slowly process what you are going through. God has the power to bring new life when all we see is death; to bring life to dry bones.

Mighty God, you rule the swelling of the sea. As these waves of loss and grief rise and crash around me, hold me still and steady in your love. As the waters surround my feet, may your Spirit anchor me to you. Jesus wept when his friend died, and I weep now, but I trust in your redemption plans. Death is never the end of the story when it comes to living a life with you. Amen.

OCTOBER

22. LAZARUS, ARISE! – PART 1

On his arrival, Jesus found that Lazarus had already been in the tomb for four days. **John 11:17**

Perhaps one of the most poignant stories within the Gospels is the story of Lazarus, who had first-hand experience of the miraculous power of Jesus Christ.

Jesus is sent word that his friend Lazarus is desperately sick, and instead of running to the rescue, Jesus remains in his current location for another two days. By the time Jesus decided to arrive on the scene, Lazarus was not only dead, but had been dead for four whole days. That doesn't sound like the beginning of a resurrection story!

Four days devoid of all signs of life whatsoever. That is a long time dead, and yet Lazarus breathed again. Jesus could have packed his belongings and rushed to his friend's side while he was still breathing, but he foresaw the miracle on the horizon, a miracle that was made even more spectacular because of how bleak the outcome looked. Jesus was in no doubt that this whole experience would bring glory to God in the end and that people would tell this story forever.

RN

23. LAZARUS, ARISE! – PART 2

But do not forget this one thing, dear friends: with the Lᴏʀᴅ a day is like a thousand years, and a thousand years are like a day. The Lᴏʀᴅ is not slow in keeping his promise, as some understand slowness. **2 Peter 3:8–9**

Jesus always knew that Lazarus' death wasn't the end of the story. And yet, for everyone else on the ground – for Mary, Martha and the rest of Lazarus' friends and family – the anguish of those four days must have been excruciating.

Those feelings will be shared with every family member, friend or loved one who has waited by a hospital bed, on the end of a phone, in a waiting room or even in another country waiting for news of a loved one's health. Those four days must have felt like an eternity, but time is not under our control but God's. God's being 'on time' is often our 'too late', but as the clock ticks and the pressure mounts, remember that nothing is too far gone for God to bring breakthrough.

I don't have a magic wand that I can wave to absolve the suffering of the 'four days' you may be experiencing. Only to say that in those dark moments, Christ remains. As bleak as the outcome is, the story is not always written in the way we think it might be, but there is a plan in play. This plan may make no sense to us, but God is already on the other side, ushering his ending in.

RN

24. LAZARUS, ARISE! – PART 3

He has made everything beautiful in its time. **Ecclesiastes 3:11**

When it comes to the natural world, almost everything that passes away is followed by new life, but sometimes there is a space in between the two states – it takes time for new seeds to be planted.

It is the same with us: what we do in the transitional time between death and life is significant. The perceived 'void', where we feel like we are not heard or seen and that God has forsaken us, can have a massive impact on the trajectory of our lives and dictate the spiritual depths we descend to.

Jesus Christ was well aware of the anguish experienced by everyone surrounding Lazarus' untimely death. He was fully aware of the situation, to the point that he was moved to tears on his arrival at Lazarus' tomb (John 11:35). Even though the whole village thought it was too late for Lazarus to live, despite the outlook, Jesus remained in control. He knew how to navigate the space between perceived death and promised new life with an unwavering faith in the God we were born to follow.

Do you find yourself in one of these 'in between' spaces today? Has something died, whether it be a relationship or a dream, that you'd long to see come back to life? Ask God to help you keep trusting in the liminal space, trusting him to author the end of the story in precisely the way it's meant to go.

RN

25. LAZARUS, ARISE! – PART 4

Jesus said to her, 'I am the resurrection and the life. The one who believes in me will live, even though they die; and whoever lives by believing in me will never die. Do you believe this?' **John 11:25-6**

Sometimes, hearing that 'God is in control' can be a bitter pill to swallow at a moment where it feels like our world is crumbling. But in light of Lazarus' story, in my darkest moments, mourning the loss of something I hold dear, I am forced to reflect: how do I trust that God is in control enough to enable me to carry love, hope and grace in the face of death?

Am I navigating this season with self-compassion, or, in my pain or impatience, am I rashly burning everything to the ground – my self-worth, my relationships, my opportunities?

Experiencing pain doesn't give us a free pass to inflict it. If we do, we only end up harming ourselves and those around us. We may need to seek God's forgiveness and guidance on how to bring restoration.

Whatever pain you are experiencing today, how do Jesus' assurances in today's passage help you look at your present hardship in light of eternity? Do you truly believe God is in control? It's OK if the answer to this question is currently 'no'. I encourage you to spend some time in prayer, asking God to reveal his steadfast and life-giving nature to you at this time.

RN

26. LAZARUS, ARISE! - PART 5

*The angel said to the women, 'Do not be afraid, for I know that you are looking
for Jesus, who was crucified. He is not here; he has risen, just as he said. Come
and see the place where he lay.'* **Matthew 28:5-6**

When Mary Magdalene and Mary the mother of James approached the tomb of
Jesus Christ in Matthew's Gospel, they had already endured a whole world of
suffering.

I am struck by the strength and bravery it took for these women to have
stared death in the face at the cross (as told in John 19:25), watching someone
they loved so dearly be humiliated, and then visiting the tomb despite
their grief.

For each of these women, Christ represented not just the Saviour of the
world, but also someone with whom they had experienced a close personal
relationship. His mother Mary watched the son she had carried in her womb
and raised and loved for more than thirty years being killed and presented as
a fraud and criminal. And Mary Magdalene witnessed the suffering of the One
who had brought her such freedom.

Despite all this, today we read how the pain endured by these women at the
cross was transformed into joy as they became the key witnesses to a miracle
beyond their (and our) wildest dreams.

In what situations in your life today do you feel like death is having the final
word? Ask God to reveal to you the flickers of light and new life he is birthing
in you and around you as a result.

RN

27. REMAIN, DESPITE THE PAIN

For we believe that Jesus died and rose again, and so we believe that God will bring with Jesus those who have fallen asleep in him. **1 Thessalonians 4:14**

The gift buried within the depths of our moments of grief, behind the great suffering, is beholding a glimpse of God that we never thought possible – bearing witness to the miracle of the new.

Now, the miracle will inevitably be different from what has passed, but the question I ask myself is, am I willing to put myself in a vulnerable enough position to watch something (or someone) I love die? To be there through the worst, in the darkest of nights, till death do us part?

It's one thing to remain when we're surrounded by joy, when life is thriving; it's easy to sit in a garden in the full bloom of summertime, but am I prepared to sit in the same space in winter when the flowers have faded and the trees are naked and bare?

In the face of death, of anguish, am I prepared to stand side by side in love, to resiliently hold the hand of those at the edge? Would I be so bold, like those women at Jesus' tomb, who gave witness to death? And if I were to do so, can I trust that in time my pain would be redeemed as I beheld the miraculous, death-defying transformational glory of God?

RN

28. *SELAH* – NEW LIFE

Death does not have the final say. While we experience it in all aspects of our lives, we must learn to acknowledge the pain and yet still see God at work within it. With Jesus, where there is death, there is new life. Can we reshape death to see it as a step that leads to resurrection life through the finished work of Christ, who died for us on the cross?

What in your life have you written off as dead and gone, that may be in the process of resurrection? Spend some time today reflecting on the past week and the circumstances this topic may have brought up for you. Ask God to show you where he is already at work, ushering in new life.

Jesus Christ, you are the resurrection and the life. You conquered death and showed me that though the darkness may last for a night, hope is always on the horizon. You can make everything beautiful in its time. Even this. Amen.

29. DEATH IS NOT THE END

And I heard a loud voice from the throne saying, 'Look! God's dwelling-place is now among the people, and he will dwell with them. They will be his people, and God himself will be with them and be their God. "He will wipe every tear from their eyes. There will be no more death" or mourning or crying or pain, for the old order of things has passed away.' **Revelation 21:3-4**

As we have been reflecting this month, death can bring with it a heaviness that can feel hard to carry. What's more, this weight can be multiplied substantially when we are not prepared to accept death and dying as part of our earthly reality. As heavy as the weight of death is, we must hold on to the knowledge that death is not the end. What a glorious hope we have in Jesus Christ!

Since the days of Isaiah, God has foretold of the 'new heavens and a new earth' (Isaiah 65:17; 66:22) that he has planned for the whole of humanity who put their trust in Jesus. This is a place of perfection at the end of the age, when all things are restored. In the space where all things are reunited with God, there will be no separation, no poverty, no hatred, no sickness, no war, no loneliness, no tears and no pain.

What a wonderful inheritance the children of God have! This knowledge of where we are headed should bring us hope in the darkest of times. It also empowers us to share this hope with those who don't yet know Jesus, whether through our prayers, our words or our actions.

RN

30. ARISE FROM THE ASHES

He said to me: 'It is done. I am the Alpha and the Omega, the Beginning and the End. To the thirsty I will give water without cost from the spring of the water of life.' **Revelation 21:6**

The world Jesus came to save includes every single human being who has ever lived, no matter their heritage, circumstances or life experience. Jesus is the personification of the unbreakable Spirit of God, experiencing the fullness of death, carrying all of creation in his heart as he descended to the depths to conquer death, and then resurrected to ascend once more to be at God's right hand.

What an image – someone fighting their way to the very bottom, to the very pits of hell, only to make it through to the other side victorious! To rise from the ashes anew despite experiencing death. Jesus demonstrates the pathway we too will take, one that reconnects humanity with eternal life, the way God has always intended it to be.

As terrifying as it may seem, death is not the end; there is life beyond. There is more depth in a single breath than we could ever imagine, and when our final breath on this earth is taken, we are assured that through the life, death and resurrection of Christ, there is an eternity for us to behold.

RN

31. 365/360 REFLECTION

This month our reflections have touched on relationships, death and our relationship with death. We've seen how ignoring pain and suffering can be damaging, as can overlooking the sacrifice and hard work needed to maintain healthy relationships that brim with love and forgiveness.

There is a price of fellowship and intimacy, but the gifts are incalculable. There is the pain of death and suffering in this world, but we know through Christ that death is not the end.

The Bible speaks of comfort for all those who mourn. Commit to spending some time today reading through a section of the Bible and even memorising some of the verses that have stood out to you this past month. Then ask God to show you how you can play your part in providing safe spaces for those around you to grieve, to lament and to find healing.

NOVEMBER

1. DARE TO DREAM

And it shall come to pass afterwards,
that I will pour out my Spirit on all flesh;
your sons and your daughters shall prophesy,
your old men shall dream dreams,
and your young men shall see visions.
Even on the male and female servants
in those days I will pour out my Spirit. **Joel 2:28-9 (ESVUK)**

Dreams are non-exclusive. It doesn't matter how young or old you are, your geographical location or nationality, everyone is given the licence to dream. Nor are fulfilled dreams an exclusive phenomenon. God doesn't reserve that right for any particular people group or demographic, so why do we sometimes exclude ourselves from the camp of those people whose dreams come true?

In the face of social media and the global comparison this can bring, the tornado of thoughts tearing through our minds can be that we're too old or that dreams are saved for the select few (not us!).

The truth is that God has made his Spirit accessible to all people, no matter what race, gender or financial background. That Spirit carries the seeds of dreams, and they are planted in the hearts of every human being walking around this planet, so if you think you're exempt, you're wrong!

What dreams might God be planting in your heart today? Are there dreams of days gone by that have been forgotten in the busyness and disappointments of life? Might it be time to dream them again?

RN

2. ALL-ACCESS PASS TO DREAMING

No, this is what was spoken by the prophet Joel:
'In the last days, God says,
I will pour out my Spirit on all people.
Your sons and daughters will prophesy,
your young men will see visions,
your old men will dream dreams.' **Acts 2:16–17**

In Acts, Peter reiterates these words from the prophet Joel to the crowd in Jerusalem. Peter invites everyone to the party. No one gathered in that multicultural array of humans is excluded from experiencing the Spirit of God, or from the Spirit giving birth to dreams within them.

Peter declares that the children among them, irrespective of gender, will have the ability to prophesy about the future and orchestrate change. He states that the younger generation present will have visions and carry insight beyond their years. Lastly, Peter points to those in the crowd considered in the latter years of their lives, and claims that God has not forgotten them either, that irrespective of their age, they will not lose the power to dream dreams.

To dream with God is to invite ourselves into a heavenly conversation about what the future of our lives could look like. It's one of the most beautiful steps of faith to take. To dare to dream. To risk our hopes on what could be.

You are a dreamer, by default, because the Spirit who contains the mysteries of the universe lives within you. Let that truth resonate through your heart and mind as you go about your day.

RN

3. DANIEL, THE DREAM INTERPRETER – PART 1

This made the king so angry and furious that he ordered the execution of all the wise men of Babylon. So the decree was issued to put the wise men to death, and men were sent to look for Daniel and his friends to put them to death.
Daniel 2:12–13

Daniel is in a hot mess. It's not his fault. He and his close friends, Hananiah, Mishael and Azariah, are fighting against the clock because the king of Babylon has decreed that all wise men, magicians and sorcerers in the kingdom are to be killed unless they solve a particular problem. It's essentially an episode of *Countdown* where the punishment for time running out is death; the stakes are high!

Problems and pressure are part and parcel of the expansive lives we were created to live. The stakes that Daniel faced were extreme, but we've all experienced pressure, whether it's in a tense boardroom meeting, an explosive family environment or a work call gone wrong.

Daniel sees himself as creative problem solver, and we need to take a page out of his book when faced with a hard deadline. He doesn't buckle, he doesn't waver, he doesn't hide. He remembers that despite his talent, his gifting, his competency and wisdom, there is one who is greater, smarter and wiser than him: God. And rather than running for the exit, Daniel demonstrates what we all need to do in times of extreme pressure: he exchanges a lifeline and calls on a friend.

RN

4. DANIEL, THE DREAM INTERPRETER – PART 2

Then Daniel returned to his house and explained the matter to his friends Hananiah, Mishael and Azariah. He urged them to plead for mercy from the God of heaven concerning this mystery, so that he and his friends might not be executed with the rest of the wise men of Babylon. During the night the mystery was revealed to Daniel in a vision. Then Daniel praised the God of heaven.
Daniel 2:17–19

We may not be in the times of Babylon, but we too can find ourselves in a pressure cooker as we try to discover the 'secret' to our own lives, seek the meaning of our own dreams and search for answers to the questions that keep us up at night.

When Daniel is looking for his answer, he knows the first place he needs to look.

He returns home, he confides in his closest friends and he comes before God. Daniel actively carves out time, doesn't give in to panic, and seeks compassion from the God of heaven regarding this secret. Is that the first place I run to when I am in search of the secrets to my own path? As Daniel declares, 'He reveals deep and hidden things; he knows what lies in darkness, and light dwells with him' (Daniel 2:22).

If God is the one who reveals profound and hidden things, then surely that is the first door I should be knocking on when my future is cloudy and I'm looking for the right next step to take. The stakes can seem high, the pressure may feel intense, but let's take a moment to be still and to seek an audience with the One who reveals the profound and hidden things of this life and the next.

RN

5. MADE FOR PURPOSE

Your hands made me and formed me;
give me understanding to learn your commands. **Psalm 119:73**

Having a clear discernible talent for all things musical at a young age made pursuing my personal dreams a little easier. I've always been comfortable being the centre of attention when it comes to entertainment. If you've got a clear and obvious gifting, building dreams around that particular talent isn't necessarily rocket science, but what if your gifting is not as obvious, and the pathway is not as discernible. What then?

All of us have incalculable potential deep within us.

The creative spark is not reserved for those in the entertainment or music industry. We all carry skills, talents and hidden attributes, 'superpowers' as it were, and we need to take the time to scratch a little deeper to unlock them.

All of us have been created for a multitude of purposes, not just to fulfil one practical task, to occupy one career path or to experience one major event. Life is far too vast for us to hang all our hopes on one destination (other than Jesus!), and we can become so obsessed with finding that one thing we're good at that we miss or completely ignore all the things that make us truly unique.

RN

6. PRAYER FOR DREAMERS

During the night the mystery was revealed to Daniel in a vision. Then Daniel praised the God of heaven and said:
'Praise be to the name of God for ever and ever;
wisdom and power are his.
He changes times and seasons;
he deposes kings and raises up others.
He gives wisdom to the wise
and knowledge to the discerning.
He reveals deep and hidden things;
he knows what lies in darkness,
and light dwells with him.' **Daniel 2:20-2**

If you're searching for purpose, for a dream to be birthed within your heart or for a light of inspiration to descend from the heavens, this prayer is a great one to meditate on today.

We might be tempted to rush through these pages in search of the answer, but this is not a textbook for 'doing life right'. The only one who holds the secrets that we desire and the One who can reveal the deep and hidden things within us is God.

Today, I want to invite you to prayerfully read this passage a number of times. First read through the passage slowly. Then reflect on what stands out to you. Read it a second time, praying through the passage with God, in communion with him. And third, read the passage and then rest in silence.

RN

7. *SELAH* – DON'T DISCOUNT YOURSELF FROM DREAMING

God knows the desires of our hearts and knows the pathway to us experiencing joy, fulfilment and purpose as we live our lives in communion with him.

Spend time today reflecting on the things in life that energise you and bring you joy; maybe those passions can lead you to a life more in tune with who God designed you to be. Is there a dream, an idea or a vision buried deep within you that you've ignored or repressed?

In the same breath, it is also good to remind ourselves that dreams don't need to look big in the world's eyes for them to be big to God. In a world so full of hate-talk and polarisation, sometimes the big dream is simply being kind to someone who is not like us or extending forgiveness to someone that the world says doesn't deserve it. Don't discount yourself from dreaming the deepest desires of your heart. God has good works planned for each and every one of us.

Heavenly Father, you reveal the deep and hidden things. You know what lies in darkness, and light dwells with you. Reveal to me the hidden dreams of my heart, enlighten me and lead me towards your purpose for me in an unhurried way that brings glory to you. I thank you and praise you. Amen.

8. GOD-DREAM

Joseph had a dream, and when he told it to his brothers, they hated him all the more. He said to them, 'Listen to this dream I had: we were binding sheaves of corn out in the field when suddenly my sheaf rose and stood upright, while your sheaves gathered round mine and bowed down to it.' **Genesis 37:5-7**

Over the next six days we are going to look at the fears Joseph had to overcome on his life journey. When he was seventeen, his father gave him a multicoloured coat which made him stand out among his brothers, causing them to be insanely jealous of him. (This was not helped by the fact that this coat was just an example of the many ways that Joseph was his father's favourite son!)

Then, Joseph had a dream that his brothers would bow down to him. Very naively, he shared it with them, and this had a huge impact on his life. One of the big questions today's verse raises for us is, how do we know if a dream is from the Holy Spirit or a result of the cheese we ate last night?

There are some simple truths that can help us discern whether something is from God or not. First, a God-dream always aligns with the Bible. Knowing and dwelling in the Bible can provide the framework by which we can check all our decisions. Second, God-dreams can intimidate us slightly because they can't usually be done in our own strength, and it's up to God (not us) if they are to become a reality. Joseph's brothers hated him so much that this dream could only become a reality with God's power.

Have you had a God-dream – a dream so big that you must rely on him completely to bring it into being? Write it down (if you haven't already) and pray about it today.

DB

9. REJECTION IS REAL

Then they said to one another, 'Look, this dreamer is coming! Come therefore, let us now kill him and cast him into some pit; and we shall say, "Some wild beast has devoured him." We shall see what will become of his dreams!'
Genesis 37:19-20 (NKJV)

Joseph encountered huge rejection from his siblings because of his dreams - in fact, they were so angry when he told them about them that they wanted to kill him. Although hopefully no one wants to murder us, rejection is unfortunately part of life and will happen to us all.

Rejection is more often than not just around the corner: when we try to get into that college, get that job or that promotion, or when we ask that person out. How do we live without fear of rejection? For me, I try to centre myself on the fact that even though this person has rejected me, Jesus always accepts me. I remind myself that he knows my every thought and action - past, present and future - and still loves, protects and provides for me.

Rejection hurts, and no one but Jesus can heal the wound it creates in us. His unconditional love is the only antidote.

It's also important to remember that sometimes rejection makes a lot more sense in hindsight. Over time, I have realised that if I had not been rejected for certain things and by certain people, I would not be where I am now, so I am grateful for what I get to do and who I get to do it with. God redeems everything and works it for our good, so he can turn our rejections into blessings.

DB

10. LEAD BY EXAMPLE

Now Joseph had been taken down to Egypt. Potiphar, an Egyptian who was one of Pharaoh's officials, the captain of the guard, bought him from the Ishmaelites who had taken him there.

The Lord was with Joseph so that he prospered, and he lived in the house of his Egyptian master... So Potiphar left everything he had in Joseph's care; with Joseph in charge, he did not concern himself with anything except the food he ate.
Genesis 39:1, 2, 6

Joseph now lived in Potiphar's palace. He had not allowed fear to paralyse or stop him. He sensed that God could use him anywhere. His leadership skills and desire to see Potiphar succeed saw him promoted to overseer of all his boss's affairs. Joseph didn't have books on leadership; he had his relationship with God and was led by his example.

At the time of writing, there is a trend called 'quietly quitting', where people do the bare minimum at work. I get not having a boss who values you, or wanting to spend extra time with family and friends; however, if Joseph had quietly quit, if Jesus had quietly quit, if anyone in the Bible called by God had quietly quit, we wouldn't be reading about them today.

We are chosen to make a difference. I am not suggesting we work longer hours, but rather that we spend more time with Jesus, resulting in us demonstrating love, joy, peace, patience, goodness, kindness, gentleness and self-control in spaces that lack them.

Our day-to-day lives might feel mundane, but the miraculous is always possible when we believe God can use us where we are. Pray and look for opportunities to lead by example today!

DB

11. LEVEL UP

Now Joseph was well-built and handsome, and after a while his master's wife took notice of Joseph and said, 'Come to bed with me!' **Genesis 39:6–7**

Joseph was making improvements in the palace, and everyone liked and appreciated him, including his boss's wife. This woman is likely to have been beautiful, so Joseph's refusal to sleep with her was not because she was unattractive, but because he was more attracted to the call of God on his life and in honouring his boss. In revenge for his refusal, Potiphar's wife accused Joseph of trying to rape her and he was sent to prison. He'd acted with integrity and made the right choice, but ended up in the wrong place, the last place he would ever want to be. Imagine the fear and betrayal he felt.

We might not end up in prison, but this 'right action, wrong place' feeling can happen to us. We can honour God and be obedient, yet things don't always go in our favour. We don't compromise our values at work, we don't cover up the lie, we don't say yes when we should say no, but it doesn't always seem to work out in the moment when we keep our integrity intact. Remember, God knows everything, and no person can thwart his plans for us. Have we been unfairly treated? Let's give it to God and trust him for our future restoration.

DB

12. PRISON PROMOTION

But while Joseph was there in the prison, the Lord was with him; he showed him kindness and granted him favour in the eyes of the prison warder. So the warder put Joseph in charge of all those held in the prison, and he was made responsible for all that was done there. The warder paid no attention to anything under Joseph's care, because the Lord was with Joseph and gave him success in whatever he did. **Genesis 39:20-3**

Now I don't know what I would do if I were to be thrown unjustly into prison, but I'd probably do my best to get by, stay quiet and simply survive. In stark contrast to how many of us would face the hardship described in today's verse, we see that Joseph looked at every obstacle as an opportunity to serve God and give him glory. He listened to others, served them and soon found himself in charge of the care of all the prisoners.

Sometimes when we are in a bad situation, whether that be with our finances, relationships or health, we can think God has abandoned us. This couldn't be further from the truth. It's in our hardest and darkest moments, when we fear abandonment, that God assures us he is with us.

God was with Joseph in the palace, and he was with him in the prison.

Whatever our situation is right now, however fearful it seems and alone we feel, we can be assured that God is with us. Not only can he meet us where we are, but he can also turn the situation around so that people can experience his goodness. Are we in a prison situation right now? Are we close to giving up and quitting? Ask God if he can use us in that situation for his glory.

DB

13. NUMBER TWO

The plan seemed good to Pharaoh and to all his officials. So Pharaoh asked them, 'Can we find anyone like this man, one in whom is the spirit of God?' Then Pharaoh said to Joseph, 'Since God has made all this known to you, there is no one so discerning and wise as you. You shall be in charge of my palace, and all my people are to submit to your orders. Only with respect to the throne will I be greater than you.' **Genesis 41:37–40**

While Joseph was in prison, he helped two prisoners correctly interpret their dreams. Two years later, one of them was with Pharaoh, who could find no one to interpret his troubling dreams. They sent for Joseph, and he successfully interpreted the dreams and offered a strategy to deal with the problem they raised. Joseph was promoted to number two in the land, to put the strategy in place, and before long Joseph's brothers ended up coming before him in Egypt to buy food in a time of famine. Not recognising him, they bowed down in respect – just like Joseph's dream had prophesied. We might think that Joseph would take revenge on them, but he had been put in this position by God because he demonstrated God's character. Joseph forgave them, blessed them and sent them back with provisions.

Joseph was seventeen when he was sold into slavery and thirty when he became second only to the king. For thirteen years he had hardships and fears to overcome, but he never gave up, and because of that, he could be seen to do God's will in any situation.

No matter where we are, and whatever we are going through, Joseph's story teaches us to never give up or doubt the words God has spoken over us. Is there a word or promise over your life that God wants to remind you of today as you trust him for your future?

DB

14. *SELAH* – FASTING

If we find ourselves seemingly 'stuck', like Joseph, seeking to do all the right things but thrown into a situation we can't see the way out of regardless, the spiritual practice of fasting can provide the opportunity for spiritual clarity. Whether it be abstaining from food until sundown, fasting from coffee or taking a break from the noise of social media, take the time to strip away temporary gratification as you seek God's divine wisdom and deliverance over the circumstances you face today.

In what areas of your life do you feel trapped and need to be set free from imprisonment? Ask God to meet you in all these places.

Lord God, as you were with Joseph, you are with me. Lord, you are with all those who feel trapped, who feel rejected, who feel alone. God, you are our deliverer, our rescuer and our salvation. Even in the prisons we find ourselves in, you never leave us nor forsake us. Nothing can separate us from your love. Please remind me of this truth today. Amen.

15. FLOODED WITH IMAGINATION

And [I pray] that the eyes of your heart [the very center and core of your being]
may be enlightened [flooded with light by the Holy Spirit], so that you will
know and cherish the hope [the divine guarantee, the confident expectation]
to which He has called you, the riches of His glorious inheritance in the saints
(God's people), and [so that you will begin to know] what the immeasurable and
unlimited and surpassing greatness of His [active, spiritual] power is in us who
believe. **Ephesians 1:18–19 (AMP)**

As Paul prayed for the Ephesians, I too pray for you, that today God begins to
open the eyes of your heart. This Amplified translation makes for awesome
reading: '[I pray] that the eyes of your heart... may be... [flooded with light
by the Holy Spirit].' What a prayer, that our souls are illuminated by God and
awoken to everything that is stored within us.

These verses remind me of God's unlimited capacity to create, and he chooses
to do this through our very flesh and bones, pouring his dreams and visions
into our hearts and minds.

Today, I pray you'll receive enlightenment about the dreams to which he has
called you that our God will begin to reveal the riches of his inheritance buried
deep with you. They are there, whether you believe it or not! The seeds of
promise are within you, even if they are hiding beneath the soil.

RN

16. EVERYTHING STARTS SMALL

The Lord is not slow in keeping his promise, as some understand slowness.
Instead, he is patient with you, not wanting anyone to perish, but everyone to
come to repentance. **2 Peter 3:9**

Everything starts small. Like any seed, no matter how big the fruit or tall the tree, it begins small enough to sit within our hands. These humble beginnings even echo the very beginning of time. Everything requires time to grow, and our dreams are no different.

Small starts are a blessing; they enable us to cultivate slowly, to build and grow with it, and to maintain the right environment for flourishing. Our lack of patience and our desire to have instant results or success can result in pursuing passions obsessively, at the expense of our emotional, physical and spiritual health - not to mention the added frustration and disappointment when we are constantly met with the reality that everything, no matter how fast or hard we run, takes time.

We need to dispel the instant gratification mentality that is plaguing our culture.

Nothing is instant, and if it is, like a firework fading in the night, it rarely stands the test of time. It is very rare that we have a dream that is established in the very next moment, without patience, work, prayer and determination being applied. So take heart, good things take time to grow.

RN

17. EVERY SEED NEEDS WATER

*Who dares despise the day of small things, since the seven eyes of the L*ORD *that range throughout the earth will rejoice when they see the chosen capstone in the hand of Zerubbabel?* **Zechariah 4:10**

Those seeds that are hidden beneath the surface, the dreams that land in our hearts or stir within our minds, will not become mighty redwoods overnight. Our expectations have to be measured when fostering our dreams, particularly when it comes to the timing of them.

While frustration is understandable, we have to be careful not to despise or resent the days of small beginnings. If we become obsessed with the days of overflow – a time or milestone in the future where we feel like we'll be a 'success' – we'll not apply the foundations needed to sustain our dreams to full term. Without proper care and nurturing, those seeds will wither away before they even break through the earth. And we have to plant these seeds with God as our gardener.

There is a saying in the music industry that it takes ten years to make an overnight success; I would push it even further to say it takes ten years to have moderate success in such a fiercely competitive arena. Patience is key, so rather than looking to the heavens asking why you're not floating above the clouds, cast your eyes with gratitude to the ground, and pour your energy into nurturing the seedlings that are about to sprout.

RN

18. PROTECTING YOUR DREAMS

I am convinced and confident of this very thing, that He who has begun a good work in you will [continue to] perfect and complete it until the day of Christ Jesus [the time of His return]. **Philippians 1:6 (AMP)**

Our dreams, especially in their infancy, are fragile and need to be protected. I cannot count the amount of times I've shared an idea or a dream in its early stages, only to be told I was mad.

These promises, visions and dreams are delicate when they're being born within us and as we begin to build confidence in them. Major blows in the early days can do critical damage to our confidence and determination to continue.

Becoming mindful of the intimate spaces in which we make our dreams known is an important consideration as we begin to pursue our dreams. We cannot be so naive as to believe that everyone will be supportive, understanding and encouraging. Not everyone can see the gaps that we see in the market that need to be filled or hear the cries of the people in need. Not everyone will share the spark of imagination that we have had.

What we can be confident of is that the One who planted the seeds of a God-dream in our hearts has all the patience in the world and will continue to perfect, to mould and to nurture these dreams until the day when all of our dreams come true at the end of time. He'll keep going until all our creativity, ambition and innovation is satisfied in the One who made it all.

RN

19. NOISE-CANCELLING HEADPHONES

So faith comes from hearing, and hearing through the word of Christ.
Romans 10:17 (ESVUK)

Fear can kill faith, but it's also true that faith kills fear.

Today's verse says faith comes from hearing Christ's words, not necessarily the words of other people. There are many self-help podcasts and books that promise to help us tackle our fears, but Christ's words do not merely seek to modify our outward behaviour; rather, they bring about an internal heart transformation, a renewed way of thinking that empowers us to live more freely, like Jesus.

If we want to grow in faith, it is important that we listen only to those who speak God's truth to us.

We must discern how much power and authority to give to others to speak into our lives. People's words are creative, and when people speak negative words about us and we allow them into our heads and hearts, they can inject devastating doses of fear into our thoughts, actions and dreams.

The journey we are on involves having the courage to detox, divert or challenge any voices causing our fear to escalate. Today, I pray that the Holy Spirit will give you spiritual noise-cancelling headphones so that you can't hear the words of those who would discourage or intimidate you.

Today, may you only hear Christ's words encouraging you to be who he has called you to be.

DB

20. SEED VS TREE PEOPLE

May the favour of the LORD our God rest on us;
establish the work of our hands for us -
yes, establish the work of our hands. **Psalm 90:17**

Not everyone can see what we see, but we must continue with the work regardless. There is, for example, in my experience a big difference between 'seed people' and 'tree people' (though, disclaimer: we often interchange between them depending on our circumstances).

Seed people can be shown a seed, an infant dream, and use their imagination to see the fruit that will emerge in the centuries to come after planting that very seed. Tree people cannot make sense of the seed's potential but rather need to wait until they see the full tree - the finished picture - become a reality before their very eyes.

Seed people catch the vision early and may only need to see a piece of the puzzle in order to understand the big picture. You can show seed people a dream, an idea, a barren area of land, and they can use the power of their imagination to see the forest that is to come.

We must brace ourselves that not everyone is going to understand us, catch the vision that we have caught or champion our dreams, and that's OK. Let us lose ourselves in the gardening of our field of dreams, and not occupy ourselves with the thoughts and opinions of others.

RN

21. *SELAH* – WALK, DON'T RUN

Every seed starts small, and maybe you've been waiting for the 'big idea' to come, not realising that it's been sitting there as a seed in your mind the whole time. We've reflected this week on the fact that such seeds do not become trees overnight, but rather need to be planted, watered and nurtured in the right soil. They also need the great Gardener, our God, to see them grow and flourish.

What are some of the seed ideas you have had that may need watering? Ask God to highlight these to you, as well as what practical conditions you may need to put in place to see them grow.

Heavenly Father, you rejoice to see the work begin, so I pray that you bless the work of my hand, and give me the wisdom and enthusiasm to grow this seed to maturity. Father, you make all things beautiful in your time. Please grant me the patience to steward well this dream you've sown in me and the wisdom to know what dreams to let go and which ones to water and watch grow. Amen.

22. FEAR HANDLER

For the word of God is alive and active. Sharper than any double-edged sword, it penetrates even to dividing soul and spirit, joints and marrow; it judges the thoughts and attitudes of the heart. **Hebrews 4:12**

There is a reason why the 365 devotionals in this book – all focused on freedom from living in fear – are taken from the Bible, rather than simply being a collection of the top motivational sayings or catchy social media quotes. It's because God's word contains a different power entirely.

God's word has been given to us to help us overcome fear, darkness and evil in the world. God's word is truth and enables us to come against the lies and deception the enemy wants to entrap us with, given half a chance. God's words applied to our lives by faith become alive and active and empower us against fear and temptation.

Jesus faced every temptation to give way to materialism, greed and pride and every attack against his identity as God's Son by actively cutting down the enemy's lies and half-truths with the word of God (Matthew 4:1-11).

The enemy seeks to disempower us through deceptions that attack our hearts, minds and emotions. God's word gives us the truth. And we must decide who we will agree with in any moment or situation. Think of any worries or fears you are wrestling with today and see what God's word says about them. Declare his truth out loud and feel the strength come into your weak knees!

DB

23. DREAMS ARE EXPENSIVE

Lazy people want much but get little,
but those who work hard will prosper. **Proverbs 13:4 (NLT)**

Every technological innovation, cultural advancement or timeless piece of
art began as a vision in someone's mind. Even God, at the beginning of time,
floating above the earth in Genesis 1, called a 'good' universe into being from
nothing.

A moment of inspiration, a vision, a flash of what the future could be:
everything has a starting place. But after those sparks of creative genius, what
ensues is the struggle to give those dreams the breath of life. The question is,
are we willing to count the cost to see the dream realised?

I don't think that this generation, or the ones that will follow, will struggle with
having dreams. We are incredibly aspirational, and our short attention spans
have us firing 10,000 thoughts a minute; we are on an endless quest for stimuli
that will satisfy. We are constantly inspired, quick to pivot and overloaded with
reference points. But the question is, when the challenges to our dreams come,
will we be willing to pay the cost to keep going for God?

RN

24. EXCESS BAGGAGE

But blessed is the one who trusts in the LORD,
whose confidence is in him.
They will be like a tree planted by the water
that sends out its roots by the stream.
It does not fear when heat comes;
its leaves are always green.
It has no worries in a year of drought
and never fails to bear fruit. **Jeremiah 17:7–8**

Whether we fly with easyJet or by private jet, there is a necessary baggage allowance. When we go over the allowed weight for the hold, we have to lose some things, leaving them at the airport, stuffing them into hand luggage or wearing lots of layers of clothing! We don't like losing our excess baggage, but at the end of the day it's a heavy weight that is preventing us from going where we need to go.

Fear, in many ways, is like excess baggage. It's a heavy weight we carry around. I don't know what fears are holding you back today, but as we have seen throughout our reflections to date, everything God has for you is on the other side of fear.

Fear and anxiety can make us think the battle is too hard, but God encourages us that he will fight for us and fight with us. Writer and preacher A. W. Tozer is quoted as saying, 'Christians should be the boldest people in the world – not cocky and sure of ourselves, but sure of Him.'[17] This is possible when we are deeply rooted in God. Pray about this today.

DB

---

[17] A. W. Tozer, Twitter, 25 July 2015, twitter.com/TozerAW/status/625020224736104448 (accessed 20 April 2023).

25. THE COST OF DREAMS

Suppose one of you wants to build a tower. Won't you first sit down and estimate the cost to see if you have enough money to complete it? **Luke 14:28**

Jesus talks specifically about the cost of being a disciple, of being a student of his teachings and a follower of the Way. If someone wants to build a tower, surely they would sit down and estimate the cost to see if they had enough to see it through? How many of us have sat down and honestly counted the cost of the life we wish we could have when it comes to dreaming with God? Or do we spend more time daydreaming than being the accountant for our dreams?

For many of us, our struggle will not be the anxiety arising from a lack of dreams, but with the effort required to make those dreams a reality. Because more times than not, dreams take blood, sweat and tears to be realised. If you fear that the process of dream-chasing will be hard, I am here to agree that it will be. Dreams, visions, goals, ideas, need to be built from the ground up, brick by brick, in order for them to emerge from the recesses of our minds. Hard work is inescapable.

Can we be known as a generation that is willing to pay the cost of bringing our ideas to life? The change we so desperately seek in the world, and in our lives, will only come to pass if we are willing to set fear aside and fight for what God is truly putting on our hearts.

RN

26. GOD WALKS WITH US

Do not be afraid, for I am with you;
I will bring your children from the east
and gather you from the west.
I will say to the north, 'Give them up!'
and to the south, 'Do not hold them back.' **Isaiah 43:5-6**

Having the right intentions is admirable, but if our intentions are not followed by actions, then those intentions are futile. In the light of these reflections on dreams, the visions that are planted into our hearts can remain lofty, unattainable ambitions that never develop beyond tools for escapism if we are not prepared to put in the effort.

We should be the ones working hard to make our dreams come alive, and we should be further encouraged that God is more than willing to match our efforts. God is a massive fan of ours and is ready and willing to surpass the investment we put into our dreams, especially if they align with establishing his plan of love for all creation.

God calls us to not be afraid, because he is right there on the journey alongside us, bringing us from the east to the west as we walk towards the fulfilment of our destinies. If we have to get to the top of a mountain, God will climb with us; if the treasure is at the bottom of the ocean, God will join us in the dive. But, ultimately, God can only support what we've set in motion. God won't drag us down the road; we have to take the first step and put our faith into action.

RN

27. FEAR OF BEING INADEQUATE

*Then Moses said to the Israelites, 'See, the L*ᴏʀᴅ *has chosen Bezalel son of Uri, the son of Hur, of the tribe of Judah, and he has filled him with the Spirit of God, with wisdom, with understanding, with knowledge and with all kinds of skills – to make artistic designs for work in gold, silver and bronze, to cut and set stones, to work in wood and to engage in all kinds of artistic crafts.* **Exodus 35:30–3**

People can believe that if they haven't got a 'pastoral role' in the church or some kind of 'ministry', they aren't as useful to God or his kingdom.

We can think that being a pastor or ministry leader is the pinnacle of a Jesus-centred life, and other roles and responsibilities are less adequate. Here, we see the first mention of the Holy Spirit filling and anointing a guy called Bezalel, in order for him to do creative, artistic work. The same Spirit that gave Samson supernatural strength and Gideon the courage to lead helped Bezalel to design and craft. We are all equally valuable in making a difference and advancing the kingdom.

God can anoint and empower us for supernatural, Spirit-led work inside or outside a church building and organisation. We don't get value from roles and titles; our value is in being a child of God, using our God-given gifts, skills and talents for his glory. Sometimes our fears and insecurities make us doubt our importance to God and his purpose on earth. Today, be encouraged that God has anointed you and positioned you exactly where you are for a reason.

DB

28. *SELAH* – PAUSE AND LISTEN

There is a price to be paid to forge the lives we deeply crave.

Today, can you create a moment to ask yourself whether you are willing to count the cost of following Jesus, wherever he may lead you? Jesus asks us to take up our cross and follow him. He does not ask us to do this as a stranger who stands at a distance, but rather as a loving Father who knows that he has so much more to offer us than the things of this world that we desperately try to cling to.

Spend time today soaking in God's presence and love and ask him to loosen your grip on anything you are holding on to too tightly. With an open heart and open hands, ask him to fill you with desires and dreams that he longs to see you become a part of today.

'Blessed is the one who trusts in the Lord, whose confidence is in him' (Jeremiah 17:7). This day I put all my trust in you. I will not be anxious, though I may be navigating a desert season, and I will not lose sight of you in the times of overflow. I put my faith and all my trust in the God who rules in every season. Amen.

29. DREAM ARCHITECTS

For the Spirit God gave us does not make us timid, but gives us power, love and self-discipline. **2 Timothy 1:7**

Sometimes when God gives us a dream, pursuing it will feel as easy as sailing on a windy day. And yet, the reality for many of us is that we'll have to put in the hard work and persevere when the going gets hard. Praying over our plans and dreams is essential, but don't be surprised if God gives you a very practical next step to follow. It might be scheduling time to read, to research, to practise, to network. We may have to go and learn from the people in the industries we want to enter into and study the practices that have enabled others to go that step further than we have on the journey to date. We have to get really practical to bring these dreams to life.

Buy a diary, set some goals, book that personal trainer, invest in further education. Go on a retreat, still yourself to align your spirit with God, call a mentor or reach out to someone who is a little further along the journey. What's stopping you?

Let us not be lofty dreamers alone, but may we be Spirit-filled dream architects, visionaries who go on to change culture, shape our communities and experience the peace that flows when we operate from the depths of our purpose.

RN

30. 365/360 REFLECTION

Looking back on the month that has passed, we have reflected on our dreams, desires and hopes for our lives and the lives of those around us. We have seen that everything starts small, needs to be nurtured and will take time to grow. We have also seen, most importantly of all, that we're in partnership with an expert gardener in God. Are you ready to get down on bended knees in the mud and sow the seed that God has put within you?

If you're dream searching, take some time to reflect on what energises you. The ideas, activities or moments that give you joy. What spaces give you a sense of peace? Or is there a social, creative or cultural problem you feel a burning desire deep within you to bring a solution to?

Today, let's set aside some time to ask God to search our hearts and minds and direct them towards Christ and the things he would long to see in this world.

DECEMBER

1. RESURRECTION

But Christ has indeed been raised from the dead, the firstfruits of those who have fallen asleep. For since death came through a man, the resurrection of the dead comes also through a man. For as in Adam all die, so in Christ all will be made alive. But each in turn: Christ, the firstfruits; then, when he comes, those who belong to him. Then the end will come, when he hands over the kingdom to God the Father after he has destroyed all dominion, authority and power. For he must reign until he has put all his enemies under his feet. The last enemy to be destroyed is death. **1 Corinthians 15:20-6**

We believe that death is not the end.

Christ has indeed been raised from the dead, demonstrating the resurrective nature of all creation through Christ. The more time I spend on earth, the more I realise that we can't skip through the seasons of life. We cannot break the pattern embedded into the fabric of time and space.

Old things must pass away before the new is established.

Jesus couldn't skip the crucifixion process; he endured every moment of that descent, felt every twinge in his muscles and experienced every restricted breath on the cross. Being a follower of Christ, a disciple following in his footsteps, means that we too have to taste the experience of death in order to dine at the table of resurrection.

RN

DECEMBER

2. THE DAWN WILL BREAK

Christ Jesus who died – more than that, who was raised to life – is at the right hand of God and is also interceding for us. **Romans 8:34**

When we are trapped in the present, surrounded by destruction, and it seems like there's no hope to be found and nothing on the horizon, we have to trust that the story doesn't end there.

God has not abandoned us to our situation. Christ's story is the evidence that death is one step towards inevitable resurrection in him.

Up close and in the moment, Jesus' death on the cross paints the most harrowing of images. He was left to die alone, bruised and bloodied, and it looked like all hope was gone. When we, too, are face to face with death, in the midst of the chaos of losing something or someone, it can feel like an all-consuming fire. There seems to be no way out through the black smoke of fear. We may feel bruised and bloodied and on the edge of giving up, but we must hold on. In time, God's time, resurrection comes, healing comes, restoration comes.

God is not defeated by death, and neither is the Spirit of Christ within us. Even if there are no signs of life, even if it's been years since the sun has shone in your life, the dawn will break. If there's one thing I can promise you, it is that.

Hold on, resurrection is coming.

RN

3. CHRIST CONQUERED DEATH

'But, LORD,' said Martha, the sister of the dead man, 'by this time there is a bad odour, for he has been there four days.'
Then Jesus said, 'Did I not tell you that if you believe, you will see the glory of God?' **John 11:39-40**

Not to be confused with the Buddhist concept of reincarnation, resurrection is written into the fabric of the universe. It's how God has programmed reality, this cycle of new life, growth, maturity, death and then new life again.

God's creation, the first story we read in the Bible, embodies this truth. The flowers, the animals, even the water cycle moves to a renewable pattern (well, until humans move in and disrupt things!): precipitation, collection, evaporation, condensation and back to precipitation again. Over and over. They said I'd never use my GCSE Science knowledge but look at me now!

This cycle is also present in the relationship that is God, and integral to who Jesus Christ said he was. There is no escaping it – Jesus Christ claims to have risen from the dead. No matter how much we try to avoid the claim, or try to make it casual, it is a wild statement. One that, if true, changes everything about life as we know it.

If we trust that he is who he says he is, then we have one of the greatest tools for facing our fears. If nothing truly dies when it's held in Christ's hands, then we should move with boldness towards our fears. Failure is not the end of the story. Heartbreak is not the end of the story. Death is not the end.

RN

4. CHRIST, THE RESURRECTOR

When he had said this, Jesus called in a loud voice, 'Lazarus, come out!' The dead man came out, his hands and feet wrapped with strips of linen, and a cloth around his face.
Jesus said to them, 'Take off the grave clothes and let him go.' **John 11:43-4**

C. S. Lewis explains in his book *Mere Christianity* that we have to make a choice. Either Jesus was and is the Son of God, or he is mad, or he is something worse than that.[18] The truth is, Jesus made many countercultural claims. If they were not true, we would indeed have to conclude that he was mad or bad. Whether we can even fully grasp the mystery around his claims about eternal life or not, we should spend time in prayer asking God to plant this promise of eternity deep within our hearts.

Unravelling the mystery of God and the power of the resurrected Christ is a journey of faith that will take a lifetime, but we don't need to understand everything in order to begin applying these truths in our day-to-day lives. God gave his Son, not only to die on the cross for us but also as a human example of how to live life to the full; he knew we would never grasp how to live out God's goodness in the world if we couldn't see someone who looked like us do it first.

The accounts of Jesus' life in the Gospels make for fascinating and foundational reading for those of us who want to face our fears the way Jesus did. Why not dive deeper into the Gospel of John today and take a fresh look at Jesus' response to Lazarus' illness and death?

RN

[18] C. S. Lewis, *Mere Christianity* (London: William Collins, 2012), p. 52.

5. GOD'S WILL, NOT OUR WILL

Many are the plans in a person's heart,
but it is the LORD's purpose that prevails. **Proverbs 19:21**

Sometimes the root of our fears and worries is our unmet expectations. There is a picture within our mind of what we have lost, and we expect that the very same thing is going to be brought back to life again. When we realise that the thing we lost is truly gone, disappointment can flood in.

We lose a particular person in our lives, a relationship comes to an end or a career opportunity falls through that hits us financially, and we hope we will regain what we have lost tenfold. When the 'new thing' isn't what we'd hoped or expected, we might begin to question whether God is even at work. Did God not hear my petition? Did I say the wrong prayer? Did I not believe enough?

Today's scripture reminds us that we cannot achieve godly outcomes in our own power. 'It is the LORD's purpose that prevails', and he is always at work. The tricky part is surrendering and being aware that God's plan isn't always our plan.

Sometimes we invite God to step into our suffering, call for fire from heaven to come down and bring revival, but we provide a list of very particular parameters for the miracle we expect that look more like 'my will be done' than 'your will be done'.

RN

6. THE FINE ART OF LETTING GO

No one sews a patch of unshrunk cloth on an old garment, for the patch will pull away from the garment, making the tear worse. Neither do people pour new wine into old wineskins. If they do, the skins will burst; the wine will run out, and the wineskins will be ruined. No, they pour new wine into new wineskins, and both are preserved. **Matthew 9:16–17**

Letting go of the tight grip on our lives, on our expectations, liberates us from frustrations and unmet dreams. God is doing something. He does not merely patch up the old and make do. In his fullness he is able to create new life in a way we could never imagine.

Truly letting something go means letting every drop of it go and giving it completely over to God. God is good, and God wants us to experience that goodness in all its fullness; it's just not always in accordance with our own plans.

As we surrender on our knees, asking for 'new life', for 'new wine', we must look beyond our own desires and expectations, as they can blind us and rob us of the joy of the very 'new thing' right before us that God is asking us to steward today.

Remember, what is being resurrected in our lives may look different from what has died. We may be different following spiritual deaths too. Do we trust that what is being resurrected is part of the grand design of God's will? Don't let your expectations prohibit you from experiencing the miraculous.

RN

7. *SELAH* – RESURRECTION LIFE

Resurrection can look like death if we don't give God enough time to work out his plans.

We must open our minds to be able to see the pain and suffering we endure, but also hold firm to the expectation that God will use this to transform ourselves or our circumstances for good.

Spend some time in silence today, whether that be one minute or fifteen, to exercise hearing the still voice of God that cannot and will not be defeated by death. Have you witnessed situations or moments where the resurrection power of God has been on display? Ask God to help you bring these to mind. Perhaps there is an action you need to take to help you remember this today – whether that be writing the breakthrough down in your journal or carrying around a sign of new life, like a flower or a refined stone, to remind you that God is always at work in you and your life.

Dear God, 'many are the plans in a person's heart, but it is the Lord's purpose that prevails' (Proverbs 19:21). I step aside and usher your will in to my life and pray for the establishment of your heavenly kingdom here on this earth. Even when I am faced with what looks like death or destruction, I know that you are still with me, and I know that your hope is mine to hold on to. Amen.

8. AMBASSADORS OF RESURRECTION – PART 1

We are therefore Christ's ambassadors, as though God were making his appeal through us. We implore you on Christ's behalf: be reconciled to God.
2 Corinthians 5:20

Christ has no body now but yours. No hands, no feet on earth but yours. Yours are the eyes through which he looks with compassion on this world. Yours are the feet with which he walks to do good. Yours are the hands through which he blesses all the world.

These words are taken from a poem written by sixteenth-century Spanish mystic St Teresa of Ávila.

These few lines truly bring to life the notion that Christ's resurrection was only the beginning and that the work he wants to do in this world is not yet finished.

We can see from these words and from today's scripture, taken from 2 Corinthians, that our job as Christians is not just about relying on what was done by Jesus on the cross; rather, Christ's resurrection requires participation on our part. I have been saying, 'I am a partner, not a passenger,' a lot to myself lately. Christ has risen, and we are invited to have this same Spirit dwelling within us, therefore we are the evidence of that miraculous resurrection power here and now.

St Teresa declares that we are the hands and feet of Christ. We are the means for Jesus to show his compassion and the vehicle through which people will experience his love. We are the ambassadors of resurrection in our communities, and God is making his appeal through us.

RN

9. AMBASSADORS OF RESURRECTION - PART 2

And he died for all, that those who live should no longer live for themselves but for him who died for them and was raised again. **2 Corinthians 5:15**

Embracing the idea that Christ has no hands or feet on earth but ours means accepting our responsibility to bring forth the change and transformation that was prophesied in Scripture.

Through the Holy Spirit's power working within us, we have an incredible amount of influence over our own experience of reality. Therefore, we have more power than we sometimes give ourselves credit for when it comes to bringing about change and ushering in a new dawn in our lives. If we wait for someone else to do it, we may find ourselves waiting forever.

How else will your workplace become less toxic? How else will your personal relationships experience new depths of love and compassion? How else will creation be restored in light of humankind's destructive consumption of raw materials?

Before Christ ascended, he commissioned humanity to be the living embodiment of the gospel message, to become God's people on the ground, and challenged us to live each moment as if we were ambassadors of the 'new eternal life' that is available for all.

RN

10. THE BATTLE IS OVER

God has ascended with a shout,
The Lord, with the sound of a trumpet.
Sing praises to God, sing praises;
Sing praises to our King, sing praises.
For God is the King of all the earth;
Sing praises with a psalm of wisdom. **Psalm 47:5–7 (NASB)**

Resurrection is cause for celebration! To be joyful, to sing a new song unto the Lord. The truth that death is not the end is good news, right? Do you know that truth today in your body, in your bones?

Spending our days worrying or lashing ourselves for mistakes gone by will have us overlooking the celebrations required in the present. There is so much to show gratitude for, if only we pause long enough to see it.

Praise is not dependent on things going well or the outcome not looking bleak. Praise is something we can do regardless of our circumstances; it means raising our gaze above the things we are facing to fix our eyes on Jesus, even for a moment, in order to see his perspective on all things.

I have to admit, I can be one to wallow in self-reflection and can sink into the depths of melancholy all too easily, but as much as it is OK to acknowledge what we are truly feeling, praise is the pathway to moving us on to firmer footing and towards brighter days.

The 'fight' has already been won; before you took your first breath, you were a winner in Christ.

RN

11. BREAK FREE, GET UP AND DANCE

Praise the LORD.
Praise God in his sanctuary;
praise him in his mighty heavens.
Praise him for his acts of power;
praise him for his surpassing greatness.
Praise him with the sounding of the trumpet,
praise him with the harp and lyre.
Praise him with tambourine and dancing,
praise him with the strings and pipe,
praise him with the clash of cymbals,
praise him with resounding cymbals.
Let everything that has breath praise the LORD.
Praise the LORD. **Psalm 150**

As you know by now, I was eighteen when I first met Jesus. When I experienced his grace, love, mercy and freedom, I knew my life had changed. I was joyful and passionate. And yet there was still no way I was going to jump up and down in worship like those nutcrackers in the service! I sat at the back judgmentally and tried to be super cool. Looking back, I cringe at how much I feared people's perceptions of me. Soon after, God spoke to me through a leader who asked me why I cared so much about what people thought of me, because Jesus loved me and had already accepted me. It hit home. God is looking for real, unashamed lovers of Jesus, so much so that they lose their fear of others and are free to worship.

Where fear of others is holding us back from praising God, maybe we need to take a step out of our comfort zones and allow God to help us break free as we worship him using any moves we can make!

DB

12. ALLOW YOURSELF JOY!

Because of the LORD's great love we are not consumed,
for his compassions never fail.
They are new every morning;
great is your faithfulness. **Lamentations 3:22-3**

I love moments of communal worship in church, but sometimes I can find my attention drifting away from God and towards the happiness shining from people's eyes, and the cynic within me can start to rise up. From this moment on, I am not a part of the crowd but a metaphorical bystander whose cynicism is preventing me from experiencing the priceless joy that can be found in praising Jesus.

Sometimes I find it's hard to switch off and lose myself to the fanfare.

Now I'm not saying we should play along and throw our hands in the air during worship if it's not an authentic response to what the Spirit is doing within us; we do not all have to be extroverted or express our faith in the same way. But the mistake is in thinking that we have to feel a certain way before we praise. Instead, praise is a powerful weapon that we can use to get our fearful hearts to fixate on God and not on our worries.

Don't let the cynic in you deny the joy of the Lord that is your strength within you. Even if you don't feel like it, I encourage you to begin singing, shouting and dancing for the Lord, and see how the posture of your heart can change in the process.

RN

13. THE BIGGER PLAN

Lift up your eyes and look to the heavens:
who created all these?
He who brings out the starry host one by one
and calls forth each of them by name.
Because of his great power and mighty strength,
not one of them is missing. **Isaiah 40:26**

Death, resurrection, eternal life. We may think they only hold significance in relation to our personal salvation, but that's only part of the picture. Beyond our personal island is a whole ocean, and there are galaxies beyond that too. God has a plan, a purpose, a resurrection story for every atom he has created, and being obsessed with our personal stories robs us of beholding God's beautiful plan to restore the heavens and the earth.

Of course, how each of us operates on the private island called 'our life' is of infinite importance to God. God sees every hair on our head, and cares about us endlessly, but there is more going on than getting a ticket to the 'good place'. Jesus died for the whole world. From every single baby ever to be born to every single person who will ever breathe oxygen.

It's about you, yes, but it's not *only* about you.

Lift up your eyes and look to the heavens. Step outside yourself for a moment and witness the world around you. We're invited to take part in the greatest story to ever unfold.

RN

14. *SELAH* – HANDS AND FEET

Over the last week, we've been looking at what it means to be Jesus' hands and feet here on earth. Let's spend this moment reflecting on what has stirred within us as we've read this week's devotionals. Is there an area of your life or your character where you think God may be wanting to work? Is there an area of your thought-life that may have become too self-centred rather than God-centred? Ask God to reveal these places and to help you fix your eyes on Jesus, and in doing so to turn your love and attention out to the hurting world around you.

As I lift up my eyes and look to the heavens, I see the splendour of your works all around me, God. You are not bound by time, by space or by death. Your light never fades, God. I pray you soften my heart, so that I am able to be an extension of your loving kindness. I pray that I can humbly embody the Spirt of Christ today, and that every step I make echoes the reality that you are alive! Amen.

15. EVERYTHING IS CONNECTED

For God so loved the world that he gave his one and only Son, that whoever believes in him shall not perish but have eternal life. **John 3:16**

This radical gospel centres on our loving God extending the invitation of new life to all creation. To all living creatures, to every single human being we walked past today, to the coffee shop barista who always spells our name wrong, to the lady who awkwardly smiled at us on the bus, to our most feared enemy and to our closest friend.

I can lose sight of that and turn my faith into a completely isolated and individual mission of self-improvement. God is very patient and continues to do an incredible work within us despite our selfish motives. We must think bigger if we're ever going to catch up with God's vision. We are a priceless puzzle piece among a tapestry of priceless puzzle pieces.

The only way we can even begin to behold such a work of art is by stepping outside ourselves, taking a break from the roles we play in the different spheres of our lives and opening our eyes to the true mystery unfolding around us. Everything is connected, rooted in the same loving Father who began the universe. Our personal resurrection is part of God's space-wide plan of restoration; now that is surely worth lifting our eyes from ourselves and to God for?

RN

16. JESUS IS ALIVE

Many have undertaken to draw up an account of the things that have been fulfilled among us, just as they were handed down to us by those who from the first were eyewitnesses and servants of the word. **Luke 1:1-2**

The resurrection of Jesus Christ was the catalyst that sparked a movement that went on to change the very course of human history. I've spent a lot of time daydreaming, trying to transport myself back to that time in history to truly grasp what was going on!

The palpable sense of expectation that must have been swirling on the ground when word began to spread from person to person that *Jesus is alive.* This incredibly electrifying, mind-boggling, faith-shifting story is so dangerous that people would die telling it. Despite my fears surrounding my faith, two thousand years ago something real happened.

The biggest leap of faith, and therefore one of the biggest fears we must face, is to believe in God's faithfulness to us, to believe that God is working for us and not against us, and that the same Christ who rose all those years ago, that same fearless Spirit of love, lives within us now.

RN

17. A LIFE THAT NEVER PERISHES, SPOILS OR FADES

Praise be to the God and Father of our LORD Jesus Christ! In his great mercy he has given us new birth into a living hope through the resurrection of Jesus Christ from the dead, and into an inheritance that can never perish, spoil or fade. **1 Peter 1:3-4**

How we see God ultimately shapes how we see ourselves.

Whether we believe in an intentional Creator or think we've been engineered with a particular purpose, or that we're all just floating around this dust cloud insignificantly, our belief systems frame how we process and address the fears we face each day.

Whether we believe fear is a necessary tension to overcome, or something we have to fight and wrestle with, or whether we believe we have the power to make a difference to our life: all this hinges on who we believe ourselves to be and why we are ultimately here on this earth.

To stare fear in the face with confidence, we must become aware of the authority that Jesus has placed within us to boldly go where he is asking us to go. As today's verse shows us, we have been birthed into a living hope 'through the resurrection of Jesus Christ from the dead, and into an inheritance that can never perish, spoil or fade'. As you ruminate on these almighty words, why not ask God to help the truth of them anchor you to your authority in him today?

RN

18. A CHILD IS BORN

For to us a child is born,
to us a son is given,
and the government will be on his shoulders.
And he will be called
Wonderful Counsellor, Mighty God,
Everlasting Father, Prince of Peace. **Isaiah 9:6**

It's been mentioned already, but 'Do not be afraid' is littered throughout Scripture. One of the key sentiments God has communicated with humans reaching towards him over thousands of years is, do not live in fear, do not be governed by terror and do not be afraid.

Today's verse tells of a prophecy shared years and years ago that speaks of the coming of Jesus Christ, not as a warrior or a king in the way the people of the day expected, but as a meek and mild baby boy. Even so, as the prophecy states, this baby was to be called 'Wonderful Counsellor, Mighty God, Everlasting Father, Prince of Peace'. It seems so unlikely that God would use a tiny baby to save all of humanity, but the Bible shows us that he so often chooses the least, the last and the lost to be his means of ushering in the kingdom of God here on earth.

Are you feeling meek? Not strong enough to dust yourself off and go again? Rest assured that with God, the small, the mild and the hurting can be used in his great plan to bring peace to the world.

RN

19. HE IS RISEN!

The angel said to the women, 'Do not be afraid, for I know that you are looking for Jesus, who was crucified. He is not here; he has risen, just as he said. Come see the place where he lay.' **Matthew 28:5-6**

When the two Marys went to Jesus' tomb and found him gone, they were told by an angel that they were not to fear because Jesus had risen. Imagine leaving everything to follow Jesus, stepping into all he called us to, and then he's killed and it's all over. Imagine the fear, worry, uncertainty, insecurity and humiliation we would be feeling on top of the grief of losing a loved one. Then we hear, 'He is risen.' If Jesus hadn't risen, he would be like any other prophet or legendary figure - a great guy with strong values who cared about people.

This verse shows Jesus isn't that - he has risen, conquering death, and the cause of it (sin), so that we can have a relationship with God and spend eternity with him.

This means we don't need to live with a fear of death. Dying can hurt; loss and separation is painful, and I'm not making light of that, but there is so much more on the other side of death for those who die loving Jesus. God promises resurrection life in a new body that won't deteriorate, with God and other loved ones in a renewed creation where there is no pain, tears or suffering, for ever. And though he has great works for us to do here and now, our ultimate destination in heaven should motivate us to move with boldness in our day-to-day lives.

DB

20. SLEEP WELL

You will not fear the terror of night,
nor the arrow that flies by day. **Psalm 91:5**

When a therapist is asked how to battle anxiety, they give suggestions like taking regular exercise, cutting out caffeine and alcohol, journalling and meditating with deep breathing. One thing they all recommend is lots of sleep. This is difficult because anxiety prevents sleep. For some of us, negative thoughts running through our mind late at night seem impossible to stop.

In today's verse the fear of terror in the night is linked to arrows that flew in the day. What happens in the day has an impact on our mind and affects our sleep.

One thing we can do to stop what happens in the day affecting us at night is to pause to question where these 'arrows' are coming from. If it's social media, we can reduce our time on it before sleep. If it's a person, we can see them less. Many arrows fly at us at school, university or work, and avoiding those places is not an option, but praying that God would protect us in those places is.

My wife and I often talk about the 'arrows' we've faced during the day and process them together in the evening. Then we pray and give them to God. We don't allow the negative thoughts to circle around our minds as we drift off to sleep - only to be woken a few hours later by our baby boy!

Try giving God some of the arrows you've faced today and ask for his gift of sleep tonight.

DB

21. *SELAH* – ALIVE AND WELL

Christ is alive, but sometimes we are blinded to the joy of this truth in our everyday walk.

Each morning you rise from your bed and take a breath is a gift, no matter what it is you are facing or fearing. Take some time this evening to look back on your day and to note down a handful of things you are grateful for. They may be few and far between, but there will be at least one! Often, once you start listing things you are thankful for – a new day, the sunshine, air in your lungs – you find your mind becomes awoken to the many blessings that you encounter each day.

Jesus, thank you that you are alive and that you are still working for me! Through your life, your death and your resurrection you became our living hope and invited us into an inheritance that can never perish, spoil or fade. Today I celebrate you and acknowledge that the Spirit you sent as our companion and advocate now lives in me – the very same Spirit that conquered the grave! Amen.

22. OVERWHELMED OR OVERCOME?

Be not overcome of evil, but overcome evil with good. **Romans 12:21** (ASV)

People don't seem to fear evil as much as they once did; thanks to online streaming platforms, many forms of evil have now become kind of 'cool', from *Stranger Things* to true crime documentaries.

What used to be considered evil is now entertainment as we become numb or desensitised to it, but that does not mean evil doesn't exist. We need only click on a news app to hear some real-life horror stories, which sadden our hearts and deplete our hope. So what do we do about evil?

This scripture shows us where to begin: 'Be not overcome of evil, but overcome evil with good.' God is good and there is no evil in him, so when we encounter darkness, it is his light that we are to shine out. When we experience evil, we are to respond with goodness, with things lovely, pure and true. When someone gossips about us, we speak well of others. When someone takes from us, we give to someone else. If someone lies about us, we speak truth about others. If someone discourages us, we encourage others. If someone hurts us, we forgive them. The list goes on.

In these ways we break the influence of evil in our lives and transform the culture around us with good. This sounds difficult, but Jesus was always countercultural in what he modelled, and he can help us bring heaven to earth. What evil can we overcome with good today?

DB

23. WHEN I SEE NO CHANGE

Being confident of this very thing, that he who began a good work in you will perfect it until the day of Jesus Christ. **Philippians 1:6** (ASV)

Jesus has begun a great work of transformation in us. But maybe today we feel like nothing has changed, and the transformation we long to see is taking too long.

Often when I load up my old computer I am confronted with the spinning wheel of doom, which leaves me powerless to do anything except wait for the computer to sort out the internal problem. Then after a few minutes it disappears and everything's working again. Nothing much seems to have changed on the outside, but inside everything has changed. Things shut down, refresh, restart. And it can often be the same with our lives.

Sometimes we don't notice a massive change that is occurring on the inside until we are confronted with a moment where we notice everything on the outside is working better than it did before. In between those moments of realisation, God is still working in us to make us more like Jesus every day. We might not always see the change, but often our friends, family and colleagues do.

Be encouraged today that we don't need to fear not being a 'good-enough Christian'. If we have surrendered our lives to Jesus, he will make sure we are becoming more like him, provided we seek to engage with him and have a willing heart to be shaped by him. Every day we spend time with Jesus, more change takes place, which affects our lives and the lives of the people around us.

DB

24. UNCANCELLED

By faith the prostitute Rahab, because she welcomed the spies, was not killed with those who were disobedient. **Hebrews 11:31**

Since the dawn of social media, what has now become known as 'cancel culture' can affect every human, regardless of age, status and heritage. Cancel culture says, 'Because you have done wrong, you can no longer do what you were doing, and we are taking power away from you.'

Personally, I can't stand injustice and I'm glad when I hear that wrongdoing has been exposed and people are free from toxic and painful situations. At the same time, people I know and love have made mistakes and are afforded no second chances from the masses – or even from people close to them.

Our God is a God of justice, but he is also a God of second chances. When we are grateful for God's mercy and forgiveness, this enables us to show mercy to others.

In today's verses we read about how Rahab, a prostitute, helped God's people with his plan, even though she believed her lifestyle would disqualify her from playing a part in God's great narrative. In reality, God did want to use her to play a significant role in his plan, and she received mercy and salvation as a result. Not only that, but thanks to the gift of the Bible, her story is still shared today.

No matter what we have done in the past, nothing can separate us from God's love if we turn to him. By grace we have been saved, through faith, as a gift of God (see Ephesians 2:8). We didn't get cancelled, but Jesus cancelled our sin and shame on the cross. What greater reason is there to worship him today?

DB

25. DAILY DECISIONS

Search me, God, and know my heart;
test me and know my anxious thoughts.
See if there is any offensive way in me,
and lead me in the way everlasting. **Psalm 139:23-4**

It takes humility to ask God to search our hearts and thoughts, to ask him to reveal the areas that we need to give to him to transform.

Humility comes from the same root as the word 'human'. Humility is knowing that God is God, and we are not! Humility is leaning into his power rather than our own strength and ability. Humility is knowing that his ways are better than our ways, so in response we surrender and lean into his guidance.

Sometimes it's hard to make decisions in our day-to-day life, whether they be seemingly small ones, like who to spend our time with, or obviously bigger ones, like who to marry. Fear of getting things wrong can plague our decision making if we're not careful.

For me, when I am faced with a decision, I often ask God to reveal to me which of these two options would require the most faith. With less of me and more of God in my decision making, I find that I often see more of his power at work in my life as a result.

Spend some time with God today. Give him your thoughts and need for guidance and ask him to reveal anything that needs to change in you as you seek to walk in his ways.

DB

26. FEAR GOD OR PEOPLE

The fear of the Lord is the beginning of knowledge,
but fools despise wisdom and instruction. **Proverbs 1:7**

God gave us the gift of 86,400 seconds today. The question we have been asking ourselves throughout many of the daily devotionals in this book is, how many of those seconds are we going to spend fearing people and how many are we going to spend fearing God?

As we have seen, fearing God does not mean that we are terrified of him. Nor does it mean that we run away and hide in the places we think he might not be able to find us (a futile attempt, as we see if read Psalm 139!). Nicky Gumbel, founder of Alpha, has shared with me that if we truly fear God in the biblical sense of having a holy respect for him, we need not fear anything else. Fear of God is not a negative thing. In reality, it's the most positive fear we could ever have.

Fear of God is the beginning of wisdom and the antidote to the fear of people. It causes us to run towards God rather than away from him. In him we gain knowledge and wisdom to live life well and in loving service to others. Every second we give to spending time with God, in worship, in prayer, in his word, is not wasted but invested in the only relationship that can truly fight fear.

Let's spend some of our valuable seconds with the Lord now!

DB

27. FEAR OF ASKING QUESTIONS

So then, just as you received Christ Jesus as Lord*, continue to live your lives in him, rooted and built up in him, strengthened in the faith as you were taught, and overflowing with thankfulness.* **Colossians 2:6–7**

I first met my wife, Charlie, at a Christian summer festival for teens and young adults. She was nineteen and I was twenty-one. The first question I ever asked her was where she'd got her jeans! Since then, we haven't stopped asking each other questions. The more I find out about her, the more I fall in love with her.

Asking questions is an important part of building and growing a relationship.

Elisabeth Elliot said, 'Faith does not eliminate questions. But faith knows where to take them.'[19] We might fear asking questions about the Bible or about God, but we can trust God to love us and our many questions. What he wants is to spend time with us, and as long as we are putting our questions to him and to those who will point us back to him, then questions are a good thing, regardless of whether we find our answers in this life or the next.

I have personally found the best way to process my questions is with trusted friends from my church community. What questions do we have today? Who can we trust to ask some of the big questions about life, meaning and purpose so that we can grow in our relationship with Jesus? He is not afraid of our questions, so we should not be afraid to ask them.

DB

[19] Elisabeth Elliot, *A Chance to Die: The life and legacy of Amy Carmichael*, www.goodreads.com/work/quotes/121523-a-chance-to-die-the-life-and-legacy-of-amy-carmichael (accessed 20 April 2023).

DECEMBER

28. *SELAH* – PAUSE AND THINK

As we come to the end of this devotional, it's important that we continue to make regular space to soak in the words of Scripture. Is there a particular verse or reflection in this book that has stood out to you? Turn back to it now and read it afresh: why do you think this verse stood out to you? Does reading it again now reveal any insights into how you have grown in your journey this year?

Holy God, thank you that you are always here to guide me and teach me. Help me, in the silence, to acknowledge the Spirit stirring within me, and where and who you are pulling my attention towards. Give me the courage today to face my fears, and to boldly walk by faith. Amen.

29. TAKE THE MESSAGE OUTSIDE

Humble yourselves, therefore, under God's mighty hand, that he may lift you up in due time. Cast all your anxiety on him, because he cares for you.
1 Peter 5:6-7

John Wesley, a preacher and revivalist, was one of many brothers and sisters in the Wesley household. John and his brother Charles were used significantly by God throughout their lives. Despite John's early steps in ministry failing miserably, he was sure of his calling and persevered. God used everything John Wesley got wrong in his early ministry to teach him, and lifted him up when the time was right for the Methodist movement to be born through him.

John was a man of prayer and fasting, deeply hungry for the things of God. The Holy Spirit dwells where he is wanted, and it was clear through John's actions and pursuit of God that he wanted Jesus, and desperately wanted other people to experience his love - no matter what background people came from.

As John preached a message of inclusivity (and Charles wrote hymns, the worship songs of the day), not everyone agreed with him. As a result, some churches didn't allow him to preach, so he took the message outside, and this new movement continued to grow.

John Wesley must have been afraid, like you and me, but he chose to face fear and opposition so that everyone could hear the good news of Jesus. What areas of our friendship groups or wider communities desperately need to hear the gospel? How might we go about spending time with Jesus to empower us to speak out when needed?

DB

394

30. PRAISE, PRAISE, PRAISE

Enter his gates with thanksgiving
and his courts with praise;
give thanks to him and praise his name.
For the LORD is good and his love endures forever;
his faithfulness continues through all generations. **Psalm 100:4–5**

When we sing, or remain still in a position of worship, our soul joins the billions that have gone before us who also trusted in God despite their circumstances, in the face of their fears.

We have seen throughout this 365 devotional that worship goes far beyond songs and singing, but this verse reminds us that core to the Christian tradition, spanning the denominations in which we worship, is a call to 'enter his gates with thanksgiving and his courts with praise'. Through singing, we move our eyes from ourselves and on to God. And face to face with the God of creation, we have the opportunity to put our fears into context.

Heaven has a habit of shrinking our earthly concerns down to size.

So you may not have the best voice in the world or may not be blessed with any rhythm whatsoever, but as we have been learning over the last year, moments of transformative worship are not about skill or craft, but about authenticity and transparency. Lend your voice to the choir of saints, singing despite their situations. We are part of a wonderful history of worshippers.

RN

31. THE END IS THE BEGINNING

Therefore go and make disciples of all nations, baptising them in the name of the Father and of the Son and of the Holy Spirit, and teaching them to obey everything I have commanded you. And surely I am with you always, to the very end of the age. **Matthew 28:19-20**

We firmly believe that the key to living a more courageous life is found in Jesus Christ, and there seems no better way to bring this book to a close than with Jesus' final words to his disciples. Famously referred to as the Great Commission, these words are still our commission today.

Since these words were first uttered, the Church of Jesus-followers across the world has grown dramatically. Many different faces in many different places seek to become more like Jesus and carry the good news about him to everyone, every day and everywhere.

Our becoming like Jesus makes the world a better place as we become more loving, joyous, peacemaking, patient, good, faithful and self-controlled. Jesus sends us out into the world, not to promote our own names or build our own empires, not to fill buildings or start church programmes, but rather to make him visible to a broken, hurting world.

As we have seen throughout these pages, fear can too often stop us from fulfilling the call. From the fear of embarrassment and not being good enough to the fear of rejection or failure or disappointment, we can find many reasons not to step up and out in being Jesus' hands and feet in our circles and communities. And yet, we have one fear that can overcome them all.

AFTERWORD

The Bible tells us that 'perfect love drives out fear' (1 John 4:18), and Jesus demonstrated this perfect love on the cross when he died to absolve us of our sins. When we fear God, standing in holy reverence before him, our human worries are shrunk down to size and our confidence in who Christ says we are is bolstered. We hope that in reading these reflections you have felt your fears reducing and your fear of God increasing, empowering you to show God's love to your friends, family, colleagues, community, village, town, city, nation, region and the world.

The truth is, conquering fear may take a lifetime - perhaps we'll only be truly fearless in heaven? But that doesn't mean we can't experience more and more of God's kingdom here on earth. Keep going as you step into more and more victory in him. This is only the beginning, and as you invite others on this journey into courageous living, maybe you can be thinking about who you might want to pass this devotional on to. Or maybe you want to turn to the first page and begin all over again.

Either way, we want to thank you for walking through this year with us. May our next year, like this one, be filled with less fear and more hope as we walk with faith in the knowledge of the Father's love for us; the one perfect love that has the power to cast out all fear.

Lots of love, Dan and Rocky

SCRIPTURE ACKNOWLEDGEMENTS

NOTES

NOTES

NOTES

NOTES

NOTES